From South Central to Southside

In the series *Studies in Transgression*,
edited by David Brotherton

ALSO IN THIS SERIES:

Philip Kretsedemas and Jamella N. Gow, eds., *Modern Migrations, Black Interrogations: Revisioning Migrants and Mobilities through the Critique of Antiblackness*

Robert D. Weide, *Divide & Conquer: Race, Gangs, Identity, and Conflict*

John C. Quicker and Akil S. Batani-Khalfani, *Before Crips: Fussin', Cussin', and Discussin' among South Los Angeles Juvenile Gangs*

John M. Hagedorn, *Gangs on Trial: Challenging Stereotypes and Demonization in the Courts*

Series previously published by Columbia University Press

Adam Baird

From South Central to Southside

Gang Transnationalism, Masculinity, and Disorganized Violence in Belize City

Foreword by Philippe Bourgois

TEMPLE UNIVERSITY PRESS
Philadelphia • Rome • Tokyo

TEMPLE UNIVERSITY PRESS
Philadelphia, Pennsylvania 19122
tupress.temple.edu

Copyright © 2024 by Temple University—Of The Commonwealth System
 of Higher Education
All rights reserved
Published 2024

Library of Congress Cataloging-in-Publication Data
Names: Baird, Adam (Adam David Scourfield), author. | Bourgois, Philippe
 I., 1956– writer of foreword.
Title: From South Central to Southside : gang transnationalism,
 masculinity, and disorganized violence in Belize City / Adam Baird ;
 foreword by Philippe Bourgois.
Other titles: Studies in transgression.
Description: Philadelphia : Temple University Press, 2024. | Series:
 Studies in transgression | Includes bibliographical references and
 index. | Summary: "This book looks at violent gang cultures in Belize
 City, arguing that hegemonic masculinities imported from American gang
 cultures through deportation and popular media evolved in a context of
 postcolonial extreme poverty and disorganized urban life to drive a
 deadly culture of gendered violence"— Provided by publisher.
Identifiers: LCCN 2023059601 (print) | LCCN 2023059602 (ebook) | ISBN
 9781439923337 (cloth) | ISBN 9781439923344 (paperback) | ISBN
 9781439923351 (pdf)
Subjects: LCSH: Gangs—Belize—Belize City. | Violence—Belize—Belize
 City. | Young men—Belize—Belize City—Social conditions. | Gang
 members—Belize—Belize City. | Belize City (Belize)—Social conditions.
Classification: LCC HV6439.B42 B357 2024 (print) | LCC HV6439.B42 (ebook)
 | DDC 364.106/6097282—dc23/eng/20240318
LC record available at https://lccn.loc.gov/2023059601
LC ebook record available at https://lccn.loc.gov/2023059602

♾ The paper used in this publication meets the requirements of the
American National Standard for Information Sciences—Permanence
of Paper for Printed Library Materials, ANSI Z39.48-1992

Printed in the United States of America

9 8 7 6 5 4 3 2 1

For Dad

Contents

	Foreword by Philippe Bourgois	ix
	Preface	xv
	Introduction: Welcome to Southside	1
1.	Establishment: From South Central to Southside	21
2.	Response: The Janus Face of the State	35
3.	Escalation: Disorganized Violence and the Homicide Boom	66
4.	Adaptation: The Syncretistic Gang	94
5.	Interventions: The Challenges Ahead	127
	Conclusion: Reconfiguration	165
	Notes	175
	References	179
	Index	193

Foreword

Philippe Bourgois

This powerful, vividly ethnographic documentation of tragic rates of internecine gang murders and routinized gang rape—in the idyllic, off-the-beaten track Caribbean tourist destination of Belize—is profoundly upsetting and moving. It calls out to us all for witnessing, engagement, and remediation. Living in Los Angeles, the Hollywood-ized gang capital of the Americas, I find myself thinking repeatedly about Adam Baird's book months after having read it, pained by the vulnerability of the Belizeans he presents and the global colonial and ongoing imperial and neoliberal political economic forces he picks apart. He forces us to confront both the local and the global political economic forces implicating all of us. Most persuasively, he highlights the toxicity of the culturally mimetic flows of "Crips vs Bloods" Black-on-Black-on-Brown hyperviolent masculinities of territoriality and ephemeral microprofiteering boomeranging across the Americas and, via social media and narcotics/guns exports, throughout much of the globe.

Most important, Baird shows us how this peculiarly brutal Central American/Caribbean version of criminal interpersonal violence is rooted and actively sustained, even dynamized, by an ongoing history of U.S./British/opportunistic corporate profits, extractive accumulation, and interminable colonial through post–Cold War geopolitical interventions. He also describes the everyday details and failed premises of the well-intentioned—but "drop in the bucket," ineffective attempts at remediation and "reform." This violence continues to thrive on the starving undocumented Global South/North and East/West labor migrations, "zero-tolerance" racisms and deportations, and Caribbean shantytown Horatio Alger delusions colliding naively with the cynical out-of-control rapacity of our era of predatory neoliberal capitalism.

Even international development banks and idealistic nongovernmental aid and multilateral development organizations pursuing free market and reformist fantasies have subsidized the mediocrity of local-level corruption and global-level neglect, amid a denial of the urgent need for a structural reduction in the injustice of rising levels of North/South global inequalities. In recent years, ongoing corruption has meant that international cooperation for the poorest living on the "Southside" of Belize City has dried up. These transhistorical processes have created what he conceptualizes as "chronic vulnerability" (see Introduction) in "Southside," the socioeconomic deprivations necessary for spiraling gang violence. He shows us how the latest boom and bust of resource extractivism-as-usual and ferociously populist hyperconsumerism fan ever more deadly regimes of growing class and white supremacist inequalities and have turned the U.S.-Central American/Caribbean imperial backyard (the birthplace of plantation slavery and boom-and-bust extractive resources export-oriented bonanzas during the Industrial Revolution in Europe and the United States) into a genuine cesspool of capitalism even in the furthest sideshow eddies of this troubled region. The gunshots, cadavers, weeping victims, and mourning families are obscured from the legions of oblivious foreign tourists gaping at Belize's natural beauty, crystal clear sea, beaches, and charismatic cultural diversity and friendly face-to-face interactive style. The suffering generated by poverty, and what one of Baird's interlocutors in Chapter 1 criticizes as "corruption in high places" and what Baird multiple times refers to as the "partial Rule of Law in Belize," remains out of sight, out of mind.

Baird is a skilled writer and sociological and political economy analyst. His language is both accessible and scholarly and strives to "speak truth to power." At the same time, he is empathetically ethnographic highlighting the human stakes of structural inequalities in the everyday lived experience of the poor. He has the courage to describe the routinization of interpersonal criminal brutality on street corners and the muddy swampy neighborhoods while focusing his moral and theoretical critique on the "structural inequality, abandonment, and the unmitigated corruption that leads to failures of development for the poorest" (see Chapter 2) and foreign capital—that is, "those in power"—rather than the low income victim/perpetrators he interviews and sometimes befriends. He is refreshingly well read in the literatures on gangs, gender violence, and masculinity studies and both the anglophone Caribbean and Spanish-speaking Central American political economies and cultural formations.

By the time you have finished reading this book, Baird will have demonstrated in engaging human terms how such an objectively beautiful corner of the world has become so overrun by internecine firearm violence under neoliberal capitalism. He is focusing specifically on the cruelties and undeserved irrational privileges of men who are the perpetrators who are simultaneously also victims. They and their families are trapped in an economically unsustainable nation buffeted by British colonialism and U.S. imperialism because their deepwater ports and innumerable shallow swamps have for multiple centuries been used by opportunistic pirates, smugglers, and slave traders and, more recently, narcotics traffickers, exacerbated by an influx of Blood and Crip gang member deportees from Los Angeles imported because of U.S. zero tolerance policing and immigration policies inflected with racism. The fragile economic base of Belize has promoted corruption and street-level logics of retributive interpersonal violence. At the same time, Baird forces us to confront, no holds barred, the most brutal manifestations of toxic masculinity: firearm murder, narcotics addiction, and rape. These are the ulcers of colonialism and neoliberalism that no one dares notice, or that we are all too ashamed to discuss openly, but that demand transparency and accountability and are easily visible to whoever is willing to see the high stakes of globalized injustice and local level desperation.

The author is not just another uselessly critical academic scholar. He is an applied researcher dedicated to reducing gang violence and creating internationally funded development programs to mitigate the traumatic effects of gang violence, unemployment, absolute poverty and chronic poverty. For these reasons he has been visiting and working in the notoriously gang-impacted swampy "Southside" neighborhoods of Belize City since 2011. He reveals the underbelly of underfunded and unstable nongovernmental organizations plagued by public sector neglect and corruption. He explicitly critiques the bad faith of the usually lighter-skinned elite political families who ineffectively dominate electoral democratic politics in Belize. They only pay lip service to the everyday crisis of the urban Creole poor and ignore the incompetence of their governmental institutions as well as the pettier corruption of police officers. They sweep the suffering of their people under the rug of embarrassment and their ongoing privileges.

Baird quotes frequently from the Belizean organic intellectuals and independent self-funded researchers and critical thinkers he has befriended over the years. He especially admires the unsung spontaneous heroes—primarily women—who engage in an age-old Belizean informal practice of fostering vulnerable babies and young children from gang-impacted families. Most memorable to me is a four-year-old little girl rendered mute from having witnessed, or suffered, too much gang-related trauma for a human being to process and who only communicates through her slightly older brother through her facial expressions (see Chapter 4). Their mother had presumably been swept off her feet by addiction. Baird works with the mother and daughter who are now caring for this pair of just-out-of-toddlerhood children. These women are veteran foster caregivers with an insightful critique of how brutally the habitus of girls are so often distorted in subordination to the privilege of older boys and men. They explain powerfully how they know this because they have a much easier time comforting and putting back onto an educational prosocial track little boys through their practices of informal foster care and affection than they do helping little girls and preadolescent women from the gang-devastated families they assist through the goodness of their heart and the hard work of nurturing them in their home. These children and their mother are just a few more victims of the latest waves of narcotics and firearms passing through this waystation. Belize is merely one marginal stop out of innumerable other marginal Central American stops in the prohibitionism-generated paths that snake millions of dollars' worth of primarily cocaine to more profitable markets up north to feed the U.S. appetites for imported psychoactive drugs. Baird argues that international drug trafficking is controlled by a few families along the coast together with a select white-collar elite. "Southside" gangs are largely excluded from this lucrative trade apart from their occasional smuggling services, and only a few crumbs of the profits from the tons of transshipped cocaine that pass through Belize are ever diverted to them. Nevertheless, they are continuously scapegoated as the nation's criminals by the powerful, and drugs, particularly marijuana, are far more easily accessible in mud-poor neighborhoods than stable supplies of running water or electricity. Baird also makes sure we realize that 80 percent of homicides in Belize are committed with firearms despite 100 percent of that weaponry being fabricated internationally.

All Central American nations face the geopolitical curse of proximity and economic unsustainability in the dominating shadow of the neoliberal behemoth that is the United States, which is the richest, most militarily powerful nation in the world but shamefully has an annual murder rate six to ten times higher than that of any other wealthy nation on the planet. The other Central American nations also propel large proportions of their able-bodied youth to underpaid and undocumented employment into the lowest rungs of the entry-level labor force in the United States, where their skin color and penury force them to live in the most violent, impoverished, and segregated neighborhoods. Many of these youths have the bad luck of growing up in the gang capital of Los Angeles. Many Belizeans have also entrepreneurially ventured off as merchant marine sailors and obedient luxury deckhands and have jumped ship in Brooklyn, New York, or into the even more iconically "lumpengangsta" violence of Jamaican shantytowns (see Chapter 2), or the ports of other economically unstable/unviable nations of the formerly British-controlled Caribbean islands.

Hundreds of thousands of Central Americans have been deported home by U.S. authorities, but the tiny size of Belize gives its deportees a disproportionately toxic impact in the intimate settings of enduring face-to-face neighborhood networks. As a result, Belize has been saddled by a particularly virulent "made in USA" reggae-inflected transnational gang violence. Economically fragile men blighted by historically rooted "chronic vulnerability" desperately scramble among themselves for masculine recognition with nothing but the imported fancy cars they crash while high or drunk. Baird describes the teetering shacks on stilts that these men live in and introduces us to them as they complain to him about how frequently their front yards get flooded in hurricane season and the resultant backed up sodden putrid garbage. This toxic brew is exacerbated by prohibitionism, racist longings for the legitimacy of whiter skin, the routinized petty and large-scale corruption of politicians, legions of predatory foreign corporations, and local profiteers predatorily gobbling up any remaining overlooked natural resources that can still be extracted from the peri-urban swampland of the "Southside" neighborhoods of Belize City.

What is especially fascinating about the uniqueness of the Belizean case as a former British colony in the contemporary U.S. imperial backyard of its heartland empire is the impact of the virulence of U.S. racism against Blacks reflecting back onto Belize. It is obviously not a coincidence that virtually all the Central American Caribbean rim nations vie with one another for the ignominy of having the world's highest annual homicide rate. Similarly, it is notable that all these nations are multiculturally diverse gems trapped in a pressure cooker of cultures and histories of oppression and resistance. Their region was forged by the global winds of plantation slavery, and logging slavery in the case of Belize, buccaneers, escaped slaves, U.S. multinational corporate booms-and-busts, and U.S. military invasions. As Baird shows, these forces have respawned Afro-indigenous and creolized European unique, but eminently mutually recognizable, all-American cultures that are overflowing with licit and illicit entrepreneurial energy. Most importantly, this book is a powerful and ethnographically rich contribution to a broader critique of masculinist violence, oligarchical mediocrity, and the contradictory diversities of white supremacist racism in Central America and the Caribbean.

Preface

I first went to Belize in 2011 invited by the UN to design a gang intervention project. I was taken by surprise. What gangs? Isn't Belize a Caribbean tourist destination? I had just spent the previous year working on urban violence in Medellín's most notorious neighborhoods and had taken UNDP staff around some of the worst-affected areas. My name had been passed along. They thought it would be a good idea to come and share some of that experience with their staff. To be honest, I knew nothing about Belize, other than it was a former British colony, somehow both Central American and Caribbean. None of the academics I knew who worked on gangs in the region, and I knew a lot, had said a word about the country. I was intrigued but did not expect to find much of a problem, or at least, nothing like I was used to working with.

Then I visited Southside Belize City, looked up the homicide rates, and blinked. Wait, what? Viscerally, the poverty felt worse than Medellín. The marshlands that became scorched earth in the dry months, the flimsy wooden houses, plank gangways, the trash piles, people's clothes often in tatters, children running barefoot, the total absence of infrastructure bar a menacing tangle of electric cables above every corner. Maybe it was something to do with the searing heat? And, per capita, it was more violent than Medellín. Who would have thought? Very few, it turns out. Most of all, what the hell were the Bloods and Crips doing here? I had read copious amounts about transnational *mara* gangs in the region, but nothing about *colors* gangs making the journey. It was discombobulating to see blue and red "rags" and be reminded of N.W.A.'s *Straight Outta Compton* album from my teenage years. This was Belize, a backwater, yet there were young men *cripin'* at a tiny run-down street called Majestic Alley, a stone's throw from the dock that takes tourists to the cays.

South Central LA had come to Southside.

I scrambled around searching for academic literature, reports, anything on what was going on and found nothing. Well, almost nothing. There was a solitary publication on male youth exclusion by Herbert Gayle, who I found out was not Belizean, but a Jamaican living in Kingston, so I could not even sit down and talk to him. But what luck. I focused on masculinities too, so using Gayle's local knowledge, I poured in the learning from my Ph.D. based on Medellín and set about frantically stitching together a "male" focused gang intervention project, the deadline looming like a sword of Damocles at the end of the week. Exhausted after submission and a midnight oil session sorting out the project budget with the UNDP deputy representative, I walked past Majestic Alley and got on a boat to Caye Caulker an hour's ride away. The pristine sands and crystal waters were a world apart. Later I flew back to Medellín, but the Belizean experience lingered. It bothered me that no one had written about the severe violence there. I was guilty of that, too, so I resolved to go back. Not as an intrepid white hero-researcher, but because I was frustrated, angry even, that Southside's plight was invisible outside of Belize.

It turns out that getting research funding "just to go to the beach" is harder than expected. I did not return to Belize until 2016 when my university at the time, Coventry in the United Kingdom, gave me a small pot of money to prime national contacts for a funding bid. I made connections at the University of Belize and did a few research interviews on the side. Then, a year later, after some rejected bids, I won another small grant from the British Academy and the Leverhulme Trust,[1] enough to take me back twice if I spread it thinly. A couple of years after that, the UNDP, who I had stayed in touch with, invited me over to help put on a conference in the capital, Belmopan. Then, in 2020, I was invited to take part on a European Research Council project collecting gang member life histories.[2] Again, I managed to squeeze two trips out of money meant for one. By then I was living conveniently next door in Guatemala, which helped. I had quit academia and followed my wife, who had taken a new job working with refugees, disheartened after a large project I was due to lead comparing "gang negotiations" across Latin America was canceled unceremoniously.[3] I calculated that I had also chipped in a substantial amount of my own money to make the fieldwork happen, but I'm not complaining. Finally, by 2022, I had stitched together enough research trips to fill a book.

What I found strange about conducting research in Belize were the people. They are polite to a fault, distant, family oriented, and small "c" conservative. I used to joke, that in Medellín by the time I had taken a taxi down from the airport into town, the driver had invited me to his house for dinner to meet the family, out for beers, and offered to show me around town. In over a decade of visiting, I made friends with Belizeans, but they never invited me anywhere socially, not even for a coffee. Culturally, it is a world apart. I asked my Caribbean friends from Jamaica and Trinidad about this. Is it because I am white, British, too alien? No. They said, it was actually quite normal. It did make relationship building challenging though. It takes a long time to get under Belize's skin, reminding me that all ethnographies are unpredictable endeavors, they can be wild rides that sometimes feel "broken" (Contreras 2019). Yet imperfections, frustrations and breakthroughs are part of the process. After several years of knowing alias "Angel," who was well aware of my research agenda, he admitted to me that he was a founder of the Majestic Alley Crips in the 1980s. "Why didn't you tell me this years ago?!" "I din' trus' you." Frustrating? Yes. But a colleague reminded me it is a privilege to be let in and this should be marked down as a success. So it proved, as Angel went on to become one of my key confidants and features throughout this book.

What is Belize City really like? For that you will need to read the book or visit for yourself. But, let me put it in the bleak words of a former gang member turned youth worker, a friend who sadly passed away in 2023. He chose to be anonymized as "Mr. T." I asked him why there is so much violence in the city? He paused, drew a solemn breath, and said, "We should tear down de ghettos an' start again. Nothin' will eva change 'til de living conditions change. Dese kids [who end up in gangs] live in a single room wid a pissbucket in de corner wid their siblings an' mum."

I had been thinking about ideas like "social terrain" and the impact of vulnerability for a while. Mr. T made me think some more. The gang violence I had come to research in the region over the years, including Trinidad and Tobago, and Jamaica, in addition to what I had read about gangs the world over, was trying to tell me something about commonality. They were all different, yet linked by shared experiences, common problems, made up of the same demographic. How could that be reflected in an analytical framework to make sense of violence? I had thought up a conceptual narrative by the time I heard Josh Dublin, a criminal justice reform advocate, on a podcast. What he said was succinct yet spoke volumes. "The vast majority of incarcerated people in New York State came from . . . seven basic neighborhoods, right? And these were neighborhoods that were all impoverished, that were all plagued with what we call 'crime generative factors,' from substance abuse, to dilapidated housing to just, um, poverty, right?"[4] It felt like he was confirming what I had been thinking: *gang violence in the United States and Belize comes from the same place.* Historically vulnerable populations, starting from slavery, are made violent by brutally unequal societies. If sections of society are held back, bullied, abandoned, squeezed, excluded, and scapegoated for society's woes, accumulatively over generations, we should not be surprised that one day they erupt into a self-consuming violence, as Southside Belize City did two decades ago.

From South Central to Southside

Introduction

Welcome to Southside

Why read this book unless you have a specific interest in Belize? Although Belize City—with a population of some sixty thousand—is small by comparison with Los Angeles, San Salvador, Guatemala City, or Tegucigalpa, its examination reveals why gang transnationalism becomes established in some places but not others. This case study on how community transitions-to-violence take place provides a window into cities that have seen dramatic rises in urban violence in recent years. Fundamentally, "chronic vulnerability" is a precondition for continuously high levels of social violence. The examination of the social terrain in the poor Southside area of Belize City shows how this vulnerability was a prerequisite to the late 1990s homicide boom and how vulnerability and violence are profoundly gendered.

The Belizean case is an enlightening study for gang researchers and urban-violence scholars more broadly. Of course, this book does not claim to provide wholesale answers to the intractable problem of urban violence; rather, it provides a window into these processes through which we gain insights and a conceptual framework transferable to contexts that suffer similar social, economic, and political marginalization. Contrary to facile assumptions that the rise of transnational drug trafficking through Belize is responsible for increasingly organized and armed gang violence on the streets, the truth of the matter is different. A combination of gang disorganization, structural exclusion, and transnational cultures of masculinity combined to fuel the story of Belize City's descent into violence, a story that has global implications.

Those who live, work, or conduct research with vulnerable populations understand that high levels of violence are nothing short of devastating to communities. The better we understand these processes, the better position we will be in collectively to challenge them and roll them back. We have yet to collect knowledge from the Belizean transition to violence, given the dearth of literature in circulation on the subject. What might we learn?

The gang-led homicide surge in Belize is one of the most vertiginous in modern history. Those interested in the dynamics of U.S. gangs as a transnational phenomenon more broadly—not just the Bloods and Crips but others covered in the gang transnationalism literature such as the *mara* gangs and the Almighty Latin Kings and Queens (Brotherton 2015; Brotherton and Gude 2020)—will benefit from understanding how U.S. gang cultures took root in Belize and how they evolved. This is the first book that covers the role of U.S. Blood and Crip gang transnationalism in the genesis of Belizean gangs. The Central American location makes comparisons particularly relevant not only to the maras in neighboring countries, as seen in recent works by the likes of Dudley (2020) and Wolf (2017), but also to those in the Caribbean, where Belizean-style "garrison politics" to borrow a term from Jamaican scholarship, reflect wider regional dynamics. The way U.S. gangs establish themselves and flourish in foreign countries that are culturally distinct underscores the gang as a dexterous, adaptable, and syncretistic social organization, something we can best appreciate when U.S. gang culture is studied out of context: in this case, dropped into Southside.

Why does transnational gang culture successfully take root and grow in some communities and not others? Or more informally, why Southside, why not your own backyard? Gang-led homicide booms are not entirely unpredictable. In fact, if we combine the correct social ingredients, we can actually predict where homicide booms may occur, and it is very clear where they will not. To be loquacious, there is a certain social alchemy to the generation of violence. Admittedly, the real world is messy, contradictory, and confounding, and we should rightly be circumspect of deductive frameworks that claim to predict violence. However, the argument that "chronic vulnerability," defined later in detail, is a prerequisite to severe levels of social violence runs counter to the supposedly objective explanation that drugs and organized crime drive spikes in social violence.[1] Alone, they are not a sufficient explanation. Violence is determined by the social terrain, above all else. In the Belizean case, drugs have been unimportant in the rise of violence because transshipment networks are hermetically contained within families, tight groups of white-collar criminals, and, frequently, members of the Belizean Police Department (BPD), organizing sea-to-land transshipment routes, what I called *surf 'n' turf* trafficking in my field diary, or nighttime plane landings on the nation's highways far from the city. These networks are at pains to avoid street gangs. Methodologically, this approach was inductive, which will make a useful comparison with empirically grounded studies of violent communities elsewhere.

This proposition brings us back to the vulnerability of the social terrain as an essential component of gang "success," dovetailing with recent calls from multilateral agencies to focus on the role fragility plays in fueling conflict. The OECD *States of Fragility* report (2020) speaks to this directly, as does the World Bank Group's five-year *Strategy for Fragility, Conflict, and Violence* (2020), which builds on their joint report *Pathways to Peace* with the United Nations (2018).

Vitally, vulnerability and violence are gendered, as seen in the social dynamics on Southside. Statistically, poor young men are far more susceptible to joining gangs and killing each other the world over, as exemplified in the recent compendium of gang studies by Brotherton and Gude (2021). This precarity is defined later in the book as *masculine vulnerability*. Comparatively, *feminine vulnerability* is analyzed in the same setting, enabling us to understand how men and women are distinctly affected by, and respond to, gangs, violence, and exclusion. Considering how gender leads individuals to strategize for survival differently helps us understand the way violence propagates and victimizes on Southside—and, consequently, how we might respond in a gender-sensitive way to reduce violence. This framework is eminently transferable to other violent urban contexts because gangs are an overwhelmingly poor male enterprise across the world, though one where women play an important yet often overlooked role. The concepts of *chronic vulnerability* and, consequently, masculine vulnerability were incorporated into a report by the United Nations Office on Drugs and Crime (UNODC), based on my earlier publication (Baird 2020a), and presented in an issue paper to the United Nations Convention against Transnational Organized Crime for adoption as a global resolution by member states in 2021.

I first traveled to Belize back in 2011, fresh out of my Ph.D. studies, hired as a consultant by the United Nations Development Program (UNDP) to design a crime reduction project pitched to the U.S. Embassy. I knew very little about Belize before I arrived, like many readers here I would hazard to guess. Even for scholars of Latin America and the Caribbean, the country tends to slip beneath our radars. This is probably because Belize, located on the Caribbean Sea sharing borders with Mexico to the north and Guatemala to the west, is inconspicuous with a small population of approximately four hundred and ten thousand. It certainly does not spring to mind when thinking about gang violence in the region. Belize City, the former capital on the coast, is the largest town in the country by far, yet it scarcely has sixty thousand inhabitants, small enough to have a distinct village feel to it. The country is unique. It is a member of the Central American Integration System, the Community of Latin American and Caribbean States, and the Caribbean Community and Common Market. It is also a fledgling nation: a former colony named British Honduras in 1878, later Belize in 1973, although the country did not gain independence until 1981. The etymology of "Belize" is likely found in the Mayan word *baliz*, meaning "muddy waters," given the prevalence of swamps, lakes, and lagoons across the country (Fowler and Bunck 2012, p. 73). Belize chose to remain part of the British Commonwealth, a status that remains unchanged to this day. Assad Shoman, former Belizean minister, said that the decision not to become a republic was motivated by historical Guatemalan claims to Belizean territory and that the prevailing wisdom "held strongly that it would be safer to keep the Queen as Head of State" (2011, p. 310).

Visitors to the country are often surprised by the still-in-service red British letter boxes dotted around the city and the youthful image of a 1970s Queen Elizabeth II stamped on banknotes and coinage. Tellingly, for this multicultural and idiosyncratic country, in 1978, the Belizean dollar adorned with the Queen's head was pegged to the U.S. dollar, not sterling, at a rate of BZ$2 to US$1. The country is predominantly known as a tourist destination and with good reason. It has a spectacular natural and cultural heritage: from diving the perfectly circular Cousteau-discovered Great Blue Hole to sampling Creole cuisine, enjoying Garifuna dance and music, or scaling the Mayan ruins inland at Xunantunich or Caracol. Although rightly popularized as a tourist paradise, as it is touted on ubiquitous, yet unimaginatively sloganed, *UnBelizeable* T-shirts, there is another side to the country. Less known is the chronic violence that concentrates in the gang-saturated Southside of Belize City. But this is *new violence*. In such a beautiful country, it feels like a paradise lost.

At independence, Belize's homicide rate was entirely unremarkable. Startlingly, by 2017, rates reached forty-five per one hundred thousand, exceeding that of Mexico and making Belize comparable to its noisy Northern Triangle neighbors: El Salvador, Guatemala, and Honduras (Peirce 2017). Yet, despite having one of the highest homicide rates in the world, studies on gang violence in the city are extremely rare.

When I made my first research-specific trip to Belize in 2016, I took with me a working hypothesis to shape the exploratory fieldwork. It went something like this: The sharp rise of Belize's murder rate in the 1990s coincided with the increasing transshipment of drugs through the country; this led to a trickle down of drugs into Belize City, which galvanized gang violence and generated increasingly weaponized and violent masculine identities. I expected to find confirmatory evidence of a drugs and gun supply chain leading straight to the streets, lit up by the violence of disenfranchised young men in ever-more-organized criminal gangs. There were certainly guns. However, the youth gangs I found were unusually young compared to my research experiences in Medellín and the Port of Spain. They were often made up of children and were palpably anomic, prone to splintering, and not obviously embedded in organized crime in any meaningful way. There was disorder and unpredictability tied to interpersonal disputes, or *beefs*, on the streets, which often turned lethal. Interestingly, it gradually became apparent that street gangs were not directly linked to the broader arc of transnational drug flows. Not only that, but street youths were actively *excluded* from the trade by traffickers, although the national press driving a moral panic around gangs have never flagged this. What, then, accounts for the rise of gangs if drug trafficking was not a front-and-center cause as orthodoxy would have us believe?

Contemporary weaponization clearly multiplied the capacity for lethal gang violence, but, upon investigation, it was clear that gun smuggling had a markedly different political economy than cocaine trafficking. In effect, drug transshipment does not adequately explain Belize's violence. This led me to explore other explanations by focusing more keenly on the fragility of the social terrain, where poverty and exclusion provided the conditions on Southside necessary for transnational gangs to embed and proliferate. These gangs armed and expanded across Belize City rapidly, and the later splintering of a once-established gang order sparked an unprecedented homicide boom at the turn of the millennium, from which the country has never recovered. What's more, gang identities have proved to be culturally syncretistic; they evolved away from the Blood and Crip transnational prototype imported from the United States. While elements still lingered, such as the red (Blood) and blue (Crip) *rags* they wore and much of the Americanized gangsta lexicon, gang members had become a unique mix that was more Creole—a word itself that implies blend and fusion—than U.S. gang culture. It was distinctly Belizean.

Despite being culturally syncretistic and splintering into a bewildering mosaic of gangs across the city, their gender demographics remain consistent. Above all, violent masculinities persist. Gangs in Belize are overwhelmingly made up of young Black and Brown men from poor neighborhoods. Although Creoles are only 25 percent of the national population, they are far more likely to murder and be murdered than any other demographic group (Statistical Institute of Belize 2021). This raised sociological questions: How can gangs be so culturally fluid yet maintain such a rigid gender order? And if we can somehow interrupt violent masculinities, surely that would mean the end of the homicide boom? We should be rightly skeptical of silver bullet propositions, but gang interventions the world over tend to be gender blind and are most certainly masculinities blind. Surely, then, a masculinities reading of the *rise* and *continuity* of gang violence is a prospect worthy of further exploration.

Belize's gangs are not organized around the multiple illegal markets such as extortion, loan sharking, money laundering, or other transnational crimes witnessed among some mara gangs in neighboring Central American countries, or the more organized gangs in Kingston or Port of Spain. It is confounding, when gazing at the chaotic street violence of today, to hear stories from elder locals about the recent past, when the early Blood and Crip *Generals*—gang leaders—exercised social influence, controlled the use of guns, placed normative parameters on gang-member behavior, and were the central interlocutors in the clientelist political party politics that still define Southside today. Gangs had, for all intents and purposes, slipped from *organized* to *disorganized*, a process that made them more violent. This was a visceral counternarrative to most literature on street gangs in the region, which argues, in one form or another, that gangs become increasingly violent as they connect to overarching organized criminal networks (e.g., Dudley 2011). Such narratives feed a discourse that the ever-institutionalizing gang is the cause of violence and that policies and interventions should necessarily dismantle their structure. Conversely, violence on Southside was rife partly because the old General-led control had disintegrated. The necro-politics of the street were now characterized by multiplying, sporadic, and heavily weaponized beefs. These initial observations upended the rather simplistic hypothesis I had taken into Belize City and reframed the research.

Gang Violence in Belize City

Below the Haulover Creek that bisects Belize City, despite some notable and historic buildings toward the shore and downtown areas, Southside comprises ramshackle neighborhoods, many of which are built on unforgiving peri-urban swamplands that bake and crack in dry season, kicking up choking dust-clouds. Southside, including the notorious downtown street north of swing bridge called Majestic Alley, more recently joined by new generation gangs along North Front Street and the Pickstock Street area known as 'Jungle,' has played host to gangs since the early 1980s, after which fighting dramatically increased between 1999 and 2000 driving up the national homicide rate.

Belize is a country characterized by elitism and inequality inherited from the colonial encounter, and Southside residents are perennially at the bottom of the country's socioeconomic strata (UNICEF Belize 2011; Warnecke-Berger 2019, p. 197). The country has a rich mixed heritage, with sizable Mayan, Spanish, Garifuna (Afro-Indigenous), and mestizo populations. The Creole minority of predominantly West African descent is, rather uniquely, disparately spread across the country's social, economic, and political classes. A number of the political elite and the majority of Southside's poorest residents are Creole, although the meaning of *Creole* in Belize is broad and encompassing. Southside Creoles tend to be darker skinned, elite Creoles lighter skinned. As Gayle, Hampton, and Mortis say, given Southside's demographics, it is unsurprising that most gang members are Black and Brown (2016, p. 192). One dark-skinned gang leader I met in the city went by a number of street aliases, one of which was the prosaic "Black Boy."

In the twentieth century, most of the inhabitants of Belize Town in British Honduras, as it was then known, were poor. Their plight was compounded by the Great Depression of the 1930s and the catastrophic hurricane that destroyed most of the town in 1931 (Bolland 1997, p. 270). Subsequent economic decline led to intense poverty and widespread unemployment, and people reacted by organizing into trade unions, creating the Great Workers Union of the 1940s and, from there, the People's Committee, to demand independence. However, after the Second World War, the colony's economy further contracted, and, in 1949, Britain decided to devalue the British Honduras dollar, deepening the crisis and social unrest. The trade union along with the popular agitation for independence "provided the crucial base for the rapid development of the People's United Party [PUP] after 1950" (Bolland 1997, p. 271), which would later win the country's first ever elections under universal suffrage, in 1954, although with limited powers as a colony.

In 1961 Hurricane Hattie laid waste to the coastline sparking a national emergency. The subsequent housing crisis burdened already fragile livelihoods and prompted a remarkable exodus north, where some 30 percent of the entire population migrated to the United States (Vernon 2000). The migratory flow was not stymied by the wave of optimism that accompanied George Cadle Price, the new leader of the PUP, as he pressured Britain into allowing British Honduras self-governance and a new constitution in 1964. Consequently, in 1973, the country was renamed Belize, finally becoming fully independent on September 21, 1981, in a peaceful transition of power. Historic migration to the United States was fundamental for the later deportation of Bloods and Crips, with their red and blue *colors*, back to Belize City, marking the beginning of the country's contemporary gang culture.

While Belize shares the Northern Triangle "deportation model" of gang transnationalism, it most noticeably diverges along the lines of ethnicity and language. The Creole and, to a lesser extent, Garifuna migrants that joined gangs, understandably gravitated toward the English-speaking African American Bloods and Crips, not the Spanish-speaking Latino 18th Street (in Spanish known as Calle 18 or Barrio 18) and MS-13 "mara" gangs, thus defining the gang culture and identity of future returnees. While it is likely that some Spanish-speaking Mayan or mestizo Belizeans will have joined Latino gangs in the United States, there are no studies of this. Speculatively, given that these populations are predominantly inland in Belize, they have been less susceptible to the mass displacements caused by coastal hurricanes such as Hattie that forced the Creole population north. Those who joined the Bloods and Crips in the United States were deported for the first time in the early 1980s. These were the pioneers of gang transnationalism in Belize, predating the emergence of the maras in Central America by several years.

Newly deported Bloods and Crips encountered a nascent democratic system. There was limited institutional capacity to enforce the rule of law, and the two main parties, the United Democratic Party (UDP) and the PUP, utilized political clientelism and patronage, damaging electoral tactics, and governance practices that would come to define future Belizean politics and civic practices. By the end of the 1980s, two main factions, the George Street Bloods and the Majestic Alley Crips, were well established with Generals drawn into these clientelist networks. The 1990s security policies and policing swung neurotically between, on the one hand, crackdowns by the newly created, militarized, and later notorious Gang Suppression Unit (GSU; renamed Gi3 in 2020) and army deployments to the streets and, on the other hand, gang negotiation and reintegration programs such as the Bird's Isle Declaration, organized through the prime minister's office and supported by the state-created Conscious Youth Development Program (CYDP).

Reflecting ineffectual and punitive *mano dura*—heavy-handed—policies toward maras in Northern Triangle countries, GSU armed responses tended to corrode human rights and increase community violence rather than quell it, while negotiated approaches suffered from underfunding and unsustainability as gangland beefs would consistently break fragile truces. The end of the 1990s marked the beginning of Belize's homicide boom. Murder rates rose nationally from 9 per one hundred thousand in 1995, to 33 in 2002, peaking at 43 in 2012, before settling in the high 30s (Peirce 2017). If there were two main gang factions in the 1990s on George Street and Majestic Alley, by 2008, these had expanded or fragmented to over thirty gangs in the city (Haylock 2013). In 2017, Belize City's homicide rate reached 99 per one hundred thousand, placing it among the top-ten most violent cities in the world. Murders on Southside that year reached an unprecedented 128 per one hundred thousand (Arciaga Young and King 2019). The Jamaican academic Herbert Gayle stated that homicide on Southside is more severe than elsewhere in the Caribbean, and Belizean intellectual and broadcaster Nuri Muhammad described it as an urban poor young Black male phenomenon (Gayle, Hampton, and Mortis 2016; Muhammad 2015).

Chronic Vulnerability

Mexican "narco" violence is often extreme, but occurs sporadically and unpredictably across the country, rather than being location specific and continually affecting the same population. If we consider where homicide consistently occurs, the highest rates in Latin America and the Caribbean are persistently found in the poorest neighborhoods of cities with significant gang populations and, occasionally, in crime hot spots in downtown areas. A long list of scholars in the Caribbean confirm this (e.g., Bennett 2017; L. Evans and Jaffe 2020; Kerrigan 2019; Pawelz 2018; Townsend 2009), and Knight has specifically connected historic Caribbean-wide socioeconomic marginalization to modern violence (2019). My own work has compared specific social terrains in the Port of Spain with those in Belize City, ones that are similarly affected by transhistorical, accumulated forms of poverty, exclusion, and oppression, making them propitious sites for transitions to violence, which happened in both cities around the year 2000 (Baird 2020a). That this takes place at the urban margins so consistently, an internecine, self-consuming violence *among* excluded populations, is demonstrated across the literature. For example, an edited collection by Auyero, Bourgois, and Scheper-Hughes (2015), indicates the exceptionalism of these contexts to violent turns. Arguing that particular social terrains are not only susceptible to, but *necessary* for, a transition to violence is a bold claim that requires substantiation.

Chronic vulnerability is a "shoulders of giants" progression reaching back to Émile Durkheim's foundational observations that deviancy should be understood as a challenge to the normalized repressiveness of the state (1895/2007); it is socially generated and historically accumulated impoverishment. Although this may feel somewhat doctrinaire to the reader, chronic vulnerability hypothesizes that if social, economic, and political exclusions are counteracted, chronic violence will subsequently recede. The concept draws further inspiration from, and should be understood as complementary to, Pearce's notion of "chronic violence" as a three-dimensional phenomenon—temporal, spatial, and intense (2007). Likewise, chronic vulnerability is conceptualized in three-dimensions, (1) across generations (temporal), (2) concentrated in the same neighborhoods or locations (spatial), and (3) at high levels (intense). Additionally, analytical intersections are vital, such as the race, age, and gender lenses used in this book. In academically aspirational terms, there is scope for any number of intersections to be applied in future research, limited only by our imagination.

In sum, the central claim then, is this: *Chronic violence only emerges from contexts of chronic vulnerability.* While external influences such as transnational organized crime, including drugs and weapons trafficking, can shape pathways to violence, they cannot alone, or somehow objectively, create it.

If they could, we would expect to find homicide booms occurring equally, at random, across the global drugs supply chain. This is a conclusion Matthew Bishop, Dylan Kerrigan, and I came to when studying gangs and drug trafficking in Trinidad, asking why so many young men were seemingly "Breaking Bad" (Baird, Bishop, and Kerrigan 2022). The culminating chapter of this book develops this notion into a theory of change based on tackling chronic vulnerability to reduce both *actual* and *potential* chronic violence. Within context, this can be understood as an urban gang-centric approach of targeting fragility to reduce conflict, championed by the OECD, United Nations, and World Bank referenced earlier.

Old Belize

It is useful, comparatively, to highlight that the eastern Port of Spain in Trinidad and the Southside of Belize City have unique realities yet share several defining characteristics. Both are affected by histories of colonialism and slavery (Bolland 1997; Kerrigan 2016; Knight 2019), where the dehumanization of the enslaved and the "coloniality of power" (Quijano 2000) meant that Black and Brown populations emerged from bondage and indentureship into peri-urban yards comprising informal wooden settlements that would become the poorest neighborhoods of their respective capital cities (Belmopan did not became Belize's administrative capital until 1961). Belize City is a port town and has been the largest settlement in the country since the mid-1800s. When slavery ended in 1838, over 90 percent of the population in the settlement was of African or part African descent, the poorest sections of town being south of the river (Bolland 1997, p. 267). What is now Southside was originally built by the poor and slaves themselves, springing up behind old Back Street toward the swampy interior of the present-day Martin's area, far from the cooling sea breeze of the shoreline where the affluent white British settlers lived. This place used to be called Eboe Town, also *Igbo*, named after the slaves trafficked out of western Africa:

> Consisting of numerous yards, flanked with long rows of what are called negro houses, being simply separate rooms under one long roof, which used to be appropriated to slaves, and now accommodate the poorer laborers . . . [white settlers bemoaned] a very large assemblage of Negroes either free or slaves . . . who have resorted to certain appointed huts situated in different parts of the Swamps on the South side of this town, whose apparent motive for which is dancing. . . Such "large parties" of African and Creole Belizeans were made possible by the dense settlement pattern in Belize Town. (Bolland 1997, p. 65)

After the Treaty of Madrid in 1670, British and Spanish powers agreed to suppress piracy, leading buccaneers, privateers, and otherwise pirates of the Caribbean, to change tack from plundering Spanish trade ships carrying the highly prized logwood used in dying wool back in Britain (Shoman 2011, pp. 15–16), to becoming loggers, or "cutters" themselves. This shift led to British settlements appearing in the 1650s in the Bay of Honduras—incorporating the Belizean coast—inhabitants henceforth being known as *Baymen*.

In the 1760s, the logwood market collapsed due to a glut in supply, so the Baymen turned to mahogany, which continues to be exported from Belize to the present day. The signing of the Convention of London in 1786 between the British and the Spanish meant that the British could settle and log wood in the region as long as they acknowledged Spanish sovereignty and agreed not to build forts or create governments or plantation agriculture. However, the convention was short lived.

This coastal region was highly disputed between the British and the Spanish at the time, leading to numerous battles culminating in a pivotal event in Belizean history, the Battle of St. George's Caye, where Baymen alongside African slaves, finally ousted the Spanish on September 10, 1798, now a national holiday. However, the notion that "Congoes, Nangoes, Mongolas, Ashantees, Eboes and other African tribes" (Bolland 1997, p. 67) and Creole slaves brought from neighboring Caribbean islands, particularly Jamaica, somehow fought shoulder to shoulder in harmony with their slave masters is highly disputed. Many slaves had, in fact, already fled into Spanish Honduran territory in the years running up to the battle, yet the slaves' malcontent with British colonial masters has been airbrushed from history, an inconvenient truth not remembered in national holiday celebrations (see, e.g., Shoman 2011, pp. 35–37). Since that point in time, Belize became a de facto British colony, but only formally became known as "British Honduras" in 1862, and, for the next one hundred years, was primarily used to exploit timber from the New World to be sold in the Old World for the benefit of Crown and empire.

The Baymen organized slavery for the extraction of this timber, founding a permanent settlement in the early eighteenth century at the mouth of the Belize River, which would later become Belize Town, renamed Belize City in 1943. Bolland (1997) traces slaves in the British settlement there to 1724, whom "had been imported" from Jamaica and Bermuda (p. 55). By the end of the 1700s, predominantly male slaves made up approximately three-quarters of the population. The "houseslaves" for domestic chores and artisanal work lived in relatively better conditions than "fieldslaves," who faced brutal work-life conditions until emancipation in 1838 (Bolland 1997; Shoman 2011). The division between houseslave and fieldslave laid down a marker for the class-based stratification between Creole populations still evident in current social and political structures in the country.

> The colonial legacy of racism . . . discriminates particularly against people of African descent—both Creoles and Garifuna—while relatively favoring those with lighter skins and straighter hair. Though racial discrimination has no legal sanction, for so long as somatic distinctions continue to correlate with class positions, most Creoles will find it harder to be upwardly mobile and will express the belief that the "Spanish" are overtaking them educationally and economically as well as numerically. (Bolland 1997, p. 284)

Similar historical processes have been seen across the Caribbean, notably in Haiti, where a minority group of Creole slaves became an elite class of domestic workers as cooks, servants, artisans, and so on, based at the plantation house. This was a *relatively* privileged group, mainly born in the Americas distinct from the underclass of African-born field laborers who suffered greater physical hardship and brutalization. Belize did not have an organized plantation structure around sugar or cotton colonies, creating, as Bolland records, "a unique slave society" (1997, p. 56). The extraction of mahogany led to the constant shifting of small groups of ten to fifty slave men from one inland forest location to another, female slaves and a minority of male slaves remained in settlements. Seasons were long. Logging processes meant timber was trucked by cattle to a riverbank "barquedier," a large log stockpile, in the dry season, then floated downriver in the rainy season to be squared for export. At the end of back-to-back seasons "slave men were united with each other and their families in Belize Town" (Bolland 1997, p. 56).

Given the sporadic urban interaction of slaves, who came from a range of African cultures, further including West Indians and Creole Belizeans, it became difficult for successive generations to describe themselves as anything but Creole by the end of the 1800s. This formed the foundation of future Creole culture in Belize, where "urban slaves" and "free blacks" formed into nations with their own governors or kings (Bolland 1997, p. 71). Interestingly, during festivals, different ethnic "sets," "tribes," or African "nations" would occasionally engage in faction fights, particularly among flagmen. Although there is no direct link to contemporary gangs, in the Port of Spain certain violent male identities are transhistorical and can be connected, conceptually at least, to contemporary violent male gang identities (Baird, Bishop, and Kerrigan 2022).

The way that the social stratification of slave populations evolved into a contemporary sociopolitical class division *within* Creole populations is particular to Belize. This is evident in the way a handful of surnames given to houseslaves later came to dominate as a postindependence national elite, while many descendants of the fieldslaves still live in squalor on Southside. Subsequently, Southside, like other urban margins in Caribbean countries, has been blighted by the failures of postcolonial development, then neoliberalization, which has enhanced class inequality and elitism (Kerrigan 2019; Shoman 2011). It should be noted that Southside is not uniform and has substantial well-developed buildings on the shoreline and in the downtown swing bridge area, but the poorest neighborhoods are still located there (UNICEF Belize, 2011). Many live in unplanned communities such as the Back-a-lan (back-of-land) swamplands on the outskirts of the city. The rise of gangs and violence on Southside is indivisible from its history of subjugation, continued since independence through state abandonment and political venality, meaning meager progress has been made. Vulnerability is chronic when historically rooted and contemporarily maintained.

In summary, patterns of community violence in Belize need to be understood with the past in mind. Belize's colonial experience is best understood not in relation to Central America but rather to the Caribbean, where scholars have identified historically developed patterns of violence in poor urban neighborhoods (Brereton 2010; Singh 1984; Trotman 1986). Notably, Beckles (2003) and Pemberton and Joseph (2018) connected the origins of present-day Afro-Caribbean male violence to the way slavery conditioned Afro-Caribbean masculinity to adopt a patriarchal, sexist, and violent value system reflecting that of the white male planters themselves.

Literature that discusses historical violence in Belize is, unfortunately, extremely rare. One recent exception is historian Warnecke-Berger (2017) who identifies a trend in violence dating back to the 1950s, when the homicide rate fluctuated around the twenty per one hundred thousand figure. Belize was very much a lawless frontier nation during that period, the main preoccupation being the extractive colonial project. Southside did not even have gangs to speak of until the 1980s, rather the erstwhile Base Boys, who would sell nationally grown marijuana on street corners known as *bases* (Muhammad 2015). Although I have previously evidenced an intergenerational lineage of violence (Baird 2021a), the shockingly high within-community homicide levels represented a sea change, a new violence, that only emerged in the 2000s.

Gangs and Masculinities

On Southside, the incoming transnational Blood and Crip culture, in the 1980s and 1990s, stood out as an aspirational pathway to manhood. The foreign gang arrived as a potent identity package with the power to reconfigure positions of subordination, the iconic *Original Gangsta* (OG) and *Homeboy* figures of the disenfranchised young Black man striking back at structural violence. Social terrain is, therefore, fundamental to gang transnationalism. The case of Belize City exemplifies the *global to local* dynamics of masculinities, a "transnational" masculinity (Connell and Wood 2005), between departure and destination social terrains that, while geographically and contextually diverse, share subordinations. The localization and (re)configuration of gang culture is a complex process that leads to the generation of locally—even hyperlocally reduced to a few neighborhoods—constructed variants of hegemonic masculinity. Gangs in Belize City are at once fluid and culturally syncretistic yet show unmistakable masculine continuity in terms of violent practices; in short, the vast majority of physical violence is committed by men. Gangs are ontologically imposing, shaping the very meanings of masculinity locally, and have done much to compound a street-level gender hierarchy that sells an achievable performance of power to an otherwise vulnerable community, including gang members themselves, whose deaths in service of that performance bolster homicide statistics. Young men on Southside are victims of structural constraint which makes them susceptible to the lure of gang life, a type of context-specific masculine vulnerability. This is a gendered process that sustains gangs and perpetuates victimization within the community. Tensions and blurred boundaries where victims can also be perpetrators are familiar to researchers of violent, always complex, communities (Baird 2018a; Dixit 2012; Theidon 2014) and bring to mind Jean-Paul Sartre's line from *Le Mains Sal* (1948, p. 34), we are "half victim and half accomplice, like everyone else."

Although academic literature connecting street gangs to masculinity has existed since the early twentieth century (for a superb review of the literature, see Hughes and Broidy 2024), masculinities are still relatively undervalued considering the extensive attention given to gang research more broadly, or, indeed, the bottomless well of literature on urban violence as a topic. This is somewhat surprising because street gangs share a consistent poor young urban male demographic. This does not discount female gang membership or girl gangs. In the 1980s, in the United States, Quicker (1983) conducted an in-depth study of Chicana homegirls and A. Campbell (1984) found that some 10 percent of gang members in New York City were women or girls. More recently, Mendoza-Denton's (2008) ethnography uncovered "macha" women "ready to fight" among Latina gangs in California, and Brotherton's (2015) critical appraisal of the literature on youth street gangs has shown further evidence of adult women gang leaders. Although female leadership of gangs with men in them is rare, girls and women within communities consistently relate in myriad ways with male gangs, which is normally overlooked in the literature. Previously, I have found that girls' and women's agency can be complicit in, or sanctioning of, gang practices including male violence

(Baird 2015a). However, women seldom become "one of the guys" (Panfil 2021) and participation tends to expose them to sexual violence (Aguilar Umaña and Rikkers 2012; Miller and Brunson 2000). The male composition of gangs has been observed consistently in several comprehensive reviews that span the globe (Decker and Pyrooz 2015b; Fraser 2017; Hanzen and Rodgers 2015; Peterson 2018), yet maleness is an assumed, rather than a contemplated characteristic, across much of this research.

Nevertheless, as I wrote about recently (Baird, Bishop, and Kerrigan 2022), men under socioeconomic stress have been presented as drivers of gang activity since Adler's conceptualization of protest masculinity in 1920s Chicago (Adler 1928), later, in the 1950s and 1960s, as pushback against structural constraint (Bloch and Niederhoffer 1958; Cloward and Ohlin, 1960). In the 1990s, Messerschmidt (1993, 1997) considered the relationship between masculinities and crime as structured action. These approaches are indicative of critical theory (broadly understood), where gangs are symptomatic of structural asymmetry, a male class rebellion, or even as revolutionaries (Baird and Rodgers 2015)—although, as noted by Connell (2005b), such rebellions are, more often than not, ultimately self-destructive. Over the years, in literature mainly emanating from the United States (for expansive recent collections see Brotherton and Gude 2021, and Pyrooz, Densley and Leverso 2024), gangs have been perceived as structure-like institutions (Hagedorn 2008) and socialization spaces that confer symbolic, social, and material capital on young men struggling for esteem (Fraser 2017; Mullins 2006; Mullins and Lee 2019; Shammas and Sandberg 2016). Consequently, we have progressed from presenting gangs simplistically as surrogate families by developing nuanced analyses of their function as sites of social cohesion amid chronic violence (Cruz 2014). These struggles were famously depicted by Philippe Bourgois in his East Harlem gang study *In Search of Respect* (1995). Gangs have come to be understood as bonding spaces of homosocial enactment, normatively governed by a robust collection of practices and even written rules (Anderson 2000; Bourgois 2001; Brotherton 2015), which often require ambition, intelligence, and dexterous management, as Sudhir Venkatesh vividly depicted when he became *Gang Leader for a Day* in Chicago (2008).

While no single condition determines gang emergence, marginalized urban contexts are a consistent feature. Recent data show that gangs in the urban margins drive violence across Latin America and the Caribbean, where fourteen of the twenty most homicidal countries in the world are found. Here, just 8 percent of the global population accounts for 28 percent of global murders (Igarape Institute 2024). Gary Barker (2005) wrote *Dying to Be Men*, explaining that exclusion made the gang an attractive pathway to manhood in Rio de Janeiro's *favelas*. Similarly, Veronica Zubillaga (2009) found *malandro* gang members in Caracas were also aiming to gain "respect," drawing inspiration from Bourgois. Since Adler's notion of protest masculinity, the gang has been conceptualized variously as a resistant, rebellious, or compensatory reaction to contextual threats of emasculation across the Global South, for example by Heinonen (2011) in Ethiopia or Dziewanski (2020) and Jensen (2008) in South Africa. Fundamentally, gang practices have come to be seen as indivisible from processes of socialization (Rodgers 2017) in a structure-agency dialectic where disenfranchised young men seek opportunities through the symbolic and material "masculine capitals" provided by gang life in contexts of stymied socioeconomic possibility (Baird 2018a).

This is not to deny individual agency and responsibility for violence or to reduce gang membership to victimhood or masculinities "in peril" discussed by de la Tierra (2016). Studies of gangs and masculinities have benefited from a rich vein of research that has teased out the complexities of gender in Latin America in recent years, for example, Gutmann's (1996) work in Mexico City, Viveros Vigoya (2001, 2002, 2018) and Theidon (2007) in Colombia, or Hume (2004) and Hume and Wilding (2015, 2019) in Central America and Brazil. Contemporary research has moved away from masculinist readings that essentialize male gang violence, incorporating instead multiple masculinities and relational roles with women and other members of the community. Women can advocate and participate in gang life, but this agency remains under researched, even in much gender-sensitive analysis, reflecting wider problems of denying women agency in the production—whether direct or indirect—of violence (Sjoberg and Gentry 2007). Nonetheless, conventionally, women are subordinated within the explicit and visible gang gender hierarchy and excluded from leadership positions and activities requiring the use of direct violence, which are the reserved domain of men. Not only does this have real material consequences, but women are also sexualized and victimized in ways that male gang members are not. In an exceptional and telling case, I was once told of a legendary female gang member in Medellín, Colombia, who was required to become "more *macho*" than her male counterparts to secure leadership status (Baird 2011).

One-dimensional notions of exaggerated, violent, or toxic masculinities have, therefore, been discarded for more nuanced appraisals, where gang practices are setting specific. Moncrieff Zabaleta and García Ponce de León (2018) highlight multiple male "masks" in a recent Mexican study; some are associated with individual gang performances in certain moments and places, reflecting the hypervisible gang displays I have observed at gang street parties in Colombia (Baird 2015a). Away from the gang space, behaviors can change dramatically. Violent men have been shown to be loving sons, husbands, or fathers (e.g., Fontes 2018), a phenomenon that has also been observed among combatants in conflict settings (Mäki-Rahkola and Myrttinen 2014). Gang violence is not, then, a fixed male trait: It is functional and deployed by participants to control illegal street markets or in timely demonstrations of "badness" and the "warrior-like persona" (Baird 2018a; Levenson 2013, p. 97). This has been uncovered primarily by ethnographic studies in the region where violence is understood as a situationally dependent element of a larger repertoire of gang performance. The "gang project" serves as a conduit for masculine power, status, and capital that orders the competitive internal gender hierarchy of the gang as well as that of the broader community, as I observed in my earlier trips to Southside as a "patriarchy of the streets" (Baird 2021a).

The gendered ordering process within the gang highlights the importance of the concept of hegemonic masculinity. This notion was originally developed by Raewyn Connell (2005a, 1995) as an aspirational and actual form of masculinity and concomitant practices that legitimate men's dominant position in a gender hierarchy, locating *real* men at the top by subordinating women, femininities, and nonhegemonic versions of masculinity. Although this process is traditionally understood to be ideologically driven through public spaces and social institutions, Connell and Messerschmidt's (2005) "rethinking" of hegemonic masculinity absorbs the critique of trait models and rigid typologies where the concept does not equate to a model of social reproduction, allowing for multiple hegemonic masculinities across global, regional, and local scales, while maintaining the underlying principle: the legitimation of unequal gender relations (Messerschmidt 2018, p. 48). This is exemplified in Connell's (2016) discussion that cites numerous studies—many from the Global South—to demonstrate the range of hegemonic projects and capacity for transhistorical change from colonial and postcolonial through to neoliberalization, highlighting that the key concept is now "hegemony under construction, renovation and contestation." Indeed, further rethinking of hegemonic masculinity by Connell and Messerschmidt (2005) informs the understanding of Blood and Crip gang transnationalism in this book as a form of *transnational masculinity* and underpins the analysis of comparative male vulnerability between South Central Los Angeles and Southside Belize City. This supports the arguments that chronic vulnerability creates the conditions for transitions to extreme social violence and that these processes are profoundly gendered.

In recent years, hegemonic masculinities have become bewilderingly nuanced, so we ought to be mindful of how thinly the concept is stretched. Hegemonies now include elastic, hybrid, and fleeting variants to underscore their fluid and contingent nature (Bridges and Pascoe 2018; Messerschmidt 2018). These have been used in gender interventions in South Africa (Jewkes et al. 2015; Morrell et al. 2013), to compare civil war masculinities in Sierra Leone and Sudan (Duriesmith 2016), and to examine the continuation of preexisting patriarchal logics in conflict settings (Myrttinen, Khattab, and

Naujoks 2017). However, the specific relationship between hegemonic masculinities and gangs has rarely been explored. Hagedorn (1998) identified four enactments of hegemonic masculinity in gangs in the United States: the Frat Boy, Bossman, Stud, and Gentleman. In a study of young African American men, Cobbina, Like-Haislip, and Miller (2010) found violence, respect, autonomy, and reputation indicative of the centrality of hegemonic masculinities on the streets. Similarly, an insightful study by Cooper (2009) in Cape Town described hybridized gangland masculinities that combine what it means to be a *real* man with local language, practices, and rituals based on "outlaw masculinities," when corporate or executive hegemonic masculinities are out of reach for the urban poor.

There exists much good critical work, often juxtaposed with the dominant mainstream criminological tendency, on drug trafficking, gang-related murders, and community violence throughout the Caribbean (e.g., Arias 2017; Deosaran 2017; Evans and Jaffe 2020; Jaffe 2019). There is also a substantial degree of research on multiple masculinities (and femininities), usually addressing either the historical legacies of slavery (Beckles 2003) or modern issues like sexuality, familial relations, race and ethnicity, access to public services, and sexual and gender-based violence (see, inter alia, Anderson 2012; Hosein and Parpart 2016; Reddock 2003; Sukhu 2012; Thompson 2019). However, there is much less work that brings these two concerns together by deploying an explicit masculinities framework to explain the distinctive patterns of gang-related violence in the Caribbean, beyond my work with Bishop and Kerrigan (Baird, Bishop, and Kerrigan 2022, 2023). Partial exceptions include Gayle (2009), Gayle and Mortis (2010), Gayle, Hampton, and Mortis (2016), and James and Davis (2014).

Chronic Violence

What is the connection between masculinity and continual—ergo *chronic*—violence? The race and rebellious cultural dynamics of imported Blood and Crip identities appealed to poor young Creole Belizeans as a site of opportunity, elevated gender status, and aspirational manhood. This was a model of masculinity that was "adopted, renovated, reworked and reimagined" (see Messerschmidt 2018) through the prism of local culture, being creolized by young men (on "kriolization" see Hall 2015). Evolving gang identities and the fragmentation of Blood and Crip structures in the late 1990s led to unique posttransnational gang identities. While these identities are constantly shifting, violence continues to be anchored at the intersection of class, age, race, and gender, among poor young Black and Brown men. *Violence is held constant by the competitive masculine practices of gang members.* Although Generals, gangstas, or *shottas* proved to be syncretistic identities, morphing over time as they absorbed the local cultural soup, their activities maintain their elevated status as hegemonic males. That is, the community recognizes and legitimates their identities and practices to the extent that gangstas and shottas continue atop the local gender hierarchy. Consequently, gangs continue to be perceived in aspirational terms by many up-and-coming boys and young men on Southside. This reverence is key to supplying new recruits; the gang in perpetual motion.

We should be mindful not to reduce gangs to a rigid violent male identity, recognizing that individual and collective practices are multifaceted and that masculinities are, indeed, multiple and often contradictory. This analysis draws on sociological thinking to argue that the gang displays—the gang persona and gangsta culture—established by the Bloods and Crips in Belize have a concerted, locally connected, situational, and profoundly relational hegemonic masculinity that has galvanized violence and a patriarchy of the streets. Despite the culturally syncretistic and rapid creolization and fragmentation of street gangs on Southside in recent years, the male violence inherent in gang practices persists as an expression of local hegemonic masculinity. Given that the vast majority of gang interventions are masculinities blind, understanding gang activities as a form of localized hegemonic practice is a way to rethink and reinvigorate our approach to interventions to reduce harm done to urban communities.

Book Structure

The book is organized into six chapters. Chapter 1, "Establishment: From South Central to Southside," charts the arrival of deportee Bloods and Crips to Belize City and the genesis of gang culture, arguing that gang transnationalism can be understood as a form of transnational masculinity that embeds in contexts of social vulnerability. Chapter 2, "Response: The Janus Face of the State," looks at political and state reactions to gangs in Belize City, from clientelism to crackdowns and negotiations, a contradictory melee of responses that ultimately failed. Chapter 3, "Escalation: Disorganized Violence and the Homicide Boom," counters facile assumptions that drug transshipment through Belize is behind the rise in gang violence. Rather, gang fragmentation and the *disorganization* of violence has driven up homicide rates in recent years. Chapter 4, "Adaptation: The Syncretistic Gang," focuses on the culturally syncretistic creolization process that has given rise to what has been dubbed the "posttransnational gang." While gangs are fluid and rapidly evolving groups, violence is constant. As Blood and Crip identities slipped into history, violent gang practices continue through the street-level hegemonic masculinities that those gangs first established. This chapter explores beyond masculine vulnerability, considering feminine vulnerability and gang relations on

Southside, a gender disaggregated analysis with the potential to inform future gang interventions. Chapter 5, "Interventions: The Challenges Ahead," considers the obstacles faced by contemporary gang responses. Such obstacles include "downfallness," the powerlessness of a Southside population unable to hold government and institutions to account, the negative impact of a partial rule of law applied to the poor—but not the rich—and how gang interventions have been hampered despite multiple violence reduction recommendations from multilateral institutions, academics, and others over the years. Finally, the Conclusion, "Reconfiguration," summarizes the book's key findings. Belize does not need *yet another* list of recommendations to reduce gang violence; a theory of change is put forward arguing for a focus on chronic vulnerability reduction that considers gender-based requirements.

And what of the gang intervention pitched to the U.S. Embassy in 2011? It won US$220,000 funding and the Southside Youth Success Project (SYSP) sprang to life, a masculinities-focused gang violence reduction initiative sparking the research journey that ultimately led to this book.

1

Establishment

From South Central to Southside

This chapter charts a path from South Central to Southside explaining the genesis of gangs in Belize as a consequence of gang transnationalism. There is a small yet established literature on gang transnationalism, sometimes called the gang-deportation model, predominantly from Los Angeles, that led to the emergence of the Mara Salvatrucha (MS-13) and the 18th Street gangs, collectively termed "maras," in Central America. Far less is written about Blood and Crip transnational dynamics, and next to nothing is written about their arrival in Belize. It is revealing to make the comparison between these experiences, and it surprises many that the Bloods and Crips appeared in Belize as far back as the early 1980s. Angel, a founding Crip leader, was deported back to Belize in 1981, several years before the maras made their mark in the region. Looking at these two experiences, it is immediately evident that gang transnationalism is intersectionally oriented; it follows race, class, age, and gender and is culturally and linguistically aligned. While most young male migrants from Belize to the United States *did not* join gangs, intuitively, those that did would have been Black and Brown English speakers who would gravitate toward the African American–dominated Bloods and Crips; in this same way, some young Latino male migrants gravitated toward the maras. In terms of popular rap culture in the late 1980s and early 1990s Los Angeles, we might think of African American N.W.A. versus Latino Cypress Hill. Gang membership tended to be separated along cultural and ethnic lines among both national and diaspora migrant populations, and more detailed examinations of Spanish-speaking gangs in California have identified Mexican, Chicano, Salvadorean, and other subdivisions (Martínez D'Aubuisson and Martínez D'Aubuisson 2018). Jailed, then deported, these gang members created the spark for contemporary gangs across Central America.

The emergence of transnational gangs has rightly been flagged by scholars as a subcultural phenomenon. This chapter adds the intersectional approach mentioned earlier, lending texture and depth to these analyses. Race tends to be an assumed rather than scrutinized dynamic in the literature on maras, and gender analyses are remarkable by their absence. These assumptions and absences are noteworthy. Although gang cultures can span international borders, thousands of miles apart, they are connected by class, age, gender, and race and composed of poor young men, often with shared ethnicity. Gang transnationalism can also be understood as a form of "transnational masculinity," a gendered type of cultural transfer between disenfranchised young men that connects contextually diverse, yet similarly marginalized, settings of urban exclusion.

This chapter is divided into two further sections. First, "Homelands" charts the origins of gang transnationalism, not as an exhaustive review of U.S. gangs, about which much is already written, but rather as a brief summary flagging the processes that led to Belizean-national Bloods and Crips being deported, referencing parallel experiences of Latino mara gangs, both couched within a conservative political climate of zero-tolerance gang and drug policy at the time. Second, "Newlands" discusses the genesis of the Bloods and Crips in Belize City in the 1980s and how chronic vulnerability was necessary for transnational gangs to root and flourish.

Homelands

The origins of Latino gangs and later maras, lie in Los Angeles, founded by Mexican immigrants in the poor Rampart district of the city in the 1960s. These grew significantly during the late 1970s and early 1980s as a result of the influx of Central American refugees fleeing civil wars in Guatemala, Nicaragua, and El Salvador and state brutality in Honduras. This was in addition to a steady flow of what are inhumanely termed "economic migrants," flowing north from the rest of Latin America and the Caribbean. During this period, a splinter group founded by a second wave of Salvadorean refugees became known as the Mara Salvatrucha 13 (*mara*, "friend"; *Salva*, "Salvador"; *trucha*, "cunning"; *13*, "the thirteenth letter of the alphabet 'm' signifying the criminal umbrella group Mexican Mafia") brought to life in the remarkably insightful book *El Niño de Hollywood*, a life history of a Salvadorean mara assassin, *el Niño*, written by the Martínez D'Aubuisson brothers (Martínez D'Aubuisson and Martínez D'Aubuisson 2018). They brought with them brutal violence learned as combatants deploying scorched-earth and human rights eviscerating tactics during civil wars. Among them, for example, were Nicaraguan *contras* (counterrevolutionaries) and Salvadorean paramilitaries, trained by graduates from the notorious, and since renamed U.S. military establishment, the School of the Americas. Martínez D'Aubuisson and Martínez D'Aubuisson noted the irony of these individuals trained in horrifying violence coming back to haunt the U.S. streets years later, like an attack dog turning on its handler. The maras later split into two factions along territorial lines, rapidly becoming bloody rivals with the 18th Street gang. Similarly to *El Niño de Hollywood*, in *Adiós Niño*, oral historian Deborah Levenson (2013) details these experiences across the Pico-Unión neighborhood in Los Angeles, while Dennis Rodgers and I provide a summary of the literature, covering key events from migration to deportation and the establishment of the maras in Central America (2015a).

In the Belizean case, the largest push factor for mass migration was not civil war or high levels of social violence. Hannes Warnecke-Berger has indicated that Belizean murder rates between the 1940s and the 1980s sometimes peaked over fifteen per one hundred thousand population (2017, p. 247). This is not insignificant but still a world apart from the violence of neighboring countries. The daily grind of poverty and hardship has always been a centrifugal force pushing migration (Miller Matthei 1998, p. 288); however, it was an epic natural disaster in 1961 that delivered a national shock to Belize, then British Honduras, prompting a surge of the population toward the United States. As a colony and commonwealth nation, very few made their way to the United Kingdom, too far flung a country, which to this day has no sizable Belizean diaspora. That year, Hurricane Hattie flattened Belize City so completely—many buildings were only wood structures at the time—that the capital was relocated an hour's drive inland to Belmopan, then but a village. Thousands were left homeless and some three hundred were killed. The disaster prompted a significant exodus to Los Angeles and to a lesser extent Chicago, Atlanta, Miami, and New York, in addition to the historical trickle of migrants. By the year 2000, a staggering one in three of the entire population resided in the United States, proportionally more significant than other countries in Central America (Vernon 2000). This newfound diaspora stateside supplied the individuals for later deportations of Bloods and Crips back to Belize City. Here, it should be noted that deportation is one component in our wider understanding of gang transnationalism, which incorporates a complex array of drivers, many of which are (sub)cultural, meaning that gang types can appear discursively in different contexts *without* necessarily arising as a result of deportation.

Shorty—all gang member names are pseudonyms—a former mid-ranking Blood whom I interviewed twice over the years, had reached his forty-fifth birthday by 2023. He was jailed and deported from Los Angeles, not once, but twice. When gang members are deported, they often leave behind partners, spouses, and children, and returning multiple times to the United States, followed by repeat deportations, is not uncommon. This cyclical phenomenon is not widely examined in the transnational gang literature, where the narratives tend to focus on first deportation experiences and the genesis of the mara phenomenon. Shorty missed his five children in the United States badly and, despite the risks, was planning a third run to the states. I caught up with him after he had been released from Belize Central Prison, relocating to the capital Belmopan to escape the perils of his former gang life in Belize City:

> There's a Blood block [in LA which I was part of] called Rolland Curtis, where all the Belizeans was Bloods. . . . I got seven kids, five in the States and two here. [In the States] Junior is twenty-two, twenty-three, he in jail for three years. My family [children] is mad at me [for getting deported] but what the fuck can I do? I can't fight no government. . . . I don't miss nobody [in LA] but my kids. . . . I did seven years in the feds [prison] for crossing the border and six months for hitting the police. I went to Cancun, went to Juarez, from Juarez to Tijuana, and my wife was there to pick me up with a Mexican girl in the car and they crossed me over. I only stayed for six months, 2003. I went to jail 2005 for seven years from 2005 to 2011. Jus' for crossing the border. Six months for assault. They fucked me up, but I beat them, coz they was two against one. I was chasing one and took the mace from him an' I pepper-spray his bitch ass. I was big tho, I was doin push-ups, I was real big. Plus, dey was both shorter than me, they was Mexicans, and I don't like Mexicans. . . . I was high profile, I was the Prince of the Rollin' 20s. They were trying to get me. I went to jail for everything except rape. (2022)[1]

Scholarship on Blood and Crip transnationalism is scarce. Exceptions include Hagedorn (2008) and Flores (2009) in the Americas, Johns (2014) in Australia, and Fexia (2021), Grassi (2021), Roks (2017), and Roks and Densley (2019) in Europe. In the Belizean case, apart from some of my own recent work (Baird 2021b), only Miller Matthei (1998) have considered the connectedness of Belizeans to the Bloods and Crips, although their research is now dated and focused on the Belizean disapora in Los Angeles. There is an extensive literature that focuses on responses to gangs in the United States. Orozco Flores's (2013) work on Latino gangs deals with this succinctly, and the theme appears across Decker and Pyrooz's (2015b) extensive edited *Handbook of Gangs*, and Brotherton and Gude's (2021) equally sizable collaboration, the *Routledge International Handbook of Critical Gang Studies*. What is relevant here is that U.S. deportation policies were pivotal for gang emergence in Central America.

This is a good point to turn our attention briefly to the founding and rise of the Bloods and Crips in the United States, starting in Los Angeles. The Crips emerged out of a context of economic stagnation, poverty, and racial segregation in South Central toward the end of the 1960s. Founded by Stanley "Tookie" Williams and Raymond Washington, they came from altogether more innocent street clubs of young predominantly African American men, later taking on blue rags as a symbol of identification and allegiance. Across a decade, the Crips grew into a network of *sets* involved in street-level crime, particularly drug sales. However, despite this network, fighting between different sets of Crips was common. Arguably the most significant of these conflicts started in the 1970s between the Pirus (Powerful Indestructible Revengeful United) Crips from Compton and other sets in the city. The Pirus Crips sought out other disaffected sets, consolidated them, and began to call themselves *Bloods*, initially as a moniker to address each other, then to differentiate themselves from other Crips. This grew into the key gang rivalry on the streets, and in prison, where Bloods and Crips came to be incarcerated separately.

Tookie Williams was arrested in 1979, and that same year Raymond Washington was murdered. The resulting power vacuum led to substantial infighting and spiraling gun violence between Crip sets that had acquired their own names and territorial identities, such as the Rollin' 60s, East Coast, Hoover, and the Eight Tray Crips. Crack cocaine hit the streets in the 1980s increasing gang revenues at the same time as gangsta culture boomed into a popular phenomenon. This provided Blood and Crip gang identity with a discursive power, and sets started to appear across the country, even internationally (e.g., Johns 2014; Roks 2017). Cue a powerful moral panic among the wider public, fed by conservative politics, combining a new fear of young Black and Brown men in gangs with older *war on drugs* propaganda and the inherent anti-Black racism in social policies, which Johann Hari (2015), among others, traces back to the early twentieth century.

The contemporary history of responses to street crime in the United States has disproportionately criminalized minorities (Alexander 2012). The conservative policies of the 1980s during the Reagan administration shifted the focus of criminal efforts to predominantly Black, Brown, and Latino populations. Nancy Reagan's "just say no" campaign, reaching out to children and young people, was the symbolic, sympathetic face, of the war on drugs. In reality, beneath the veneer, the invigorated war on drugs was coded into harsh new laws through the Anti-Drug Abuse Act. This act heavily penalized the possession of five grams of crack cocaine, a drug more common among Blacks and Browns, with a five-year jail sentence. Conversely cocaine, a more expensive, white middle-class narcotic—think *Wolf of Wall Street*—required an astonishing 500 grams for the same sentence (Orozco Flores 2013, p. 46). The racial discrimination of U.S. drug laws predates this, with strict penalizations of cannabis from the Nixon period that were at once antihippie, antiliberal, and antileft. Significantly, newer policies disproportionately criminalized poor Black and Brown men. In effect, the criminalization of drugs meant hefty criminalization of street gangs. The war on drugs was a de facto war against poor young Black and Brown urban people on the streets. It was at the heart of the white right-wing political project, a clear response to the nation's manufactured moral panic.

In a more contemporary example of this, in the 1990s, Rudolph Giuliani doubled down on the zero-tolerance approach during his *Fixing Broken Windows* campaign and election as New York mayor, leading to a sharp spike in incarceration rates of minority populations. The "cleaning up" of Manhattan may have been popular at the time—and, indeed, after his mayorship, Giuliani has sold his package of policies as a consultant at exorbitant prices across the globe—but the "solution" hinged upon jailing a generation of Black and Brown men, with substantial long-term consequences. Recent projections demonstrate that one-in-six Latinos, and a scarcely believable one-in-three Black and Brown males, will be imprisoned during their lives, compared to one-in-seventeen white males. These onerous figures reflect Wacquant's (1999) work on prison populations in the United States and, more recently, Alexander's (2012) outstanding contribution *The New Jim Crow* on color and mass incarceration. The description laid out in these passages here is an abridged presentation of the embedded racism of criminalization and incarceration in the United States, but it is not glib. Discursive and judicial power radically increased the scrutiny with which Black, Brown, and Latino gangs were tackled countrywide. Many whom were not nationals, such as Belizeans, were subsequently deported.

The "war on gangs" involved a series of newly created legal injunctions—a Gang Enhancement Law in the 1980s, then the notorious Clinton-backed "three-strikes" dictate in the 1990s, which handed mandatory life sentences to offenders after three crimes. If one crime was violent, it was irrelevant how trivial the other two were. These were followed up with sweeping and indiscriminate roundups on the streets, for example, in Los Angeles, *Operation Hammer* in South Central and across the Latino Rampart district. Community-police conflicts, Rodney King and the Los Angeles riots were to follow, brutalism that continues to reverberate across law enforcement structures, pertinently in the contemporary #Blacklivesmatter campaign, and at the time of writing in January 2023, with the murder of Tyre Nichols in Memphis at the hands of the police. Zero-tolerance and "wars on . . ." drugs, gangs, et cetera, was a powerful discourse, contributing to the legitimation of even harsher variants emerging in Central America soon after, most infamously known as mano dura crackdowns on gangs. Most notably, since 2022 in El Salvador over seventy thousand young men (and counting) have been put in jail, many without due process under a never-ending State of Emergency (discussed in more detail in Chapter 2). If the reader wants an example of the polar opposite to a "chronic vulnerability" based approach, this is it.

The mass incarceration in the United States that followed included substantial Central American migrant populations, soon to be deported back to countries institutionally ill-equipped to deal with a tide of gang members. Although a number of Creole and, to a lesser extent, Garifuna (Afro-Indigenous) migrants from Belize joined the Bloods and Crips, the rise of the maras in Los Angeles is contextually significant because it prompted the deportation policies that swept up Belizean gang members who may have otherwise flown under the radar. Deportations did occur in the 1980s, but these were few and far between, and there are no reliable figures for those sent back to Belize in this period. In the 1990s, the U.S. Congress passed the Illegal Immigration Reform and Immigrant Responsibility Act, whereby non–U.S. citizens sentenced to one year or more in prison were to be repatriated to their countries of origin. For example, in October 1997, twenty-seven Belizean members of the Rolling Crips and the Rolling 30s sets were deported, a period coinciding with the Bloods and Crips reaching the zenith of their powers in Belize City (Reynolds 2011).

Over the next decade, almost fifty thousand convicts were deported to Central America along with one hundred sixty thousand illegal immigrants caught without the requisite papers (Cruz 2014; UNODC 2007, pp. 40–42; Zilberg 2011). El Salvador and Guatemala were—and arguably still are—contending with legacies of postwar violence, forming the vulnerable social terrains that deported gang members inserted themselves into. Southside was also vulnerable, shaped not by postwar legacies but by colonialism, slavery, and ongoing socioeconomic and political exclusions. Notably, these countries already had precursor or proto–street gangs, the homegrown *pandillas*, that have been a historic feature of Central American societies before more organized gangs developed. *Pandillas* have been almost completely supplanted by maras in El Salvador, Honduras, and Guatemala. Similarly, in Belize City, Base Boys, which we come to later in this chapter, were superseded by the incoming Bloods and Crips.

Over a decade, between 1992 and 2002, some 1,122 individuals were sent back to Belize, the majority to the city (Warnecke-Berger 2019). Although this may sound like a small number, in terms of Belize City's population at the time, approximately forty thousand, it was significant. These were new lands for the Bloods and Crips.

Newlands

Warnecke-Berger (2017) wrote that "even though researchers have pointed to gang migration as a possible explanation for the evolution of Bloods and Crips in Belize, empirical evidence is not available and it is still unclear if leading gang members in Belize had a live history in American gangs" (p. 213). In addition to Shorty's earlier narrative, let us add some empirical detail from Angel.

With poetic timing, Angel was deported in 1981, the very year of Belizean independence, for his part in a drive-by shooting in Los Angeles. As a juvenile at the time, just seventeen years old, he was not imprisoned but rather flown straight back to Belize, where he expected to receive a sentence of some kind. "I was taken to di plane in da US, den [when I landed in Belize] *notin' happen!* [his emphasis] I jus' walk off di plane. I cum home to my aunty here in Belize City, in Majestic Alley" (2016). Institutionally, Belize was a veritable newborn and did not have the wherewithal to handle the gang influx. Angel went on to play an instrumental role in the transition of Base Boys into hardened gangstas as cofounder of the Majestic Alley Crips. Although this process began in earnest in the early 1980s, within a handful of years it had gathered momentum, and, by the end of the decade, the Crips had become firmly established as a pillar of the city's booming gang culture.

Transnational gangs tend to emerge as social forms of street-level youth groups in contexts of persistent exclusion, often stimulated by deportees but not representing some transnational organized criminal network or franchise (Rodgers and Baird 2015). The relationship between gang transnationalism and their destinations would benefit from additional conceptualization. Host terrains are not blank slates but complex settlements where historically rooted socioeconomic precarity and contextual specificities shape the inception and development of transnational gang culture. Gangs do not simply arise in whichever place deportees happen to be sent back to, rather, they require the vulnerable "social terrains" mentioned earlier to facilitate their emergence. How can the Belizean experience help us understand this process?

The cultural impact of the United States on Belize cannot be overstated. With one-in-three Belizeans in the United States sending remittances and goods parcels back, the influence is noticeable in everyday life, from clothing to kitchen appliances, and the supermarket shelves at Brodies in Belize City are dominated by U.S. brands. By comparison, colonial presence has faded into history, although there is a permanent British army base in Belize, and I have occasionally bumped into officers in fatigues around town, this is mainly for jungle training purposes and only becomes relevant on the rare occasion that border tensions flare with Guatemala and a British Navy ship deploys to the coast. Queen Elizabeth II's youthful portrait on the banknotes feels anachronistic, and that the denomination is Belizean dollars not pounds feels significant, not least because U.S. dollars can also be used freely as a parallel currency. As a visitor to Belize, one notices ubiquitous cultural cues from the United States. This made me wonder whether Belize, and specifically Southside, was in some way "culturally vulnerable" to transnational gangs emanating from the United States? The answer is, unsurprisingly, yes and no.

To pose an initial caveat: We ought to be cautious about using the notion of "cultural vulnerability" as a catchall explanation for gang transfer, but it can provide insight. As a macrophenomenon it has been outlined and problematized by Tomlinson (2003, p. 269) who said:

> Cultures in the West, specifically the United States, saw a standardized version of their cultures exported worldwide to the "weaker" cultures of the developing world that have been most threatened. Thus, the economic vulnerability of these non-western cultures is assumed to be matched by a cultural vulnerability.

Certainly, the modern identity of Belize has been profoundly molded by the external influences of migration and the "coloniality of power and Eurocentrism," where social classification was based on the idea of race (Quijano 2000). Given the population size of the country, even small movements of people can be seismic. Empirically, this sense of cultural vulnerability as a product of colonial conquest was palpable when discussing national history with Belizean academics. One lamented effusively, "Colonial history means we have been taught to embrace and value the foreign more than our own history. Everything that is great is fucking foreign. Even Jesus is foreign" (2017). Another said, "There is an inherent sense of shame about Belizean culture and history" (2017). They argued that this is compounded among the disaffected young urban poor, reflecting the local saying "boay, notin' no de goawn fi Blackman da Belize" (Black men have no options in Belize), which leads them to "embrace that [U.S.] ghetto culture because Creole culture is not held sacred. Young gang members have no recollection of history" (2017). Enter the Bloods and Crips.

Blue and red *colors* "discursively appeared" on Southside (Warnecke-Berger 2017, p. 256). In 2017, one elder Southsider said, "We were trying to imitate what we saw at the street level. To get their money, have parties, bring all the money out, all the girls out . . . it would imitate those aspects of the culture, because it was what was in front of us." Belizean scholar Nuri Muhammad wrote about the Los Angeles gangsta prototype becoming a powerful cultural signifier on Belizean streets. It is worth highlighting that few people in Belize had television sets prior to the 1980s, so the rise of television that decade enhanced the reach of the gangsta ideal. *Colors*, the LA-based Blood and Crip movie directed by Dennis Hopper in 1988, was the go-to cultural reference raised by locals when looking back at that period:

> Where did this "thing" come from? Was it foreign in origin as some say, or was it homegrown? It is difficult for some to understand that it was both foreign and local in origin at the same time. It was foreign in the sense that the media images of the gangster in the 1980s and 1990s were the Black youth of Los Angeles, New York, or Jamaica; his gait, his stance, his mannerism, and language formed a prototype that was made a global iconic figure through movies like *Colors* and *Menace 2 Society*, music videos and the recording industry. However, whilst these images were foreign in style, there were socio-economic and historical conditions for our own crop of gang activity. When we examine the gang phenomenon in Belize today, we see more than the imitation of a foreign culture, rather we see the creation of a sector of hardcore criminals with their own set of values and definitions of what society is about and what means they will use to survive in a social environment they view as increasingly hostile and unfair. These are youths who were drawn into a powerful network of quick money and corruption in high places, and it shattered their innocence of a civil and patriotic Belize. They lost hope and as a result became rebellious to the status quo. (Muhammad 2015, pp. 16–17)

Here we note a combination of elements at the genesis of gangs in Belize City; deportations acted as a spark, where cultural influences osmotically flowed from a relatively powerful South Central to a relatively powerless Southside.

However, this was not simple imitation. Muhammad (2015) refers to the combination of foreign with local, creating something new, something Belizean. This connects to the theorization by Espange (1999, 2001) and Greenblatt (2009) who have argued that, while some cultures are more hegemonic than others, they do not actually obliterate each other, rather, forms of "cultural transfer" occur where they morph and change in complex ways. Belizean Bloods and Crips were inevitably hybrid identities from the get-go, their appearance on the streets of Belize City in the 1980s a form of cultural transfer to vulnerable settings. But why *young men* in these settings?

Lending a gender perspective to the notions of cultural vulnerability and transfer, socioeconomic exclusion of the social terrain on Southside made young men susceptible to gang culture, a type of masculine vulnerability.

In a similar vein, Palillo (2020) also raised the idea of relatively powerless migrant men from sub-Saharan Africa pressed to prove their "value" by agreeing to dangerous smuggling practices, leading to a specific gendered vulnerability among these men. The notion of masculine vulnerability *does not aim to justify consequent acts of gang violence*, rather this helps cast light on why transnational gangs did not arise in wealthier Northside neighborhoods or have significant female membership, by pointing to the critical intervening role that chronically vulnerable social terrains and gender play in where and how gang transnationalism becomes established. It is an idea we come back to in Chapter 4 when discussing "gendered vulnerability" more broadly.

Masculine vulnerability stimulates agency to join gangs. Noted by Muhammad (2015) earlier, "his gait, his stance, his mannerism" underscores the "maleness" of the attractiveness of transnational gang culture. It is, then, a form of Connell and Wood's "transnational" masculinity (2005) making cultural connections between local settings of urban exclusion that may be continents apart. As I noted in my field diary at the time, *South Central* and *Southside* seemed to be, in many ways, parallel universes. On Southside, there was abundant masculine vulnerability to the foreign gang as an "identity package" with the power to radically reconfigure positions of subordination, trampled esteem, and feelings of emasculation. This was brought home to me vividly one evening as I walked through Southside with a youth worker friend of mine. I asked him why he thought young people joined gangs, and he blurted a reply in frustration, "Because dere ain't nutin' for yout' to do round here, jus smoke, drink an' fuck" (2016).

To suggest that there is a masculine vulnerability to joining gangs shared across global settings of socioeconomic exclusion may feel intuitive, but it is a significant conceptual claim. It means that social conditions lead to geographically independent, yet intersectionally connected, cohorts of gangs, bringing to mind the emotive title of John Hagedorn's book *A Word of Gangs* (2008). As a form of "transnational masculinity" linking similarly excluded young male populations along ethnic lines, Blood and Crip culture spread in a chronically vulnerable, gang fertile environment on Southside. The aforementioned "global iconic figure" of the disenfranchised young Black male gangsta striking back at structural violence was a compelling symbol in a postcolonial Belize disposed to revere the foreign.

Early deportees were said to be self-promotional. We cannot say that it was a one-way case of vulnerable youths using their agency to latch on to new and glittering gang identities; it was a more complex two-way process. Deportee Bloods and Crips gained influence by acquiring and handing out *colors* to young men and ingratiating them. Carlos, an eclectic former gang member, then prison officer, now youth worker, explained:

CARLOS: So [in the 1980s] Belizeans now have dese American [Blood and Crip] guys here who are deported, saying dis is how we have to dress. Dey would bring back a couple of barrels of clothes, and den share dat wid de guys.
AUTHOR: So, they were building, like, a cultural identity?
CARLOS: Exactly! Y'undersand? Den when clothing come in it would be basically for dat specific gang. At da time you wud wear di khaki pants and da white t-shirt, wid your red rag, den you wud be a Blood. Or red pants, red shirt, red bandana. And di Crip wud have di blue rag. Dis ting was comin' from America, y'undersand? Because we did not have da finance to purchase dem.

So, di gang leader would distribute [clothes] and he would be seen as good. "Hey! He's looking out for us!" So dat is his defense now, he is giving dem money, clothes, he protects dem, he gives dem weapons, as a form of defense. So, people [young men] start to pledge allegiance to dese guys. (2016)

While the Bloods and Crips appeared as a ghetto-to-ghetto form of cultural transfer, and without the deportee phenomenon they may well have appeared anyway, clearly gang members arriving from the United States played a galvanizing role promoting symbols of semiotic importance for emerging identities on Southside. They also transposed an oppositional and relationally constructed Bloods versus Crips conflict, one common to ganglands, mirrored over an ethnic divide, between 18th Street and Mara Salvatrucha confrontations in both the United States and Central America. It is unsurprising that two competing red and blue factions developed in Belize City in the 1980s: the George Street Bloods and the Majestic Alley Crips.

Marijuana has been smoked in Belize for generations. Long before the Bloods and Crips came to town Base Boys sold it on the streets. While they were described by some of the elder locals with historical memory as hustlers, they were not known for violence (also noted by Warnecke-Berger 2019, pp. 210–211), and no one remembered them having guns prior to independence in 1981. This absence of guns in the early days of gangs is a key point of differentiation with weapons saturated gangs in Los Angeles or the postconflict settings in neighboring Northern Triangle countries. Swing bridge over the creek also marked a territorial faultline between old Base Boy rivals, which later came to separate the Majestic Alley Crips to the north from the George Street Bloods to the south. Angel recalled the changing of the guard:

Firs we were selling weed . . . I started selling and jus doin hustling, whateva, jus to mek a buck. Dere weren't gangs den, jus guys who hang out and try to hustle. Dere weren't really any guns, we used to chase our enemies wid a stick and machete. Den we started ta walk round in blue rags, blue clothes, y'know.

My friend he started acting real gangsta da way America does it, y'know. He's da one dat decide dat Majestic Alley wud be Blue, and anyting over swing-bridge [George Street] dat's Red. (2016)

Early Blood and Crip identities quickly subsumed Base Boys. Juxtaposed against the desperate circumstances on Southside, this flashy new U.S. street culture appealed to a widening circle of young men. Aspiring gang leaders would build influence, handing out money, designating weapons. These were to protect them from blue or red rivals that, ironically, they themselves had constructed on the streets. The most successful of these aspiring leaders came to be known as "Generals," such as George "Junie Balls" McKenzie from Majestic Alley (Muhammad 2015, p. 169). Within a generation, Generals became iconic figures, and the Bloods and Crips, *the* influential model of masculine prowess for youngsters across Southside.

Conclusions

Beyond straightforward deportation-model explanations of gang transnationalism, intersectional analysis highlights the centrality of race and ethnicity, gender, language, age, and class as crucial characteristics in this process. Gang transnationalism is "successful," for want of a better word, because these characteristics are shared across international borders. *Gang transnationalism connects geographically distanced contexts with shared dynamics of chronic vulnerability.* That in itself is significant, particularly when seeking to understand how fragility leads to conflict in diverse settings. While not claiming to be a perfect model, and without excluding the chaos of happenstance, the social terrains into which gangs relocate as a transnational phenomenon are rather predictable, that is, the poor Southsides of this world, not the wealthier Northsides. The social terrain defines where gang transnationalism arises.

This process is profoundly gendered. We might rephrase the earlier italic statement as: *gang transnationalism connects geographically distanced contexts of masculine vulnerability.* A palpable susceptibility exists among young men on Southside to the lure of shiny new U.S. gang identities. Gang transnationalism is a form of class-based "transnational masculinity" that makes logical connections between men in comparable settings of exclusion: the parallel, albeit imperfectly, universes of South Central and Southside. Historic marginality meant that the foreign gang would have appealed to many as a "golden ticket" to reconfigure subordination. If not, at least it was a way out of boredom, to be part of something, to get a little cash, new clothes, a new style. That would have been very compelling in a postindependence Belize with a tendency to venerate U.S. culture.

The Bloods and Crips created a defined, tangible, and ontologically dominant culture of manhood on the streets. They became revered street-level institutions, a legitimating framework for an aspirational yet accessible form of masculinity, at a time when an impoverished young nation was finding its feet.

The next chapter considers the state reactions to the rise of gangs. To do so, it outlines a brief political history of Southside to explain how patronage and clientelism came to foster their development. Further, it considers disparate state responses, from mano dura crackdowns led by GSU, to the "Bird's Isle" gang negotiations in 1991. In all, this contradictory mélange of reactions led to the breakup of Blood and Crip leadership structures and gang multiplication, ultimately contributing to a dramatic increase in gang violence between 1999 and 2000.

2

Response

The Janus Face of the State

This chapter considers state and government reactions to gangs as they emerged on Southside in the 1980s. It is argued that the postindependence political inability to reduce the socioeconomic malaise of the social terrain fostered the conditions for the homicide boom coming over the horizon. On one hand, political parties instrumentalized gangs to implement nefarious clientelist practices, to buy and coerce votes at election time. This still goes on today, and, perversely, is highly effective, having locked the UDP into Southside constituencies over the past four decades. Although clientelism took place before the rise of gangs, their inclusion set in place the blueprint for a Belizean-style garrison politics. This continues to disenfranchise the most vulnerable Belizeans of meaningful political support and social change to this day. As one member of the international community working in Belmopan said, "The social contract is totally non-existent" (2023). On the other hand, rule of law responses, primarily through the police, have fluctuated between crackdowns, imprisoning, or killing gang leaders, while the simultaneous "taxing" of marijuana-selling gang members by the police is widespread, despite recent decriminalization of personal possession. Finally, there have been numerous negotiations with gangs historically. Some of these should be commended, particularly the ahead-of-its-time Bird's Isle negotiations in the 1990s, but too often these have been piecemeal and lead to temporary respite as opposed to sustainable change. While many men have left gangs, the socioeconomic conditions that drive gang recruitment in the city create far more willing members.

This potpourri of responses, from clientelism, to crackdowns, to negotiations, have made limited progress, not least because they are contradictory. Most notably, crackdowns focused on gang leadership—severing the head of the hydra—which contributed to splintering and *disorganized violence*, discussed in greater detail in Chapter 3. This chapter is concerned with setting the scene so the reader understands the *underlying conditions* for the homicide boom to take place. The chapter first considers "the birth of a nation," pre- and postindependence, to explain why "not a fuckin' ting has changed here on Southside in twenty years. *No ting!*" This is linked to the emergence of garrison politics, where "a garrison is an empire." After describing this setting, the chapter explores contradictory gang responses and "the Janus face of the state." Finally, we come to "the first gang negotiations" at Bird's Isle, which began a trend of interlocution with gangs that continues in various guises to this day. Unfortunately, the Bird's Isle negotiations faced an insurmountable task and, ultimately, could not prevent the homicide boom to come.

The Birth of a Nation

The earliest reference to slaves in Belize dates back to 1734, and their number gradually grew until emancipation in 1838. Houseslaves, used for domestic chores and artisanal work, lived in relatively better conditions in Belize City than the fieldslaves, who faced brutal and oppressive conditions logging mahogany and logwood in the interior of the country. The division between houseslave and fieldslave is too categorical but serves as a historical marker for the class-based stratification *within* Creole populations that can still be seen today. When speaking to Belizean academics and intellectuals, these divisions came up frequently as reference points as they sought to explain contemporary Belizean society. Male fieldslaves would return from log cutting and hauling to visit family in the city, housed in barracks or rudimentary tenements south of the river in undesirable peri-urban swamplands. One former gang member told me of a grisly finding when he was carrying out electrical work at the old Hotel Mopan between Ferrell Lane and Foreshore Street near the seafront. "Hotel Mopan was a slave house. I went to do the wiring for that building and we find chains, bones. So I stop workin' when I find out" (2022). Their dark-skinned descendants still live in this area today. One gang leader goes by the alias Black Boy in explicit reference to his skin tone. As the reader may have surmised, this area is modern-day Southside.

It is entirely uncoincidental that Southside's poverty is rooted in history. Subsequent generations south of the swing bridge have been blighted by the failures of postcolonial development, and, later, neoliberalization, which include the enhanced class inequality and elitism that hinders much of the

Caribbean (Kerrigan 2019). Chronic vulnerability in this context is transhistorical. In other contexts, it may be understood within a more compressed time frame, but, to be chronic, vulnerability must persist across generations. It is vital to recognize how and when vulnerability began—slavery and the colonial behemoth—while maintaining a healthy critique of the contemporary modern politics giving continuity to Southside's problems.

Since independence in 1981, pervasive corruption across institutions and both main political parties has meant that little progress has been made to reduce poverty in many communities. What defines the post-1981 period and, more specifically, the post-1984 elections, which ushered the UDP into Southside constituencies, is the emergence of *patronage and clientelist governance practices that adapted to the streets*: an emergence indivisible from the rise of gangs; a ghetto politics; a garrison politics; a Southside politics.

Gangs and postindependence democratic politics grew up together in Belize City, making the country unique in the Caribbean. Jamaica and Trinidad and Tobago both became independent democracies in August 1962, several decades before severe gang violence emerged in either country. While this chapter levels a critique at the role of political parties and state responses to emerging gang violence in Belize City, it is hard not to feel sympathy for Belize at this critical juncture in their history. Its nascent political system was already showing signs of corruption and mismanagement, in addition to having a genuine lack of human and financial resources and the continued exploitation by foreign capital, and then, like the swell of a thousand-year storm, it was faced with the task of dealing with the absolute poverty on Southside, just as there was a deportee influx of Blood and Crip gang members from the United States, whom the country was ill-equipped to deal with.

The birth of modern Belizean politics occurred in the aftermath of the Second World War. The 1949 devaluation of the Belizean dollar by the British consolidated an economic crisis that began with the Great Depression of the 1930s and the diminishing terms of trade for logwood. More pertinently, the stark inequality in the country between the Black and Brown workers descended from slaves and the white British overseers who controlled the means of production was being used to mobilize a national political identity that would culminate in demands for independence. That the nation's economic capital was overwhelmingly in the hands of the British provided the PUP with the political capital to mobilize widespread national support, based, like labor parties the world over, on a growing trade union movement.

The PUP was founded in 1950 out of the nationalist movement as an anticolonial party while the country was still called British Honduras. Although still a colony under the governorship of the Crown, the PUP delivered constitutional reforms that led to universal suffrage and the nation's first elections in 1954. Unsurprisingly, the PUP won the elections in a landslide, in part because there was no organized opposition to speak of until the 1970s when the UDP was established.

National hero and proindependence activist George Cadle Price became the PUP's leader in 1956 and the head of government in 1961. Under a new constitution, the United Kingdom granted British Honduras self-government in 1964, establishing a Westminster model of democracy, although the British retained control of defense and foreign affairs through a colonial governor. The country entered an effective three-decade-long single-party period as the PUP dominated national politics. On June 1, 1973, the country was officially renamed Belize, an incremental step to full independence, finally reached on September 21, 1981. At that time, Bolland notes the country had an open, dependent, and highly vulnerable economy and the government had scant power to shape the nation's future (1997, p. 260). One member of the international community working in the capital Belmopan described independence as a process negotiated with colonial authority that was singularly focused on breaking away and did not establish social or strategic planning for the most vulnerable in society at the country's inception (2023). In the first national election after independence, in 1984, the PUP was defeated by the UDP, and Manuel Esquivel replaced George Cadle Price as prime minister.

What, might you ask, has this got to do with gangs in today's Belize? The short answer is that modern Belizean politics have not alleviated poverty on Southside. For a century, literature on gangs has recognized contexts of exclusion in which gangs emerge, noted variously as socially generated epiphenomena or symptoms of social ills (Scheper-Hughes and Bourgois 2004; Thrasher 1927). Although my own work with Bishop and Kerrigan (Baird, Bishop, and Kerrigan 2022) stated that exclusion alone does not necessarily cause violence, you cannot have severe gang violence without it. This is admittedly a deterministic view that will make some academics feel hesitant, yet the aim is to position chronic vulnerability as a discourse challenge by stating that violent gangs only arise when social problems are left unresolved. While Southside began with slavery, today it represents contemporary political failures. This refutes the moralizing and political finger-pointing at gangs as the de facto problem to be quelled by force; instead, in truth-to-power fashion, it points the finger back at the politicians and other power holders in society themselves. It challenges responses in the region that target gangs with repressive measures that spend little energy on tackling structural inequality, abandonment, and the unmitigated corruption that leads to failures of development for the poorest. This is *not* an argument against policing and enforcement of the rule of law, it is an argument that states gangs are a result of the continual failure of these communities by those in power.

To borrow the postapartheid refrain from Nelson Mandela, Belize is a rainbow nation, comprising numerous ethnicities, languages, and cultures. Despite this plurality, Belizean politics remain dominated by a "hierarchic Creole society" (Bolland 1997, pp. 265–266). It is one of confounding extremes, where Creoles are both part of the political and economic elite and, at the same time, the dominant ethnic group at the polar opposite end of the socioeconomic spectrum on Southside. In one conversation I had with academic Herbert Gayle, he commented that for such an ethnically mixed country, it is striking that Creole men are found simultaneously at the top and bottom of society's economic strata. Notably, the elites are made up of a range of ethnicities.

Creoles are a shrinking minority in the country. Data from the three national censuses (1991, 2000, and 2010) show a significant rise in the mestizo—Hispanic or colloquially "Spanish," which is sometimes used as a racial slur—share of the total population since independence.[1] The 2020 census was postponed due to COVID-19 and at the time of writing in 2023 had still not been conducted. Between 1980 and 2010, the Creole percentage of the population had reduced from 40 percent to 26 percent. These changes are prompted by the duality of the centripetal migration from Central America into Belize, which rose significantly during the civil wars in El Salvador and Guatemala in the 1980s and 1990s, and the centrifugal emigration from Belize of predominantly urban Creole and Garifuna populations to the United States (see also Warnecke-Berger 2019, p. 206). One national academic said that "the mass exodus was 60s and 70s, most of Southside went [to the United States]. The [child] population was raised by grandparents or extended family . . . but if you flee to the USA, at say 15, something terrible has to be happening at home" (2021).

There are some underlying tensions based on race and ethnicity in Belize. One academic suggested that the Garifuna "other" Creoles by saying "we were never slaves, not like them" (2022). There is also a Garifuna "Settlement Day" national holiday on November 19 each year, while Creoles have nothing similar. I have spoken to Creole islanders on Caye Caulker who are resentful about land and businesses being bought up by Chinese Belizeans, and to Creoles in Belize City who have criticized jobs going to migrant Central America laborers who undercut them on wages. And, if we look back to the late 1990s, there is evidence from the United Nations High Commissioner for Refugees that Central American migrants were being racially harassed and assaulted by Creole youths (Warnecke-Berger 2017, p. 222).

Nevertheless, the increasing mestizo share of the population has fueled insecurities around the "latinization" of the country, although Creoles are still heavily represented in party politics and government, where Belize City constituencies hold a disproportionate amount of parliamentary seats compared to the wider Belizean population. Fear of latinization dovetails with historical realpolitik anxieties about Guatemalan claims that parts of southern, and in some camps the whole of, Belize, must be incorporated into Guatemala following a pre-Conquista Mayan vision of the region. Indeed, present-day Guatemalan maps only include a "temporary" dotted line in the Peten region at the border with Belize. While the dispute is ongoing, bar sporadic shooting between troops over the Sarstoon River border, it is not bellicose. By 2022, both countries had submitted their briefs to the International Criminal Court with the decision pending, which is expected to take several years. Common opinion holds that the court will rule mainly in Belize's favor. Guatemala on the other hand, stands to lose nothing but their claims to Belize. Despite, these dynamics, and to Belizean's great credit, there has never been any ethnic violence to speak of, especially when compared to the recent genocide of Indigenous Mayan populations in neighboring Guatemala (Brett 2022).

While it is rare for Creoles to speak Spanish, the mestizos I know in the city all speak English and Creole, which can come as a shock for those accustomed to Spanish-speaking Central Americans. Away from the city the Mayans I encountered spoke Spanish or English, and sometimes both, in addition to their Indigenous tongues of Ketchi, Mopan, or Yucatec. While some Garifuna living in the city no longer speak Garinagu, most along the southern coast in towns such as Dangriga and Punta Gorda speak Garinagu and English. The PUP, and the UDP in particular, are parties with historical Creole leadership, although the PUP draws on a significant rural vote, while the UDP is more centered on Belize City. However, many of today's politicians, reflecting the population, have mixed heritage. It is indicative that the 2010 census asked Belizeans to identify their "two main ethnicities," both of which are counted in population statistics. The PUP prime minister himself, Johnny Briceño elected in 2020, embodies mixed Belizean heritage.

Of all the weaknesses that plague Belizean politics, recognition must be given to the way neither leading party stokes ethnic rivalry as a campaign strategy. Given the melting pot of cultures, it is testimony to Belizeans that any racial tensions that may exist very rarely become violent.

"Not a Fuckin' Ting Has Changed Here on Southside in Twenty Years. *No Ting!*"

Of course, Belize has financial, resource, and capacity problems. It may now be a middle-income country, but it faces typical Global South challenges. We should not be distracted from the fact that the political class has failed abjectly to deliver development and even basic welfare to Southside since 1981. One evening I was walking through Southside with my friend, a local youth worker, when a car crawled by and rolled down the window letting a plume of marijuana smoke waft out. I was immediately on guard, yet the man inside was friendly and offered to give us a lift. In addition to the smoke, he had a half-bottle of rum in one hand. We declined the lift politely for obvious reasons. After the car pulled away, my friend said in frustration, "Not a fuckin' ting has changed here on Southside in twenty years. *No ting!*" I asked who the driver was—he was an off-duty police officer.

Political power and, as mentioned earlier, parliamentary seats to population are concentrated on the former capital, "politics is really just here in Belize City," reflected one national academic (2021). This is a hangover from the creation of the old capital by the former British administration that located Belize Town at the mouth of the Haulover Creek for the extraction of lumber. Today's Belize City currently has ten of the country's thirty-one political constituencies, some 30 percent of the seats in parliament.

Belizean colonial history and the emergence of national politics are covered most systematically by Nigel Bolland (1986, 1997, 2004), and more recent political history by Assad Shoman (2011), former PUP minister of foreign affairs from 2000 to 2008. These have been complemented by the work of Warnecke-Berger (2017, 2019) and the recently published article on Belize's current political economy by Ferrell and Wainwright (2022). All bar none are unequivocally damning. It is not lost on me that as a British researcher pointing the finger at the current state of affairs may lead to accusations of neocolonial scholarship. Yet, the perspectives in this book are derived from empirical fieldwork with Southsiders, politicians, civil servants, local and national experts, journalists, academics, and, of course, gang members themselves. During fieldwork, Southsiders' anger with political parties flashed to the surface the moment I raised them in conversation. Although the literature illustrated earlier may be sparse, it is unanimous in its bleak appraisal of national politics. Front and center is Shoman's tome *A History of Belize in 13 Chapters*, which is unambiguous about party failures. While the political class consolidated its own power, he notes their flagrant disdain for marginalized populations who were systematically "denied opportunities," becoming "objects of negligence and discrimination" (2011, pp. 388–389). Or as Belizean Evan X. Hyde wrote in simple terms, "Growth economics in Belize made the richest people in Belize richer, but the Belizean poor, poorer" (Ferrell and Wainwright 2022).

Although the PUP had been in government since 1964, postindependence dynamics saw a scramble for power. Ferrell and Wainwright (2022, p. 21) noted, "After the anticolonial movement finally achieved constitutional independence from Britain in 1981, Belize was governed by a capitalist state, but not a developmental one; a democracy, but a weak one." They go on to cite the first edition of Shoman's work (1987), concluding that any real process of decolonialization did not take place because the political parties, the PUP and the nascent UDP, maintained the prevailing economic and social structures, effectively preventing mass participation in political decision-making.

Given Belize's colonial history, it would be remiss not to mention the nation's ongoing pliability to foreign capital. British Belizean billionaire Michael Ashcroft is symbolic of the handover of a society from colonial masters, through postcolonial transition, to contemporary politico-economic power holders. One Belizean journalist described him to me as a "modern-day-billionaire-pirate" (2022).

> Ashcroft is arguably the single-largest player in the Belizean economy; as one of our reviewers put it, "There is no understanding of Belize's fiscal policies without taking Ashcroft into account" (Anon.). He has, at one time or another, owned the biggest bank, the telecommunications company, the shipping registry, and a television company as well as significant stakes in citrus plants, an electricity firm, and a hotel (Shoman 2011). He regularly contributes massive sums to both political parties and was rumored to have been a major donor to the 1998 PUP campaign (e.g., Shoman 2019b). The Belizean state has no ability to discipline just this one man, let alone foreign capital as a whole, in order to compel him to invest profits made in Belize back into the Belizean economy instead of repatriating them into his financial empire (Ferrell and Wainwright 2022, p. 20).

Elites that emerged in the 1960s and 1970s, "the 3 percent that the PUP represented" (Belizean researcher, 2022), dominated the country's productive resources and increasingly relied on state relationships to appropriate rents postindependence. The elites—commonly referred to as the "thirteen families"—control politics and industry simultaneously through a hermetic private-state relationship. The 3 percent were eventually partnered by a new political elite, the leaders of the UDP, who gained their position by dominating politics in Belize City.

Historically, more privileged groups have been lighter-skinned Belizeans. Mr. T, the pseudonym chosen by a dark-skinned middle-aged Creole man, a former gang member who worked at a state institution, discussed race and ethnicity dynamics. He brought to mind Bourdieu and Wacquant's *Symbolic Violence* (2004), where individuals or communities internalize and reproduce practices—in this case, the legacy of slavery—that harm or disadvantage their progress and mobility:

> MR. T: Um, Adam, I'm gonna tell you straight. What I saw happen in
> my own family, was that the children with more British, light fea-

tures, were the ones that were more privileged. Creoles were more prominent citizens than the African slaves and Indians [Mayans].
    My grandad was a very racist man. It was the strangest ting. His wife was this skin color [indicates his own dark skin tone]. He was "high-color" and he was very racist. He did not like [dark-skinned] Garifuna people. So, the culture was, keep those Garinagu people south [of the country, far from the capital].

AUTHOR: What does "high-color" mean?

MR. T: So, you see that skin tone [points to photo of group of black men, and one who has lighter-colored skin]. That we would consider "high-colored." Then, you have a little darker [points to darker-skinned men in photo]. These are all slave mentalities, where you have "maroons" [a scale of skin color] and all dat type of stuff. The color of your skin would determine the power that you wield. So, it was something where the fair skinned people were always those who were more privileged.

AUTHOR: So, would you translate those experiences into what is happening on Southside and, say, Northside?

MR. T: Northside [are] Creoles, [but] Southside, you be talking slave camp. It's still evident [today] my brother, still evident. [Southside] was just their living quarters to separate them [from the rest of society]. You see, St John's Cathedral [on Southside] was built in 1812, was built by slaves.

Most of the new political leaders from the UDP that grew within the party's hierarchy to positions of power actually came from Southside, although not all, such as former prime minister Dean Barrow. Considering Pearce and Velasco Montoya's (2022) research in Colombia, this development on Southside did not quite create the "constellation" of elites referred to in their work, rather the UDP leadership represented a second political elite alongside the PUP. Drawing on Bourdieu (1996), Pearce and Velasco Montoya highlight the principles of domination *at particular moments in history* that gave rise to a constellation of elites in Colombia (2022, p. 5). In the case of Belize, these historical moments would be: self-governance in 1964 giving rise to the PUP and suffrage; independence in 1981, allowing for the consolidation of elite control under the PUP; 1984, and the first democratic transition of political power to the UDP, a "new political elite," who enriched themselves through incessant corruption in government, cementing their seat at the top table. The leadership group of the UDP continues today, as the party reins are handed down dynastically, within families, divvied up among a few surnames that all Belize City residents can name. What is fascinating about the rise of the UDP is that it created an entirely new genre of politics,

Belizean-style garrison politics, which has been hugely successful considering the UDP domination of Southside constituencies over the past forty years.

The rise of the postindependence Belizean political system was a chance to change Southside's pattern of exclusion. Yet, rather than breaking the mold, it perpetuated subjugation. While there may be public divisions between the PUP and UDP, seen in the political squabbling broadcast daily on the *Channel 5* YouTube page, a Belizean researcher privy to elite spaces explained to me that they share overlapping business interests, family, and friendships behind closed doors (2022). Warnecke-Berger stated, "Culturally, this state-class faction behaves like traditional oligarchic elites in establishing kinship lines through intermarriage. Often, private business groups still have family members in state positions. Kinship thus is strongly interwoven with party affiliation" (2019, p. 203). The role of the political party system is to mediate between the dominators and the dominated, to give an illusion of popular autonomy, and to maintain a division of society along essentially irrelevant party lines (also see Ferrell and Wainwright 2022, p. 20). The middle classes, such as those educated at St. John's College, tend to be integrated into state institutions and political parties simultaneously, part of, and controlled by, an elite-dominated system.

Since independence, successive governments have sought to place state institutions at the service of party member interests, rather than develop institutional strength and the separation of state and government powers. Institutions were effectively subordinated to ministers' individual demands with no checks or balances, a precarious position given the small group of elites, hence interests, that commandeered the nation politically and economically. The largely "high-color" postcolonial PUP ruling class from across Belize and wealthy Northside Belize City neighborhoods was concerned with creating a capitalist state (Ferrell and Wainwright 2022) and manipulating industry and business legislation in their favor. This process was reductionist rather than a postcolonial emancipatory project, establishing the "rules of the game" for the UDP who emerged later (Bourdieu 1992, pp. 66, 81). The power grab akin to a political goldrush was straightforward: Bring state, politics, and the private sector under the control of a new national ruling class. Historian Warnecke-Berger, one of the few international scholars to analyze Belize's modern history, refers to this in Marxist economic terms as an emerging political class maneuvering for the purposes of "rent extraction" (2019, p. 202).

The transparency and accountability of political parties has always been deeply flawed. Shoman states that there were no laws governing their formation or facility for overseeing their conduct (Shoman 2011, p. 313). The PUP was typically populist, dominated by George Cadle Price between 1964 and

1984. Within the PUP, there was little participation from the membership, the party was highly personalized and marred by factional struggles, with emphasis on personalities, and infighting over loyalty and patronage (Bolland 1997, p. 277). Remarkably, the former PUP party chairman Louis Sylvestre said, "After 20 years in office, the PUP . . . has a widespread image of being corrupt, wasteful and incompetent, secretive and arrogant, prone to clientelism [and] is disorganized and discredited" (Shoman 2011, p. 313). One commentator went further, saying that during this period details of government expenditure deliberately obscured where "corruption is built into the system" (Sutherland 1998, p. 63, in Warnecke-Berger 2019, p. 203).

The PUP's internal wrangling amid the frantic rush to divvy up the country meant that Southside, perceived to be of little political or economic value, was ignored. The pursuit of elite-driven interests meant, as Ferrell and Wainwright wrote, "alternative development strategies were blocked. While the neoliberal economic model has plainly failed to fulfill the aspirations of the majority, the state has offered no tractable alternatives" (2022, p. 22). Shoman (2011) says, despite independence, no substantive economic liberation or political decolonialization ever occurred on Southside. A conversation with one Creole researcher in 2022 sums this up:

> AUTHOR: We can't say it's ongoing slavery on Southside, but there is a connection there.
> RESEARCHER: There is.
> AUTHOR: It is about exclusion and suppression that is continuing in a modern style.
> RESEARCHER: You got it. So, how will we correct that now?

How, indeed. The proverbial million-dollar question we return to in the book's Conclusion.

The PUP's corralling of political and economic power, pervasive corruption, and the clientelist abuse of the wider population meant that the party's fall from grace, when the first credible rival presented an alternative, was dramatic. The PUP lost the 1984 elections by a landslide to the UDP, a party founded barely a decade earlier in 1973. This is astonishing if we consider that just three years earlier the PUP had delivered the nation's independence, a coup de grâce if ever there was one. So pernicious was the party's behavior, that it somehow contrived to squander this abundance of electoral capital. The UDP took nine of ten seats in the city, including the whole of Southside. This was a historic moment for the country, politics reborn, a wave of optimism washing over the electorate. Locals who remember that time talked to me of the political optimism around participation, social change, and the promise of economic trickle-down through the UDP's center-right policies focusing on financial services and developing Belize into a tourism hot spot for the monied middle-class American market.

However, although the one-party political system had indeed widened, the "two political parties evolved as segments of state-class rule [and] there is little substantive difference between the respective policies of the two parties" (Warnecke-Berger 2019, p. 203). The Southside electorate had no realistic options but to choose between two very similar parties, neither of which, as they would come to learn, would bring them tangible benefits. The opportunity for change was lost, as the UDP essentially reproduced the clientelist practices of the PUP, tailoring them effectively to the Southside streets. So debased would the electoral process become, and so disillusioned the people, that the prevailing attitude among the Southsiders I spoke with in the 2020s was "we'll tek what you can" (field diary, 2021–2022). That is, selling their votes once every five years was the only time they felt they would get anything from the political process. Warnecke-Berger argues, evoking Spivak, that clientelism became "a means to co-opt subaltern groups into politics" (2019, p. 203).

Clientelist practices saw a rapid increase in financial scale during election campaigns, as the UDP created competition. Campaign costs for a single constituency were estimated at US$25,000 in 1984, soaring to US$450,000 by 2005 (Ryan 2005, p. 13, in Warnecke-Berger 2019, p. 203). Shoman is blunt with his analysis:

> [Since 1984 elections have been] won by those candidates or parties able to spend the most money, not just propaganda and mobilisation, but the outright buying of votes . . . it is well known that candidates from both political parties spend large sums of money in direct bribes to potential voters, whether it is in the form of groceries and other material goods or hard cash . . . when a party wins elections . . . it uses state resources to comply with election promises made to individuals . . . favours . . . include land, employment, contracts, scholarships, loans, housing, and others . . . this practice has increased significantly [since independence]. (2011, p. 327)

The postindependence political and economic class had appropriated the state apparatus via one of the two parties. They may be members of the PUP or UDP, or economic elites bankrolling one particular party, or sometimes hedging their bets and bankrolling both (Shoman 2011). This consolidation of power has been a coup in slow motion. In 1996, the Society for the Promotion of Education and Research declared a democratic crisis, characterized by an excessive concentration of political power, rampant corruption, and public disillusionment permeating all aspects of the political process. The Political Reform Commission found a "high centralisation of executive decision-making powers, pervasive partisanship, the absence of campaign finance regulation and the lack of effective people's participation" (Shoman 2011, p. 314).

Being in government is to orchestrate a contemporary fiefdom. The party that wins power uses public monies and lucrative contracts to repay their campaign backers and to continue to manipulate voter support through typical clientelist practices and an all-encompassing, yet blatant, network of patronage (Bolland 1997). Party control over state institutions should not be underestimated, and it is not coincidental that Belizean politicians have never been jailed for corruption, a point we return to in Chapter 5 when discussing the impact of the partial rule of law in Belize.

When there is a change of government, those in positions of authority in the civil service are sacked wholesale and job contracts are handed to party loyalists whose qualifications or credentials are of lesser concern than their political fidelity. This is not dissimilar to other Caribbean experiences. I raised this issue with a Trinidadian academic friend, and he replied prosaically, "Of course, this is the Caribbean" (ca. 2020). I have heard comments to that effect by many Belizeans over the years, particularly those trying to hold down civil service jobs. One youth worker told me that "if you don't have a degree and are in a party, you can't get ahead in Belize" (2021). He then pulled out a signed six-month rolling contract for US$25,000—a significant sum in Belize—to be paid to an individual loyal to the PUP, who at that time had recently come back into power. The contracted individual was so seldom seen at the office he was described as a "ghost," a colloquialism for a well-paid yet untouchable party loyalist who might feign work and show up occasionally, but generally do not bother, and just collect their paycheck. I met this particular "ghost" in 2016 when they had been struggling to make ends meet during the UDP administration. As a PUP loyalist, they were blacklisted from any government or state-funded position. When the PUP returned to power, they duly received their payoff. Their contract was funded from a budget line that was supposed to help disadvantaged youths.

The impact of this on the efficacy of state institutions is devastating, the pervasive way the state apparatus has been manipulated into a patronage system serving party interests is a self-perpetuating political purgatory.

> People align themselves to parties . . . not because they are blind to the corruption and uselessness of those parties, but because they know that "in Belize if you don't belong to one of the parties you can't get a job or other assistance." The situation is truly disgusting, and there seems to be no real likelihood of change. (Shoman 2011, p. 327)

To turn once more to Warnecke-Berger, "While elite rule consolidated in the hands of a state-class segmented in two competing factions, each of them being organized in a political party, the livelihoods of subaltern groups became increasingly precarious" (2019, p. 240). As Mr. T said in an interview, "Remember, deeze tings all come about from what I call a *systematic oppressive platform* that was created [his emphasis]" (2021).

"A Garrison Is an Empire"

> Houseslaves became politicians. Fieldslaves became gang bosses.
> —SOCIAL WORKER (2021)

Timing is everything. The birth of a nation, the rise of an opposition party, and the emergence of Blood and Crip transnationalism all occurred in the early 1980s. The concurrent development of gangs and postindependence politics is unique to Belize City. It gave rise to processes of contention and collaboration between political parties and gangs on the streets. A new "garrison politics" was born. For the UDP it has been tremendously effective.

What is not unique to Belize is clientelism, a practice common the world over and ubiquitous in Latin American and Caribbean slum politics. Clientelism is characterized by an asymmetrical social order that depends on relations of patronage, where the power holders wield hefty influence over subordinate populations. In its crudest from, clientelism in the run up to elections is an illegal activity where a political candidate buys votes and promises favors such as jobs, contracts, et cetera, for the faithful. There are many interacting layers to this process, and those who resist are deliberately excluded from such jobs, contracts, or other benefits. It is, unfortunately, a successful tactic wielded against disenfranchised populations whose immediate needs are often dire, leading to a short-termism where a few dollars at election time is an attractive prospect. As such, these practices depend on the absence of any meaningful social contract to be effective. Beyond this, for historically abandoned populations, a form of collective political identity, a tribal politics, and being part of something, even if it is a political veneer, is preferable to simply being ignored.

The UDP managed a landslide victory across Southside in 1984 for myriad reasons. The population was exasperated with the corruption and inefficiency of the PUP and no positive change had been seen since the birth of national governance, but, crucially, as one former politician said, the PUP were seen as "a rural party" of elites (2022). The darker-skinned Creole-dominated Southside felt unrepresented.

The UDP did not campaign on a Creole "race card," but many candidates for Southside constituencies were *from* those communities, or at least nearby in Belize City. This was a leap forward in identity politics and representation—one journalist said, even though "UDP and PUP politics are really similar, [the UDP] appeal to darker skinned ethnic Creoles more" (2022). Although Dean Barrow was not brought up on Southside, he still appealed to the Creole vote and was the most skilled politician of a generation. He went on to become prime minister for the UDP from 2008 to 2020, described by the same journalist as "the Belizean Barack Obama, a great orator. He has charisma. [I've met him many times] and he's always the smartest guy in the room. He was a top attorney. What's impressive is that he's an atheist in a right-wing religious country, but he got the church on board. He can blend to every setting" (2022). A middle-aged lady from Southside remembered the 1980s:

> AUTHOR: How did the UDP win on southside?
> LADY: Well, you have to understand that those [UDP] politicians grew out of Southside. Except for Dean Barrow. Dean Barrow came from the Royal Creole kind of family. The Royal Creoles have some white ancestry, so that is the comparison between the houseslave and the fieldslave. The Royal Creoles are like houseslaves. They interbred with the white colonialists.

While Creole voters on Southside felt more represented by the UDP, the party did not represent a sea change in the way politics were done. One national academic even dismissed the role of race politics: "It's tokenism, not racism. It doesn't matter what race you are, it's about party politics. It's all about political patronage. Some get a lot [powerful party loyalists], the rest who fall in line, get tokens" (2021). Pessimistically, the UDP are simply better positioned on Southside to operationalize clientelist practices, locking out the PUP. I spoke to numerous Belizeans about this topic, and their responses were always similar: "They [UDP] did a lot of buying of votes. They continue to buy votes. They do that a lot [taking] control of Southside for the last four or five elections," said a local researcher (2022).

Despite parties presenting policies and programs to deliver goods, services, and social welfare, and the best intentions of some individuals, the impact on Southside has been negligible. Jaded locals expect little from the state and government, so, to them, a little cash and some hollow promises at election time is better than nothing. And so, the clientelist machinery grinds on. The PUP would argue that they attempted to break with these practices in the run up to winning the 2020 general elections. However, the UDP still won the majority of Southside. Garrison politics immovable.

The connection between the fieldslaves of yesteryear coming back to the barracks after a season of logging and today's slums dominated by garrison politics is uncomfortable, yet difficult to dismiss. This echoes Spivak's (1988) famed depiction of the "subaltern," the Indigenous dispossessed in colonial society, the poorest and most marginalized "who have no platform to express their concerns and no voice to affect policy debates or demand a fairer share of society's goods" (Riach 2017). Despite the end of colonialism and the arrival of democracy, Southsiders are subaltern to this day, rendered powerless to demand their fair share, a manifestation of three-dimensional chronic vulnerability; one that is fixed in place, amid intense exclusions, across generations.

That the UDP has held fast to Southside constituencies raises obvious questions about party-gang interactions. There is no specific academic literature analyzing the relationship between political parties and gang development in Belize City. The following observations are based almost entirely on plentiful conversations with politicians, community members, civil servants, national experts, and, of course, former and current gang members.

It wasn't until the late 1980s and, in some parts of town, the early 1990s that the Bloods and Crips became a force to be reckoned with as potential interlocutors for political parties. "Gangs emerged organically," said one UDP party member, candidly, who made it clear they would only talk if they remained completely anonymous, without even a mention of their gender or age group. "They grew together with the [UDP] in a type of co-existence?" I queried. "Yes, that is accurate" (2022). When the UDP won in 1984, they took control of Albert, Collet, Mesopotamia, Pickstock, and Queen's Square constituencies on Southside; these were and are the most gang-populated places in the country. Alias Shorty was a child then, becoming a gang leader in later life. "Gangs wasn't [divided into] areas [like] Yarborough, Mesopotamia, it was just Northside and Southside back then. It was just two sides when the ground was clay, wasn't no concrete" (2022). Mr. T grew up in the notorious Martin's area: "It wasn't until the late 80s that different cliques really got started [wearing] Dickies [trousers], blue and red rags, bandanas" (2021):

> MR. T: It wasn't politics setting [gang] turf, they just went together.
> AUTHOR: But what about politics and gangs?
> MR. T: Well, the first ting you have to realize is the close-knit family-oriented structure that we have. And so, families, *divided on politics in Belize* [his emphasis], Red and Blue, UDP and PUP. So, when the gang culture came about, the political fights were like gang wars, because one crowd went to one party and one crowd went to another.
> AUTHOR: Do you think it was coincidence that the red and blue of the Bloods and Crips was the red and blue of the two parties?

MR. T: It was coincidental in the sense that the parties was there before the gangs. So, when the gangs came out, I think what the politicians saw was the opportunity to associate themselves with the color these guys wear. And that's when the bartering system [clientelism] started to happen "Come on! I have a shirt for all the guys." [politician to gang members] And also like I said, Belizeans are not loyalists because, I could be red [UDP] and ask you for a hundred dollars today, and if you give it I'll wear a blue [PUP] shirt tomorrow.

AUTHOR: So, when you're poor you have to be opportunist, right?

MR. T: Right. . . . Every election since independence, politicians have been saying "Hey Adam, how you doin' bro? I haven't seen you for a year! Don't worry, I've been busy trying to get some stuff for you guys. This BZD$50, that's for you." And it's always an opportune time [near elections] because nothing is ever happening [no support for locals on Southside outside of election run-ups]. "I'll tell you what, if you get Jason, Virgilio, and all those guys [to vote for me] you will get $50 bucks for yourself, and there'll be something [money, goods] you could give them." And so, it's a system. [So, the gang members says] "Hey, guys, *Big Man* come, jus' come!" And that in itself is something big, you know. You feel high because "he just came and spoke to me!" So, he hands out the money "here's five (BZ$) here's five, here's five." And so, there's a hundred guys on that street, so [the politician is] gonna call that street captain [gang leader]. That street captain is good for a hundred guys. These [gangs] are organized enough that if you get [the leader] you get the rest. The rest follow. Now, that whole one hundred people live on a promise [of future handouts, jobs, contracts from the politician], and everybody is "yes, yes, yes." And as soon as [the politician] wins "*LATER GUYS, I'LL BE BACK!*" [they disappear. His emphasis].

AUTHOR: "*SEE Y'ALL IN FOUR YEARS!*" [both laugh]

MR. T: "He tricked us!" And then [the politician] comes back in four years . . . (2021)

Gang/politician interactions are not exceptional but logical; they are simply a component of a wider repertoire of clientelist practices used by politicians in the community. A young man who has never been connected to gangs remembered a local election campaign in the 1990s, "A politician put BZ$20 *right in my hand*, he himself give it to me, *then later he become minister*! [chortling incredulously]" (2022). When I discussed this with a UDP party member in 2016, they very much transmitted the sense that they were doing nothing wrong because these were just standard practices: garrison politics, a normative apparatus.

Gangs become more, or less, important to politicians depending on their size and organization, which allows them to command more votes. I discussed this with two former gang members, Angel and Shorty, and also alias Vartas, still the most powerful gang leader in Belize when I met him for a second time in 2022. They all confirmed these dynamics. In a long conversation with Shorty when we first met in Belize Central Prison in 2016, he explained his role in a matter-of-fact manner: "People only vote for what they gettin' off the politicians," adding that gang leaders covet favor with politicians, indicating clientelism is a two-way street. Gang leaders themselves pocket most of the money given to them, handing a fraction of this to the "sprats," the small fish lower-ranking gang members, a fascinating insight into the dynamics of power and money in street politics. The two-way street does not mean power asymmetry between politicians and gang leaders is obsolete in any way. This was described in Belizean terms by alias Jabbar who recalled George "Junie Balls" McKenzie, the former Crip General from Majestic Alley, handing out money given to him by politicians: "When da field n***as are given privileges by da house n***as" (2021). It is this asymmetry that distinguishes Belize from a number of other ganglands in the region, where the balance of power often lies with the gang, not the local politician, or at least sways between the two. On Southside, even relatively powerful gang leaders remain subordinate, unable to escape their subaltern status.

Mr. T. said gang and political party linkages follow "the same garrison model as in Jamaica," a country that is a cultural role model for many Belizean Creoles. A "garrison" in Jamaica is an economically deprived urban area, mainly found in the capital Kingston, where the vast majority of the population vote for one of the two main parties—the Peoples National Party or the Jamaica Labour Party. Votes are usually secured by politicians mobilizing gangs or mobs to win votes through bribery, coercion, or intimidation. Politics and gang relations are often fraught, leading to frequent police-gang clashes in areas such as Tivoli Gardens. The work of Kevin Edmonds provides an excellent deep dive into these issues (2016). I once interviewed a notorious politician at his office in downtown Kingston, in 2015, the very next day as he left his office, a gang tried to machine-gun him down.

I would disagree a little with Mr. T, in that Belizean- and Jamaican-style "garrison politics" are not an identical model, in two ways: Belizean gangs rarely either challenge the politicians—there has not been a recorded case of a gang leader murdering or attempting to murder a politician as I experienced in Kingston—or are used to intimidate and bully voters. As mentioned in the previous chapter, debates in the region show that gangs as a local power coexist in complex ways with state institutions and political practices (e.g., Arias 2017; Cruz and Durán-Martínez 2016; Jaffe 2013). It is the norm in these communities that electoral power is leveraged by politicians colluding with gangs, which I have written about myself across cities in the region (Baird 2011, 2018a). This is a street-level political dialectic, horse-trading, quid pro quo.

In Belize, this system functioned most effectively during the "peak" Bloods and Crips years, until the late 1990s, when structured gangs and Generals, made for stable interlocutors. Indeed, this period saw the rise of numerous Generals such as the infamous George Herbert, a founder of the George Street Bloods, and the Crip, Junie Balls, from Majestic Alley mentioned earlier (Muhammad 2015, p. 169). However, there were several other folkloric figures such as Big Tom, Pinky, Shiny, Elmack, Kevin, and the early gang leaders from the Tillett family who went on to form a dynasty on George Street with subsequent generations taking command. In the 1990s under Herbert, the George Street Bloods were the most feared and at their most powerful. One Southsider referred to this as "the Golden Era" (2022). A man who grew up on George Street as a child remembered that "[Herbert] kept a lid on violence and robberies. Every Christmas he gave out bicycles to poor kids. . . . He was a gang leader, and he was very clever and managed everything. Then Shiny and Pinky [the next generation] rose under him" (2021). A former civil servant working on gang interventions said, "Back in the day, before Pinky and Shiny were killed, they were creating their own empire. They would identify clever kids and send them to school and even go to PTA [parent-teacher association] meetings! They'd say, 'stay in school as one day I'll need a lawyer'" (2021).

Since the 1990s, the gangs fragmented and became disorganized, a theme explored in greater detail in the next chapter to explain the post-2000 homicide boom. The organizational weakness of gangs sets Belize apart from many other gang-dominated communities in the region, such as Medellín, San Salvador, Kingston, São Paulo, and Port of Spain. Today's gangs lack the social and political power to dominate and control communities. Vartas is an outlier in Belize City, wielding significant influence in the Martin's area. Nevertheless, I first met him after I asked a member of the UDP if they could get me an interview with a gang leader; the UDP member picked up their cell phone, called Vartas, and, within minutes, he was in the office answering my questions obediently. It was clear where the balance of power lay.

The lack of organizational capacity also provides an explanation as to why gangs do not challenge the power of politicians or engage in extortion or organized crime such as money laundering and international drug trafficking. Rather like Belizean state institutions, they lack capacity. While they have some influence, they are not the old-school Generals, the stable interlocutors of lore who enriched themselves by aligning closely with politicians, like business partners, to negotiate mass vote buying. In 2016, the UDP member mentioned earlier even complained to me that gangs used to be easy to work with, "now dey jus' crazy." This gang/politician partnership suffered as gangs fragmented in the 2000s, a point I discussed with another UDP party member who chose to be anonymized as just "researcher":

> AUTHOR: What was the relationship [like between politicians] and the old Generals, Pinky, Shiny and others back in the day?
> RESEARCHER: Dere was a relationship because dese were [former prime minister] Dean Barrow's voters. Dey were security, controlled murder rates, clientelism, all kind a tings, dats why dey use dem. [Nowadays] de gangs are not self-sufficient, dey are run by dese politicians. Dey even employ dem as drivers, an' whatever. Someone has to do de nasty job and dat's where de gangs come in. De politicians control dem, dose guys can't be on deir own. Dey are not well organized, dey don't have capital.

Conversely, through territorial domination, better organized gangs in the region manipulate government and state institutions, for example, controlling municipal contracts as I discovered with my colleagues in Trinidad (Baird, Bishop, and Kerrigan 2022; 2023), or establishing agreements where the gang suppresses the homicide rate in exchange for state authorities turning a blind eye to a range of illegal money-making activities (e.g., Bergmann 2020; Feltran 2020; Rozema 2008).

State actors and politicians habitually negotiate with gangs, although the subject is taboo, both politically and for its legal opacity. Given this habituality, it stands that there is a normative understanding between politicians and gangs for vote buying at election time. It persists because it delivers, by working most effectively where great inequality exists and costing the wealthy elite relatively little to consolidate their power and privilege. Constituents on Southside have been subject to these practices for decades and have come to expect and demand little from the political process. Subaltern, yes. Lumpen, yes. The patron/client dialectic on the streets is hopelessly one sided, epitomizing disenfranchisement and the dissolution of the social contract. Little wonder Jabbar came up with the sound bite, "A garrison is an empire," implying relations of domination. The poor are easily leveraged, he continued, "The garrisons are *locked down*. [He names two well-known politicians] down George Street, they don't even canvas, and they win. . . . They are not about empowering their people, they are about keeping them dependent" (2022). Fundamentally, street politics on Southside require subordination and obedience. Turning to Mr. T once more, who said with a tone of impotence:

An' you have to understan' . . . when I look at dese political powers dat be, I realize dey have been infected in some way or another, dat dey realize "you know what, dese people, I'm going to use dem to get de power dat I need, to make myself and my family better, and den dey can eat shit and die." And dat is de craziest ting, because if you empower your people, invest in your human resource, dat is de strength of de country. De economic boom dat will happen from dat will put you on de map.

It is difficult to find an accurate descriptor for these continual processes of subjugation, but it brings to mind the Deleuzean critique of capitalism, unrelentingly consuming the whole space (Vandenberghe 2008). However it is conceptually framed, Southside has a thriving political system that extracts cheap votes, giving nothing in return, while quashing civic organization and activism. Rebellion against this exploitation does not, unfortunately, challenge structures of oppression, rather it manifests as the rage of the poor turned inward. Chronic vulnerability surfaces as chronic violence. Today's gang members are disenfranchised, depoliticized young men killing each other: *lumpengangstas*.

Belize has gaping inequality, ranked sixth most unequal out of 153 countries in the world according to Gini coefficient statistics. The overrepresentation of elite interests through political architecture is glaring, and garrison politics have played the contemporary role in the continuation of inequality. It is tragic, yet little wonder that many Belizeans still reach for the term "field-slave" to describe the collective treatment of the urban poor.

The Janus Face of the State

The 1980s were a momentous period of change in the country. Empathetically, we should not be surprised that there was a stuttering response to the emerging gang phenomenon. The UDP/PUP rivalry had recently begun and the political jostling in Belize City had ratcheted up, while state institutions had a new raft of ministerial leaders. That gangs emerged while the country was finding its feet was far from ideal, and it took until the early 1990s until the authorities put together a specifically planned response beyond simply passing the buck to the BPD.

In 1991, a Crimes Commission was set up to rapidly push through legislation to counter rising gangs. By now, there was growing public concern and violence increasingly headlined the evening news. Belizeans had never seen anything like this before. Similar to Central American countries, seen in Fontes's (2018) account from Guatemala or Martínez D'Aubuisson and Martínez D'Aubuisson's (2018) in El Salvador, the reporting stoked moral panic around gangs, leading to significant political pressure. The politically intuitive reaction to rule of law challenges is to double down on policing in affected areas, meaning the use of force, giving rise to mano dura (heavy handed) approaches. Dennis Rodgers and I reviewed the history of responses to gangs in the Latin American and Caribbean region, and mano dura is commonplace (Rodgers and Baird 2015). This tendency is interwoven with Northern Triangle countries' experiences of contending with the legacies of postwar violence, undergoing transitions to democracy from dictatorship, military oppression, and civil conflict, which has shaped the societies that deportation-model gangs inserted themselves into (Levenson 2013; Savenije and van der Borgh 2015). A range of factors are attributed to the rise of maras, such as exclusion, easy access to firearms and ammunition, connectedness to organized crime and drug trafficking, the role of politics (Berg and Carranza 2018), and the counterproductivity of militarized crackdowns (e.g., Gutierrez Rivera, Strønen, and Ystanes 2018; Wolf 2017).

> Another factor that significantly pushed Central American gangs—and in particular the maras in the Northern Triangle countries—towards a greater degree of organization, was the introduction in the early 2000s of extremely repressive anti-gang policies referred to generically as "mano dura." . . . These led to a series of extremely brutal "tit-for-tat" confrontations between state authorities and gangs in El Salvador, Honduras, and Guatemala that contributed to gangs becoming more professionalized and less visible than previously, aiding their involvement with the drugs trade. . . . Much has been made of the putative "corporatization" (see Taylor, 1990) of Central American gangs as a result both of the rising drug trade as well as in reaction to state repression (Rodgers and Baird 2015, p.479).

Despite the strong empirically based research on the limitations of mano dura, it has an enduring appeal among politicians because it is highly visible, hence newsworthy, scoring political support for the politicians that push such measures through. The most notable recent incarnation being the state of exception declared by President Nayib Bukele in El Salvador in 2022, and the flash incarceration of some seventy thousand and counting poor young men, involving the total suspension of due process and widespread abuse of human rights.[2] While a minority of those arrested are undoubtedly maras, the collateral damage, for want of a better phrase, is clear. Violence has plummeted, at least in the short-term, but at the cost of innumerable innocent poor young men being criminalized, swept up in the nets as disposable bycatch. The unsustainability and longer-term developmental impact of these policies, where gang-related crime and violence bounce back, however, have less immediate political costs, and *Bukelismo*, extreme mano dura named after the president, has proved immensely popular, hence an attractive model to copy in the region.

Gang interventions on the streets of Belize City were led by the police, a historically militaristic institution. Warnecke-Berger (2019) commented that the BPD was established to crack down on disruption during historical pre-independence labor uprisings. Bolland (1997) and later Crooks (2010) flagged the militarized focus of police training, and, in a firm indication of the government's countergang intentions, Miller Matthei recalled the first deployments of the Belizean Defense Force (BDF) to the streets in the mid-1990s (1998). The militaristic response to gangs was doubled down on with the creation of the GSU in 2010, a special taskforce within the BPD. While BDF deployments were only temporary measures, the GSU was permanent and very much at the forefront in terms of delivering crackdowns on suspected gang activity. The GSU was located away from the main Raccoon Street police station on Southside. One of the reasons for this is that many of the city's police officers themselves came from Southside, and high levels of corruption meant that interventions with gang members were often compromised by leaked information. Rather than any sophisticated gang infiltration into the police force, this was due to the tight-knit family and village-like social order. It is after all a small place.

Given the militarized tactics of the GSU, unsurprisingly, the unit was implicated in numerous incidents of abuse. It was later dissolved and reconfigured as the Gi3, in 2021, by the new police commissioner Chester Williams, with a claimed focus on investigation and intelligence gathering to mark a break with the blunt-instrument tactics of the past. However, it remains to be seen how significant this shift in modus operandi will be. It would be remiss to focus on the GSU or newfound Gi3, rather than the BPD as a whole, which faces significant challenges. Although Gayle, Hampton, and Mortis (2016) and Warnecke-Berger (2019) cite the numerous complaints that have been made to the Ombudsman's Office about the routinely excess use of force against young men, police abuse is nowhere near the lethal levels seen in Jamaica, even the United States, or the systematic human rights violations termed "social cleansing" seen in recent history in Central America, Colombia, and Brazil (Feltran 2020; Noche and Niebla 2002; Denyer Willis 2015).

Although the Belizean police do not systematically murder their own civilians, there have been a number of flash points. One was the death of Arthur Young, the leader of the Taylor's Alley Gang, in police custody, widely assumed to be an extrajudicial killing although this was never proven. The most notorious case by far, which shocked Belizeans, was the murder of four mid-ranking members of the George Street Bloods on the upstairs floor of a house at the corner of Dean and Plues Streets in January 2013. Massacres are rare in Belize, and this sent ripples through the community. Having spoken to a number of individuals across various organizations and within gangs themselves, a common allegation is that these were extrajudicial killings and questions have been raised about the absence of a coroner's inquest. Further, at the time of the murders, numerous eyewitnesses claim they saw the GSU near the premises. The police refute these claims and the crime remains unsolved (Channel 5 News 2013).[3] Mr. T reflected:

> MR. T: Yes. So, when George Street was at its most powerful, the GSU went and dey broke Shiny's hand. So, from where I was sitting, it was like, "woah, dey broke the General's hand!" Listen to me, dat man was feared in the streets by everyone. It's like, he points at you, you dead. An' da police came in an' jus' bang-up di entire group. An' da next day, dey [crying] "the police came thru here and took advantage of us" . . . den later on in the years, four of dem died in the apartment building on Dean Street.
>
> AUTHOR: That was a clear-up operation? And that raises questions about who really has the power.
>
> MR. T: [The four killed were not Generals but] dey were still "ranking officials," I knew one of da guys. Not anyone could jus' go in dere. Gaza and George Street [gang areas] was off limits. You can't jus' go in dere even the most powerful groups [opposition gangs or police] won't go in dere. Dey are very intimidating. It's like PIV [People in Violence a.k.a. Peace in the Valley/Peace in the Village gang]. PIV has always been a very intimidating gang. George Street is afraid to go in dere because of de history of brutality. "Old Monarchy" I call dem! I saw dem evolve. Then dey moved away from de principles, killing out each other, and killing neighbors.

What is important to note at this juncture in Belizean gang history is that, before police crackdowns on gangs, homicidal violence was relatively low given the Generals' control. Communities at the time considered Generals to be supportive (Gayle and Mortis 2010). Heavy-handed interventions by the police were seen as attacks on communities historically abandoned by state institutions. There was money to fund the police for entering communities mob-handed, by force, but no money for tackling child malnutrition. On any given day, gang members were being rounded up or beaten by the GSU, and, the next, they were being used by local politicians for clientelist practices. Contradictory, at best.

Both the UDP and PUP pushed through stringent anti-gang legislation, documented by Nuri Muhammad (2015, pp. 50–56). In 1990, the PUP passed the Crime Control Act I (6). Dean Barrow, leader of the opposition at the time, said it was draconian, copying British laws dealing with the IRA in Northern Ireland and the heavily criticized Jamaican "Gun Court" experience. Nonetheless, when the UDP returned to power in 1993, the party set about expanding that very same law, developing the Crime Control Act II (6), drafted by the same solicitor general, Mr. Ghian Gandhi.

A "Quick Trial Court" was established in Belize at the Magistrates Court in 1994 to process crimes against tourists, but to this day tourists have never been targeted by gang members in any systematic way, in part, because there has never been any tourism on Southside. I am often asked, "Is Belize safe to go to on vacation?" to which I have developed a standard reply that tourist destinations are very safe and violence is concentrated between gang members in the city. Instead of processing crimes against tourists, the arrests presented to the Quick Trial Court were profiled and discriminate: Poor young Creole men were targeted in police roundups on the streets and one hundred suspected gang members were ceremoniously corralled behind a rudimentary barbed wire fence in Militia Hall in 1994. The court was used to expedite them to prison after trials that lasted a matter of hours. This was the genesis point for the "overutilization" of juvenile incarceration, and today it is commonplace for young men to be held for lengthy pretrial periods on misdemeanor charges, as they say locally, *fi wan stick o weed* (for one marijuana joint; Peirce 2017, p. 5; UNDP 2012). Although, the 2017 amendment of the Misuse of Drugs Act means the personal possession of less than ten grams of marijuana has now been decriminalized, so this phrase will have to change. During the Quick Trials most had no defense as legal aid did not exist, and many were on remand for years as they did not have the means to post bail. Muhammad (2015) concludes that the manipulation of legislation, court practices, and the subsequent filling of prisons did not lead to a reduction of gang activity. I interviewed a senior police officer at the Raccoon Street police station, in 2021, who said that roundups had little impact on gangs, further noting that the toughening of gun laws in 2010—which former gang leader Shorty, mentioned frequently in this book, fell afoul of—had no impact on gun possession and circulation whatsoever.

In a comparative article on the wider Caribbean, Dylan Kerrigan and I observed that in former colonial societies founded on injustice, prisons seldom provide justice (Kerrigan and Baird 2024). Historically, prisons in the Caribbean were used by colonial administrators to control and confine the laboring population, the formerly enslaved or indentured immigrants, within plantation and agricultural extraction societies. Those of African and Asian descent were disproportionately policed and punished to deter others from engaging in "criminal" activities. In this sense, Caribbean prisons existed as a social control mechanism of racialized class-based hierarchies.

The 1990s incarceration conditions were notorious: "da piss house" holding cells in the police station and Belize Central Prison, which relocated to Hattieville a forty-five-minute drive from the city in 1993. Gayle and Mortis (2010) noted that there were no sewage facilities or drinking water and just three hundred beds for nine hundred inmates. Cells for two held up to nine prisoners and flooded when it rained, many inmates slept on wet floors with no bedding, there was no available mess hall or kitchen and no system for rubbish disposal, and there were no in-house medical facilities (p. 145).

However, in 2002, a radical and exceptional experiment took place. The prison was so dysfunctional that, remarkably, it was taken over by nonprofit the Kolbe Foundation. To have a nonprofit run a nation's main prison is unheard of, yet the transformation was pronounced. Prior to 2002, the prison could not even afford to feed its inmates. Since then, conditions have improved dramatically with a twelve-step rehabilitation program at the internal Ashcroft Rehabilitation Centre, intranet-based educational facilities, and on-site animal rearing and agriculture led by prisoners. I can attest to this, having visited the adult and Wagner's youth facilities within the prison complex, several times in recent years, and met some genuinely committed staff there. The prison has strong international standing, and, as such, is an institutional outlier in Belize. It has been researched by Whiteacre and Miller (2017, 2018), the prison director told me that one other study was ongoing (as of 2022), and it has been the subject of Raphael Rowe's Netflix series *Inside the World's Toughest Prisons*. Prison life is still obviously tough, with punishment for rule breaking leading to inmates being sent to the "Ad Seg" (segregation) bloc where all privileges are taken away. This space is not open to oversight or public scrutiny from a human rights watchdog, and other issues have included officer corruption. Despite this, Rowe concludes, "It's hard not to be impressed by this prison."

Most damning for the Belizean establishment, however, is that the prison only became a success story *after* it had been transferred out of state control. I would often ask Belizeans which institutions they thought functioned well. Although anecdotal, the standard reply was a frustrated "none of them." Yet, when pressed, I would hear comments that the prison was well regarded, that the Belize Defense Force would stand up to manipulative politicians, but, rather depressingly, that no other institution was untainted by corruption.

While the prison is functional and rehabilitative, the inmate demographic reflects social ills on the "outside." Many young Southside men transition back and forth between the ghetto, the gang, and the prison. They are constantly policed, contained, and incarcerated; even a cursory look at Belizean news on YouTube will confirm this for the reader. To paraphrase Shabazz, this "fixes Blacks spatially":

> Little has been said about the spatial geographies they lived in before entering prison. Why space because, like race, gender, class, and sexuality, spatiality is a central fundament of subject formation. Indeed, the human is always spatialized. We need look no further than Black people's fight for social justice, which has largely been composed of contestations over or within space—segregation, apartheid, slavery, the ghetto ... to understand its importance. (2009, p. 277)

Chronic vulnerability is, above all, about continuity. Southside is "outside," transposed "inside" the prison; an ongoing cycle defined by race, class, and gender (women make up a tiny fraction of incarceration rates). The social terrains prison populations are drawn from are shaped by colonial power, the brutality of slavery, and the transhistorical postcolonial failures of development and capitalism (Castells 2000); a world where urban ghettos feed the remand yards of Caribbean prisons. Here, "the racial-spatial ideologies of apartheid, segregation, and slavery, with their techniques of racial management—the ghetto, mining compounds, the reserves, projects, and prisons—that fix Black bodies and form Black subjects in space, constitute the network that Blacks have politically resisted for centuries" (Shabazz 2009, p. 292). Overlapping social-prison terrains, from Southside Belize City to western Kingston and eastern Port of Spain, are not dissimilar to experiences in the United States (Alexander 2012; SpearIt 2011, p. 90), where Black men are always "in one prison or another" (Shabazz 2009).

Throughout the 1980s, Southside was effectively abandoned by the state. Political engagement embedded clientelist mechanisms and when the state did show its face, it was in the form of indiscriminate, poorly controlled, and at times brutal policing. There was inevitable community pushback against police intervention and we should not be surprised at local support for well-organized and relatively "community friendly" gangs at the time. Petty cash handouts from Generals were routine, and predation through extortion, coercion, and threats were minor. I told one researcher that the state seemed Janus faced: bribes or batons. Admittedly, it was a leading comment on my part, yet she confirmed "You are so right. It's 'village style' politics. They send in the Gi3, but the politicians are still doing their work [using gangs as intermediaries to buy votes]" (2022). Police crackdowns, legislation changes, and mass incarceration of the 1990s ultimately failed to slow gang expansion. Confoundingly, as this was taking place, there was the first major attempt at party-led gang negotiations, which took place on Bird's Isle in 1995, a polar-opposite approach to resolving the gang crisis, to which we now turn.

The First Gang Negotiations

The village atmosphere and tight-knit family social order, arguably, more than any other dynamic, is the reason gang negotiations have been ongoing in one form or another since the 1980s. The merits of gang negotiations provoke political disagreements across the region; however, in Belize, the approach is not taboo, and negotiations have taken place for years, ranging from unofficial, piecemeal, and short term to official, organized, and long term.

Jabbar, my youth worker friend, recalled an informal set of negotiations with the police as far back as the 1980s (2016). Although a truce was brokered in these first negotiations, there are suspicions that they were used as an intelligence-gathering process to take down gang leadership rather than a genuine attempt to secure lasting violence reduction. Jabbar's suspicions came from the number of leaders arrested in the days and weeks following this truce. There have been a series of negotiation attempts, mostly led by the UDP when in government. While negotiations and police crackdowns on gangs have ebbed and flowed over the years, they have not been clearly coordinated, often running, confusingly, as parallel policies.

The first and most significant gang truce took place on Bird's Isle adjacent to Southside's southern shore, which today has a popular restaurant with views across the Caribbean Sea. It was led by then UDP deputy prime minister Dean Barrow. Jabbar said this process was facilitated by the connections Barrow had to his Mesopotamia constituency, the stronghold of the George Street Bloods. I was told that Barrow knew many of the gang members' families and even gang members themselves, so he had significant convening power.

Nuri Muhammad covers these negotiations in detail in his book *Insights into Gang Culture in Belize* (2015, pp. 75–83). A far-reaching truce was agreed on, and a document was signed by the leaders of the then fourteen gangs in the city, the eponymous "Bird's Isle Declaration," on February 19, 1995. In return for agreeing to the truce, gangs were given life skills and vocational training, a stipend, and told to stay out of trouble. Muhammad records that violence was reduced massively in the first nine months after the truce was signed. Certainly, this was a brave and experimental move by Barrow, as, previously, only the police had engaged officially with gang members. In this regard, Belize was an innovator in the Caribbean and Central American region. Credit is due here. It was a polemical yet trailblazing approach, but would ultimately prove unsustainable. The CYDP was created to facilitate the process of reintegrating participants as productive members of society, with follow-up counseling, employment, and educational opportunities, guided by a steering committee of members from the private and public sectors, NGOs, and religious groups. A secretariat was established to implement the truce agreements. Angel was one of the beneficiaries of this process, and it changed his life.

>ANGEL: When the Deputy Prime Minister Dean Barrow done truce . . .
>AUTHOR: [Interrupts] So, you got out [of the Crips] in the first gang truce?
>ANGEL: Yeah. An' I stay out. I didn't go back like some otha guys, you know, I try to develop.
>AUTHOR: So, how did you manage to stay out then, when the other guys didn't?
>ANGEL: Because da Deputy Prime Minister [Barrow] gi' me a house an' a job. An' das da job that I retire from . . .
>AUTHOR: The one we know each other from? Shit! [We first met in Belize in 2016. Angel worked his post-truce job from 1995 to 2020]. So, that was the job that came from way back then? A complete U-turn [from gang life]. But you must've also wanted to get out right?
>ANGEL: Yeah. Well, dere was so much [good] feelin' goin' on. An' the Deputy Prime Minister said he was gonna mek a change.
>AUTHOR: An amnesty?
>ANGEL: Ya, and one-on-one conversations. He help us. We have a house. A new start. A new job. But [some gang members] dey fell back because dey don't have di will, di education. . . . I didn't come from a poor family, so dat's why I tink I mek it. I come from a middle-class family, was a good ting.
>AUTHOR: You had an education?
>ANGEL: Yes! I had an education. Many o dose guys can't read and write. Ya, ya [yes, yes], I finish school.
>AUTHOR: That's really important right? If those guys can't read and write?
>ANGEL: Ya, ya, das why dey fell back. Di only ting dey know to do is shoot an' gangbang. Up to today, dere are few peoples dat survived my time . . . even here when we walk outside those streets [earlier we walked past Majestic Alley] even dese guys know I [am an] old gangster . . . you know, dey respec'.
>AUTHOR: Yeah, yous OG! [Original Gangster, we both laugh]

There is no doubting the intentions of the first gang truce; straight from the horse's mouth, Angel is a success story. Simultaneously, he flags three important challenges. First, for gang members to demobilize, they have to enter these processes in good faith; second, it takes a hefty political and economic investment to generate sufficiently robust and attractive alternatives to prevent recidivism and may include innovative interpretations of criminal justice, such as amnesties; and, finally, it is extremely challenging to get gang members onboard, for example, those with low academic achievement or trauma and addiction problems. These struggles bring to mind the refrain "you can take a horse to water, but you can't make it drink." The Achilles' heel was not the negotiated truce itself but the challenges of delivering continual reintegration and developmental support. We should not simply shoulder the blame with those working on the process at the time but recognize that demobilizing gang members is a very difficult task requiring a large dose of political and economic commitment. Understandably, many poor locals will ask why criminals, murderers even, are receiving economic and other benefits and not them or their law-abiding children? Certainly, attempts at gang demobilization across the region have delivered mixed results, some of which I investigated in Medellín, Colombia (Baird 2011), while others, in Ecuador for example, have been more successful (Brotherton and Gude 2020). Despite these challenges, the CYDP were credited with preventing large-scale gang wars as they began to work the streets, calming flare-ups.

Clearly, a number of gang members were more interested in seeing what they could get out of the process rather than engaging with personal transformation. Muhammad notes that in many cases they struggled to change individuals "gang mentality." Junie Balls was one of the Generals who took part, but he regressed and was later murdered in a gangland hit. As Muhammad says, the main issue was the lack of resources, not political will, and that the plan was only medium term, over one year, and not a permanent social strategy. The Bird's Isle gang truce finally collapsed and approximately three hundred "hardcore" gang members across nine gangs went back to business as usual. At the time, these were divided between the Crips; Ghost Town, Hoover, Lynch Mob, Kraal Road, and the Bloods; PIV, Plum Tree, Baka Town, Black Scorpion Posse, and Kick Down Fence (Muhammad 2015, p. 78).

Angel was one of the lucky ones. After the Bird's Isle negotiations fell apart, the homicide rate was about to take off. As he said, "I mek it." Many did not.

Conclusions

Tracing recent history, we see conflicted government-state responses to gangs. One the one hand, gangs were engaged: galvanized as clients of political party interests, delivering votes, or seen as interlocuters of negotiated truces to reduce crime and violence. On the other hand, they were crushed: targeted with the full force of the police, kangaroo courts, and the indiscriminate mass incarceration of poor young Creole men. Alongside the failure to deliver meaningful economic opportunities, foundering government policy and state institution responses to gangs are part of an ongoing sociohistorical process. This is not to posit contemporary life as a continuation of slavery, but to flag the indivisibility of historical from today's processes of subjugation. Southside clearly has a thriving system of embedded clientelism, which excels at suppressing meaningful political participation or representation. It is no coincidence that the most disenfranchised in Belizean society are the descendants of fieldslaves, brutality inherited from the colonial encounter. A class-based urban society pushing garrison politics has continued the pauperization of Southside. Rooted in history, violence is an outcome of the contemporary political failure that perpetuates the social terrains that gang populations are drawn from. Chronic vulnerability is a precondition for chronic violence: the rage of the poor turned inward, disenfranchised, depoliticized *lumpengangstas* killing each other.

3

Escalation

Disorganized Violence and the Homicide Boom

This chapter examines a critical juncture in Belizean gang history. In 1999 and 2000, almost two decades after Blood and Crip gangs first appeared on Southside, the homicide rate skyrocketed, making Belize one of the most violent countries in the world; by 2002, surpassing the World Health Organization's "conflict" threshold for violence at thirty homicides per one hundred thousand population, a position it maintains to this day (Chioda 2017, p. 86). Understanding Belize's homicide boom casts light on other tipping points in gang-related violence, particularly in Central America and the Caribbean, where contemporary violent democracies have seen death rates outstrip previous civil war levels (Arias and Goldstein 2010). We might simply argue that violence exists because we have gangs, after all, most homicide in the region, and certainly in Belize, coalesces among gang members. However, the homegrown protogang Base Boys, described in Chapter 1, already existed on Southside, selling marijuana and getting into fights, years before the homicide boom. When the Bloods and Crips were at the peak of their powers in the mid-1990s, homicide was still relatively low. So, the pertinent question is, Why did these gangs suddenly become so violent?

Once homicide booms occur, they establish a violent precedent and street gang culture that changes the social fabric (Baird 2020a). These changes are extremely difficult to sustainably turn back, and high levels of violence remain the Gordian knot of urban governance across the region. Rare exceptions of lasting homicide reduction, such as São Paulo or Medellín, have complex explanations, including politically taboo and largely hidden-from-view negotiated agreements between state entities and gang structures (Cruz and Durán-Martínez 2016; Feltran 2020; Hylton 2007). These challenges point to the significance of understanding and preventing homicide booms in the first place, which are too often attributed to simplistic, deductive analyses, where gangs conflated with drugs are presented as objective causes of violence. These lead to reductive policy prescriptions that work on the premise that if gangs and drugs are eradicated, some form of social harmony will ensue. In fact, when we consider the empirical evidence closely, there are always multiple factors that mediate the way communities transition to violence.

This chapter argues that we should be skeptical of assumptions that recent cocaine transshipment through Belize, also called a "bridge state" (Fowler and Bunck 2012), is responsible for sparking the violence epidemic, pointing to the disconnect between "transshipment" and "gangs." The homicide boom is explained as a consequence of the rapid fragmentation of established Blood and Crip structures, where street-level governance under the Generals gave way to widespread *disorganized* violence, fueled by an "iron river" of guns and ammunition from Guatemala that has a distinct political economy to cocaine transshipment. This is a counternarrative to prevailing assumptions that violence increases as gangs organize.

"The Game Is Tight"

The Medellín and Cali cartels pioneered cocaine trafficking through the Caribbean to the United States in the 1980s. Consequently, small island Caribbean states ratified the Vienna Convention on collaborative international laws against drugs in the region (Griffith 1997), while Jamaica was identified as *the* key transshipment route in the U.S. State Department's *International Narcotics Control Strategy Report*. Drug enforcement agencies such as the South Florida Task Force effectively shut down the Caribbean thoroughfare. This meant that traffickers seeking paths of least resistance rerouted transshipment via Central America and Mexico in the 1990s. Initially, this was through the Gulf of Mexico, then increasingly the Pacific Corridor from port towns, such as Buenaventura in Colombia, northward to the United States. Cocaine was extremely lucrative, hence the drug of choice (Bagley 2013). Since 2006, Mexican drug-trafficking organizations have reached south into neighboring Central American countries to escape domestic law enforcement pressures (Dudley 2011), yet these routes still account for the vast majority, approximately 80 percent, of all cocaine trafficked into the United States (UNODC 2012).

Anecdotally, in 2002, I spent some time on a small Colombian island in the Caribbean Sea called Providencia, or Old Providence, just a few hours by boat from the Belizean coastline. *Raizal* islanders recounted stories of making it rich reselling stockpiled gasoline at a huge markup to drug runners, who would refuel their *lancha rápida* speedboats on their way from Colombia to Central America. I distinctly remember asking a couple of young men I was stranded with on a lancha after the propellor fell off and we awaited rescue for several hours, "What about the police?" They laughed at my naivety and said, "The Mexican police are the ones who unload it." Some fishermen had even begun to transport the drugs from Providencia themselves and could make upward of US$20,000 for a few days' work. Cocaine was nothing short of a bonanza for hardup fisherfolk on the island.

This anecdote is a way to transition into a widely held assumption that crops up in the literature, that drug transshipment generates violence in the countries it passes through (e.g., UNDP 2012). One World Bank report boldly claims that drug trafficking is a driver of homicide that has "predisposed Central America to high levels of homicide" (Demombynes 2011). In 2019, the UNODC stated, "Homicide trends in the Caribbean have been influenced by violence associated with drug trafficking flows and concentrated in particular locations" (p. 27). Knight describes a historically rooted susceptibility to violence in the Caribbean, which

> has become quite vulnerable to threats from illicit trafficking and transnational organized crime and to the concatenated violence that tends to accompany this type of transnational criminal activity. Transnational crimes such as drug trafficking, the trafficking in illegal guns ... are usually accompanied domestically by increases in gangs, illicit drug trafficking, robberies, retaliation murders, rapes, and domestic violence. These expressions of violence cannot be treated independently; they are inter-related and mutually reinforcing. (2019, p. 414)

Knight is not wrong, but he is also plainly orthodox in his approach. Similarly, Demombynes's report for the World Bank argues that drug trafficking necessarily promotes "gun diffusion," assuming guns, ammunition, and drug trafficking follow the same logic and share inimical political economies. These assumptions feel intuitive but are methodologically frail because they are highly deductive, based on research using swaths of quantitative data on homicide and drug flows. In short, they identify correlation. As we know, correlation and causality are not necessarily comfortable bedfellows, and the packaging together of transnational drug trafficking with violence is too facile; it misses crucial interceding factors, namely a closer understanding of the social terrain where violence occurs. We can only scrutinize these processes by engaging those communities worst affected and, in doing so, create an empirically based and inductive picture that tells us a quite different, somewhat surprising, story in the Belizean case.

The transshipment to violence argument harks back to the categorization of drugs as a security threat and the *war on drugs* referred to in Chapter 1. This conservative discourse influenced ensuing U.S. foreign policy in Latin America and the Caribbean and, in the past two decades in Central America, has been enthusiastically rebranded by populist right-wing regimes as the *war on gangs*, skirting over the social conditions that underpin the rise of gangs in the first place (Dudley 2020; Wolf 2015). Framing drugs as an objective security threat decontextualizes the factors that mediate their impact in different sectors of society. Drugs did not play a significant role in Southside's transition to violence. Most cocaine transshipment through the country is highly organized and at pains to be low profile, actively avoiding street gangs in Belize City. By that measure, cocaine transshipment in Belize is remarkably, although not perfectly, nonviolent.

Traditionally in several countries in the Caribbean, the religious and recreational use of marijuana has not been considered a social, let alone security, problem. Equally, despite not having a strong Rastafarian culture, marijuana has been bought, sold, and widely used in Belize for decades. In the late 1980s and 1990s, the *Belizean Breeze* strain was sourced from the Orange Walk district and, although renowned for its potency, was a recreational drug normally smoked socially, and marijuana sales operated without any violence of note. One national scholar even described marijuana in positive terms as a calming influence that reduced street conflicts (2017).

During my visits to Southside, it was abundantly clear that marijuana was cheap, widespread, and smoked openly on the streets, particularly by young men. With colleagues Bishop and Kerrigan (Baird, Bishop, and Kerrigan 2022, 2023), we noted that aside from marijuana with its own distinct economy (see Klein 2016), Caribbean societies are not prodigious consumers of hard drugs such as crystal meth, fentanyl, ecstasy, or heroin. Cocaine consumption is low compared to the United States and Europe, particularly the United Kingdom and Spain, and crack cocaine consumption tends to be small and isolated, not capable of driving gang wars. This was reinforced by a study of high school students in Belize City by Briceño-Perriott, Olivera, and Esner (2013) who found that marijuana was the drug of choice and was even smoked more than cigarettes by young people. Although not the drug of choice, this is not to say cocaine and crack cannot be obtained on the streets (Hanson, Warchol, and Zupan 2004), and I was told by one gang member, "I don't like cocaine, but it's something I can get fast, in ten minutes I can get that, in three minutes, I can get that if you want it" (2022).

Strong strains of marijuana are rapidly evolving. In 2017, I was told it was called "hydro," as in, grown hydroponically for strength. In 2021, I spent the afternoon with gang members on Southside who curiously didn't pass a joint around between them, rather they had a small one each, would take two or three draws, then put it out. I asked them what was going on. They said they had progressed from hydro and now smoke Mexican "kush," which has an even higher THC level, up to a mind-bending 20 percent (considering the famed *Belizean Breeze* reached only 11 percent), so after a couple of puffs they are stoned for a long time. It was a cheap, lasting way to get high, and over the course of the few hours I was with them, they would spark up the joint, for a few puffs, then put it out for later (2021). Marijuana tends to be sold as cheap small bags, a youth worker said, "Weed is a poor man's drug, the only ting they smoke here. Poor can't afford cocaine, so it's doesn't come in [to Southside]" (2021). If there is anything approaching a public health crisis with drugs in Belize, it is not cocaine or marijuana, rather alcohol. The youth worker continued, "The poor drink 'Red Top.' Go try some, it's fucked up. Costs BZ$5 [US$2.50]." Later I bought some at the supermarket on North Front Street and tried it: a sweet, highly alcoholic, rum-based drink, that burned the throat the way cheap spirits do, sold in a small bottle that looks more like a medicine. I asked former gang leader Angel if he wanted it, he said, "I don't drink dat shit man, dat's what bums drink" (2021). Recently, a new rum-based spirit has emerged known colloquially as "Bad Man" for its high alcohol content. It is stronger than Red Top and, ominously, even cheaper.

Gangs sell marijuana from *bases* on the streets, but it is also sold by non–gang members. When I visited Shorty after he had got out of jail in 2022, we spent an afternoon at his dilapidated house in Belmopan where he relocated to get away from the "madness" of Southside. He was no longer gangbanging but was the established neighborhood marijuana dealer. As we shared a couple of beers and some fried chicken in his living room, I was struck to see the sheer number of customers walking in off the street through his wide-open front door, straight into the living room, to buy small BZ$20 bags. It was a constant flow, these were "normal" people, for want of a better phrase, just coming back from work at around 5:00 p.m. Shorty knew all of them, saying, "I don't sell to no one I don't know," and his clients seemed like his friends. One young lady stopped for a chat after she had just got off work in a call center but only had BZ$7. Shorty told her off "don't be comin' round here with small money," then reluctantly took a pinch of weed out of a bag, wrapped it in a piece of paper and handed it over. They both then laughed about it, and she said, "see you tomorrow" (ca. 2022).

Selling marijuana remains illegal, although personal possession and consumption of up to ten grams was decriminalized in November 2017. Marijuana permeates the Belizean cultural image at music events such as Smoke

Clouds Riddim by Southside artist Prophit PMO.[1] Cocaine, conversely, makes its way to wealthier tourists in beach resorts such as Caye Caulker, San Pedro, or Placencia, where I have been offered it several times walking down the sand high streets over the years. Although, Southside did have a crack epidemic in the 1990s, which is later expanded on, Arciaga Young and King's (2019) recent survey for the Inter-American Development Bank (IDB) shows that nowadays only a third (36 percent) of Southsiders said they knew people who had ever used cocaine, crack, or heroin (p. 30). In other words, marijuana is destined for local consumption. Cocaine has a different logic that does not seek out ostensibly poor inhabitants in Belize City.

The first traces of cocaine entered Belize in the late 1980s, trickling-down to the streets in limited quantities from transnational networks, then being cooked into crack. There is scant information available from this time, but elder Southsiders say this was the earliest they remember seeing cocaine and crack on the streets. Young and Woodiwiss (2019) argue that U.S. drug policies to the Caribbean in that period were "not fit for purpose," and a Belizean journalist explained the irony that crack use on Southside was actually a consequence of the regional war on drugs wiping out marijuana:

> *Belizean Breeze* was wiped out in Orange Walk wid de War on Drugs, so people turned to crack cocaine in Belize [City] as it was cheaper dan beer. Gang members drank and smoked weed. When it [weed] was wiped out wid "paraquat," dey turned to crack cocaine. As weed gone, dey were cooking crack and selling it in Belize [City]. Dere was a crack cocaine epidemic from '92 to like '97. People strung out on drugs. "Strawberries" were women on crack who would take you behind a car and do anyting you wanted for BZ$2 [US$1] to go and get a fix. (2017)

It is difficult to accurately explain the rise, fall, and impact of crack in Belize City given the absence of research on the subject; however, what is clear is that crack sales began several years before the homicide boom. This chapter is not a polemic arguing drugs are in no way connected to violence; undoubtedly, crack accelerated the unraveling of an already vulnerable social fabric and can still be found in Belize City today. This highlights that the crack epidemic did not coincide with a rapid rise in homicide rates.

Indisputably, drug sales are an economic mainstay of many street gangs across the globe (see Brotherton and Gude 2021a; Hanzen and Rodgers 2015). Additionally, there is an excellent body of contemporary scholarship in the Caribbean and Central America discussing this theme (Deosaran 2017; Edmonds 2016; Evans and Jaffe 2020; Gutierrez Rivera, Strønen, and Ystanes 2018). The literature shows that street gangs always operate locally, although some participate in nationwide and even international trafficking. This makes the distinction between "gang" and "organized crime" a common tension in the criminological field, especially as gangs are evolving, not static, entities, and real-world overlap often occurs between the two (Decker and Pyrooz 2015a). Research on *commandos* in Rio de Janeiro (Arias and Barnes 2016) and *pandillas* in Medellín flag the centrality that local drug sales can play in ganglands (Baird 2018a; Durán-Martínez 2015). Yet, for gangs in other cities, such as the Primero Comando da Capital in São Paulo, Brazil, or the maras in San Salvador, economic activities are more diverse, drugs being one facet of a smorgasbord of activities (Bergmann 2020; Feltran 2020). Briscoe and Breda (2020) have noticed that the connectedness between mara gangs in Central America and transshipment dynamics have also shifted. For example, gangs were initially only small-scale local drug vendors informally connected to transnational networks, yet, over time, some gang members "graduated" into increasingly professionalized drug trafficking. Conversely, Rodgers (2018) found that in Managua, Nicaragua, gang-based drug markets were fragile and subject to boom-and-bust, so we should not assume drugs are consistent or fundamental to gang function in transshipment countries. In other words, while gang involvement in local drug sales is a given, it is also context dependent, ranging from piecemeal small-time local sales with no connections to transnational organized crime, to gangs being considered key figures in international transshipment.

Southside gangs today are a far cry from cartel-like organizations, yet media reports link them to drug trafficking in a way that suggests they are important pivots in the international trade. There is negligible information on drug transshipment in Belize, in part, given the lack of state capacity or willingness to collect such information but also because of the tendency for scholars to overlook Belize. Fowler and Bunck's (2012) dive into archival information is a rare exception. The data we do have come from UNODC extrapolated from drug seizures from U.S. authorities, such as the State Department, and news outlets. Approximately ten tons of cocaine worth some US$75 million, or 5 percent of Belize's GDP, were transshipped through the country in 2010 (UNODC 2012), although we must assume a large margin for error in these figures. In 2018, almost a ton of cocaine was seized by Belizean security forces indicating that flows had increased significantly ("Drug Seizures Increase in Belize as More Cocaine Flows North" 2019). Transshipment tends to involve tight-knit trafficking "families," meaning either kin or small secretive groups, stretching along the coastline where drugs have historically entered, from San Pedro in the north to Punta Gorda in the south. There is a culturally attuned and very Creole form of *omertà* around drug trafficking; everyone in the village knows who the traffickers are yet say nothing. A magistrate in a northern coastal town once explained to me that *wet drop* cocaine bales are collected offshore, passing unperceived through popular tourist resorts en route to Mexico (2016).[2]

I took to calling this sea-to-land drug transshipment *surf 'n' turf* trafficking. One well-known historical example of this is the notorious George Herbert, who collected wet drops and received drug planes from the Medellín cartel in the late 1980s and early 1990s. He transported the cocaine overland to the Orange Walk district to be packed into small planes flown to the United States by his cousin or the drugs were driven up to Mexico. Herbert was running with the George Street Bloods in the city. During that period, the gang was involved in the logistics supply chain according to one middle-aged Southsider, loading and unloading cocaine from planes (2021). A small proportion of cocaine destined for wealthier markets overseas was diverted via the gangs back into Belize City driving the relatively brief crack epidemic. However, these flows were peripheral to Herbert's main business. He became rich but was eventually caught and extradited to the United States (Muhammad 2015). Similarly, my own research with colleagues in Trinidad and Tobago, across the Caribbean Sea, has shown that the Port of Spain is not a priority destination for drugs, and most cocaine never actually makes it onshore on its way to the United States or Europe (Baird, Bishop, and Kerrigan 2022, 2023).

I interviewed a member of a "family" involved in cocaine transshipment, in 2016 and 2021 in their hometown, a popular tourist destination with absolutely no visual clues that it was a drugs thoroughfare. Theirs was the typical story of a fisherman, the father in the family, finding a cocaine bale floating in the surf back in the early 1990s, and they have since gone on to become a significant player in the trade. The strategy of "keeping it tight," or "playing a tight game," has kept them off the radar of potential capture and prosecution. The fisherfolk-to-drug smugglers is a common tale in the Caribbean, although the family's first interaction with the police was more surprising. And telling.

When the father found their first bale, news spread round the village rapidly, as might be expected, reminding me of the oft quoted Colombian saying, *pueblo pequeño, infierno grande* (small village, big hell). Within hours the local police turned up at the door and turned the house upside down looking for the drugs, leaving empty-handed and furious. I asked my contact, naively, whether this was because they couldn't make an arrest, at which they laughed, "of course not." The police, even in the primal days of cocaine transshipment, were either looking to seize the drugs to sell themselves, or to extort the family, effectively taking a cut or "tax." Their fury was at losing out.

My contact told me that trafficking routes are connected to powerful individuals in the police, business, and political circles and that transshipped drugs mainly passed through Mexico by land, sea, and air, and sometimes

Guatemala. They had no knowledge of Belize trafficking directly to the United States or Europe. They continued that cocaine rarely passes through Belize City on its way out of the country and Southside is not a target market, although, of course, a number of organized traffickers live in Belize City at least some of the time. Fowler and Bunck (2012) state that international trafficking routes are "elite" and not beneficial to urban communities citing U.S. intelligence reports where "most Belizean trafficking organizations are small, tightly knit groups, and their members are often related" (p. 93). One individual who worked for a state institution was straightforward in his assessment that "big drug trafficking takes place amongst big politicians and businesspeople" (2016).

My contact told me that within their coastal village, there was one other well-connected middleman who would buy lost bales that washed up on nearby beaches, and locals knew exactly where to take them if they found them. This was demonstrated to me by a boat operator I befriended who recounted the tale of the drug plane that crashed in a national marine park in 2021, adjacent to the well-known caye I was visiting with a group of unsuspecting tourists. He said the locals quickly caught wind of the crash and scrambled out in motorboats to pick up the bales, saying "di *white grouper* [cocaine bale] di float. Di float as dey wrap in so much plastic, keep air in. . . . Den everybody knows where to tek dem in di village" (2021). This is what the locals euphemistically call *di white lobsta lottri*. Although "the game is tight" there is inevitable slippage and spillover into the village, given the inherent risks to trafficking, and the windfalls to be made out of a *white lobsta* means locals are understandably opportunist.

This opportunism is widespread in Belize. In a different location on the northern coastline, I asked a community police officer about the cocaine that had been touted to me in tourist spots Caye Caulker and San Pedro. He said that cocaine sales to tourists come from accidental finds of bales that washed up regularly on nearby beaches (2017). For example, in March 2019, 23 kilograms of cocaine were found on Northern Ambergris Caye not far from the Mexican border ("Drug Seizures Increase in Belize as More Cocaine Flows North" 2019). Given the on-the-ground information I had gathered, this seemed like a rare case of honest police beating the locals to it.

Another contact explained that trafficking brings money to the whole coastline and reeled off a series of village names. I visited one of the villages they had mentioned in 2022. It was not touristy but rather located between tourist destinations and visibly poorer than its neighbors for it. The dusty, dilapidated police station in the middle of town gave the distinct impression of a place that resolved its problems without official involvement. It was a sleepy town, and a few people were scattered around in the shade of buildings lining the street on a blisteringly hot day, several men looking worse for wear sat talking on the steps of the Chinese mini-mart, drinking blue and white labeled Belikin stout out of dark brown bottles. I asked my contact in the drug-trafficking family about the police in this particular village, a short drive from their home. They said that the officers were not locals and are rotated in and out, but such is the involvement of senior police officers in the drug trade, they are not motivated to chase down nearby trafficking families. Given their poor pay, they would rather collect kickbacks, adding that they were generally uneducated "the least intelligent guys who were bottom of my class became police officers, that's where you go" (2021). My contact continued in blasé fashion, confirming the partying and, incredibly, the role of the police. "[The village] is really poor. People there just party when they get money from a find [cocaine bale]. When they find it, they know which police to take it to and get a pay day. When the plane went down behind [names caye in national maritime park mentioned earlier], they were partying for months, until the money run out!" The police force are part of village life, poor and poorly educated, and part of the drug-trafficking ecosystem.

That said, the scale of police involvement is difficult to assess and taboo. Occasionally stories are so scandalous, they break the surface, indicating the depth of police participation. In November 2021, when I was in Belize, news broke of a drug plane that landed at night on an interior highway. There was a shoot-out between the police and the individuals unloading cocaine, who, as it turned out, were police officers and members of the armed forces. The police are consistently involved. Following a spate of plane landings in 2021, the press wrote, "Assistant Commissioner of Police Marco Vidal may not have been part of a circle of rogue cops who facilitated the landing of drug planes in Belize over the past twelve months; however, he is on administrative leave tonight for managerial shortcomings that may have enabled his men to aid and abet the movement of cocaine through the country."[3]

I was told by a retired civil servant that instances where police are caught are "fuck ups" and that the vast majority of trafficking occurs without incident and to the substantial pecuniary benefit of those involved. When I discussed this with my contact in the drug-trafficking family, they rattled off several well-known retired senior police officers who have extended property portfolios in expensive tourist areas, and they mentioned one whose elder brother was a well-known narco. In an indication of how small Belize's population is, they implicated a senior officer who I actually had a meeting with when working with the United Nations in 2011. He had retired to a sizable luxury villa by the sea, lauding his impunity in a property far beyond the reach of a police pension. This information was spoken in hushed tones, yet presented as an open secret. The whole village knew which corrupt police officers had property and where. "*Everyone* knows *exactly* what is going on," they emphasized (2021).

Reliable information about drug trafficking is hard come by, and the earlier information is admittedly bitty and anecdote heavy and certainly inadequate for a court of law, for which it is not intended. A number of officers were arrested in 2021 marking a change with the past, and the PUP sacked two hundred police officers in 2022 alone, however, there is little evidence of their facing jail time. The sense among Belizeans is that these are foot soldiers, not the orchestrators of the trade. The extent to which police are a component of a "narco-state" is a moot point and doubtlessly polemical. It requires further research, but it is entirely plausible and, one might speculate, a reason the PUP recently had to clean house, as this would not have sat well with the U.S. Embassy.

Drug Transshipment Does Not Drive Homicide, So What Does?

That ethnographic segue into the coastal drug trade in Belize was a way of adding credence to the argument that cocaine trafficking did not spark Belize's homicide boom. The locations and political economies of cocaine and marijuana are distinct. Marijuana sales are necessarily advertised in the community, while cocaine trafficking is hermetically sealed and hidden from view. Marijuana comes from Mexico sometimes routed through Guatemala, cocaine from South America. The trades involve totally different groups of people. A lot of people sell marijuana; conversely, well-organized and highly cautious cocaine trafficking restricts the number of "families" and individuals involved: "There are few competing factions," one researcher told me (2022).

Dudley has argued that gangs have historic links to drug trafficking in Belize (2011, p. 896); Fowler and Bunck (2012) report that "serious gang activity was fueled by international cocaine trafficking"; and Warnecke-Berger (2019) states that "with drug trafficking involvement, finally, the gangs were able to invest in weapons" (p. 214). Yet, these links are assumed and overstated, giving the impression that gangs are more integral to drug trafficking than they actually are. This is not to argue that there are no links whatsoever, but gangs, at best, have been only tangentially involved. George Herbert, mentioned earlier, was indeed an international trafficker in the 1990s, who involved the George Street Bloods. But this was not a starting point for the emergence of an organized gang-cartel hybrid. In fact, the opposite happened; after Herbert was extradited, transshipment links disappeared with him, demonstrating a lack of criminal institutionalization.

It is facile policyspeak to say drug transshipment caused Belize City's gang violence, and those earlier who suggest it, do not provide empirical rigor. We should appreciate Fowler and Bunck, and Warnecke-Berger's contributions, as they are thorough archive-dives and have been very useful in compiling this book; however, methodologically, they do not present primary data such as firsthand interviews with gang members, drug traffickers, or inmates in Belize.

The role of gangs was more accurately reported by the U.S. State Department in 2019:

> The Government of Belize is cognizant of the dangers posed by its status as a transit point. It is particularly concerned that growing violence in Belize is, and will increasingly be, tied to the drug trade. However, *Belize's domestic criminal concerns are focused on extremely high levels of local gang-related violence, which is not yet clearly tied to transnational organized crime* [emphasis added]. (*International Narcotics Control Strategy Report* 2019, p. 110)

Accordingly, Dudley conceded that Belizean gangs do not appear ready "to make the leap to another phase of criminal activity" (2011, p. 876). Shorty, serving time in Belize Central Prison when I first interviewed him, confirmed what the community police officer said: that cocaine only ended up on Southside streets when someone on the coast found a lost bale and brought it there. He said he did not know of *any* street gangs directly involved in the transnational organized trade (2016), and I have never heard of any accused of having a large property portfolio or a villa by the sea. I have seen Vartas's and Shorty's houses. If they are wealthy individuals, they are hiding it extremely well. Recently, a survey found that 73 percent of gang members said money earned from selling drugs was only enough to cover their, or their family's personal expenses (Arciaga Young and King 2019, p. 30), akin to drug dealers who live with their mothers observed by Venkatesh in Chicago (2008).

A 2021 *Vice News* article[4] said: "These [Belizean] gangsters aren't rich, they don't move kilos of cocaine or run large-scale extortion rackets. It's mostly nickel and dime street-level marijuana dealing that puts food on their plates. At one point, they even start asking for money for booze." Gayle and Mortis's study included interviews with twenty-three gang members (2010, pp. 314–315). They made "petty sales" of weed and sometimes other drugs, for day-to-day money, but no organized bulk trafficking, going further, saying they do not like working with drug transshipment because it is so dangerous. Shorty said most local gang members were lucky to make US$15 a day (2016). When I caught up with him on the outside, in 2022, he was dealing marijuana "successfully" and making up to BZ$200 (US$100) weekdays and BZ$400 (US$200) at the weekends:

> If you [find] a wet drop you take it to da man [sell it back into the clandestine trafficking networks], but if you get it wrong they'll com' an' kill you for it. So, you have to be smart, you can make money. But da first ting you do if you get some is *keep yo' mouth shut*. Da first ting I do with dope is buy a lot of guns. When I get dope, I've got five people, even some women, but five guns is five *shottas*. (2016)

Gang members are often performative in parts of their interviews, living up to the gangsta image, but the more an individual is interviewed, the more time the researcher spends in their company, the more the mask slips. After some time, Shorty eventually admitted that he was showing off and was talking hypothetically. He had actually never come across a cocaine bale on Southside.

During an early research trip to Belize, I remember my skepticism when the spouse of a well-known Southside politician said they longed for the good old days when the Generals were in charge, "Gangs used to be more social, now dey jus' crazy" (2016). However, after coming to understand that "jus' crazy" meant hyperfragmented gang structures and booming street violence, they were expressing concern about the traumatic impact of this on people's lives in their constituency. It was not difficult to empathize with this position, born of desperation, that created a nostalgia for the Generals of yore. But how did it come to this?

The Bloods and Crips expanded exponentially in the late 1980s and early 1990s. However, gang numbers alone do not cause spiraling homicide rates. The introduction and proliferation of guns, reinforced by the imported gun-centric gangsta culture, was fundamental in the transition to violence. At first glance a simple social equation appears: more gang members plus more firepower equals more homicide. Crudely, this is true. Yet, there are many interceding factors and processes at play. We normally find that violence increases as rival gangs organize and compete over illicit street economies, and variously against the state (e.g., Durán-Martínez 2018; Denyer Willis 2015), a type of *organized violence*. However, the Belizean case provides a countervailing example. The gang-driven homicide boom was actually caused by *disorganized violence*.

The Bloods or Crips reached their zenith in the first half of the 1990s, a period when homicide was, in fact, negligible. Of course, this does not mean that there was no lethal violence between gang members at the time; Angel told me about a number of his running partners in the Majestic Alley Crips who were killed, such as Derek "Itza" Brown in 1992. Crucially, though, the homicide boom *did not* occur when the Bloods and Crips were at their peak, rather the opposite, when their structures began to unravel.

The Blood and Crip Generals of the 1990s, looked back on nostalgically by the politician's spouse referred to at the start of this section, had the capacity to control gang structures (also argued by Muhammad 2015). They were known to keep a lid on violence using their authority as informal local mayors in combination with the machinations of party clientelism. Rather than high absolute gang numbers, the key variable for violent outcomes in Belize's case was the way gangs were organized and controlled. Counterintuitively, the suppression of violence *by gangs themselves* is a common, if fragile, phenomenon in Latin America and the Caribbean (Brotherton and Gude 2020; Feltran 2020). This has been articulated in two principal forms: *pax mafiosa*, the informal agreement on the division of illicit economies between rival groups, or *pax monopolista*, the leviathan-like domination by one organized gang that no longer needs to engage in disputes with rivals (Biderman et al. 2019).

In Belize, gun accumulation by gangs began as a trickle in the 1980s. These were sourced in-country by ambitious gang members, who showed no shortage of ingenuity in locating hard-to-source firearms. Antique rifles were unearthed from the colonial period and young men would venture into the countryside to buy side-by-side double-barreled shotguns off farmers who used them to protect their livestock from predators. There were other local sources to be found in the city, pistols and pump-action shotguns were robbed from private security guards, or *watchmen* as they are still known. Angel recalled the modest beginnings of gun procurement:

> Firs' we were selling weed, crack-cocaine hadn't even touched Belize [in the early 1980s], da cocaine came in lik after di '85. I started selling and jus' doin hustling, whateva, just to mek a buck. Dere weren't gangs den, jus' guys who hang out and try to hustle. Dere weren't really any guns, we used to chase our enemies wid a stick and machete. Den we started ta walk round in blue rags, blue clothes, y'know.
>
> Yeah, in '87, '88, we use to go fight at a local disco. If you from over di bridge, we pick a fight wid 'you, wid knife an' machete. Dey were serious fights, but not really wid guns. I tink I was about 17 maybe, I hold ma firs' gun, an' da first man dat talk big I shoot in his chest. I buy my firs' [gun] from a farmer. Den we go an' kidnap di watchman an' took his 16 [gauge shotgun] an' cut di barrel shaaff [shaft]. We call it saadaaff [sawn-off], you could stick it in your side, you run up into your enemy and you jus' bus-it [fire it] and run aff.
>
> Yeah, more money, more bigger you get. Den man come to trade gun for crack, gun for weed. So, ah [I] sell weed, but if ah have no army,

man tek it away. Ah used to pack a 9mm an' a 357. Dat's a barrel gun, it sound like a bomb explode, so everybody respec' you. *Dat's a Big Man gun y'know!* [his emphasis]. (2016)

These were humble beginnings. As described in Chapter 1, Angel was deported back to Belize in 1981, and although he was *Cripin'* back then, it was a slow start as he was more or less on his own with a handful of friends. Angel's *saadaaff* pointed to innovation through necessity and the novelty of firearms in the 1980s, and Southsiders commented to me that episodes of gunfire were still rare on the streets of the city. Although inhabitants were accustomed to some street violence, the culmination of these were knife and machete fights between Base Boys—as the scars on Angel's torso attested when he lifted his shirt to show me one day—but rarely lethal, and without gunfire it was not uncommon for mothers and aunties to venture onto the streets to break up fights.

During the 1990s, guns were trickling into the city but yet to proliferate significantly. They tended to be the sole possession of top-ranking gang members such as Generals or designated to shottas, also known as "strike men." The rank and file rarely actually *owned* guns, and, if they did use them, it was with the express permission of the gang leadership. No one could have known at the time that this was, in fact, a period of *gun control*, compared with what was to come.

The imported U.S. gangsta identities brought a subcultural trope not familiar to Southside's streets before: the glamorization of guns popularized through rap and hip-hop music, and films. Gun violence is "spectacular" (see Goldstein 2004), even in small doses, grasping the community's attention (e.g., Karandinos et al. 2015). The mothers and aunties that would break up fistfights were soon kept indoors by shots ringing out over Southside, one local told me. As Angel said, his gun sounded "like a bomb going off," which would have reverberated through the flimsy wooden shacks on Southside.

With hindsight, the Blood and Crip heyday was a period of social order on the streets. This order was weakened by three processes. First, the rapid expansion of new gang sets into peri-urban territories making control by the Generals geographically challenging. Second, the collapse of the Bird's Isle negotiations resulting in many gang members heading back to the streets. And, third, as negotiations faltered, the pendulum swung toward crackdowns that targeted gang leadership structures. This accelerated the fragmenting of the old order, contributing to a collapse of the Blood and Crip duopoly on the streets. Similarly, but on a much larger scale, previous mano dura tactics in Northern Triangle countries disrupted well-organized and vertically integrated mara structures, resulting in an uptick in violence among low-level gang members on the streets (Briscoe and Breda 2020).⁵ As one Belizean police officer said in an interview in 2021, "Gun laws were made much tougher in 2010, and we had mano dura, but that's done fuck all, it doesn't work."

There was a widely held assumption at the time, derived from U.S. *kingpin* strategy, that by targeting the leadership, criminal organizations would disintegrate. Perhaps. But removing the Generals undermined any social order on gang-controlled streets in communities forever abandoned by the state. *Vice News* interviewed jailed gang members who concurred that "the rising murder rate was tied to a criminal code that has faded as more and more of the older generation were murdered, disappeared, or ended up in prison."⁶ A journalist brought up on Southside looked back at the times when the Bloods ran with George Herbert:

> The George Street [Bloods] heyday was the late 80s to 2000, all of the 90s. George Street was the most feared, this was the George Herbert era, the golden era. Herbert lived on George Street, and he kept a lid on violence and robberies, and every Christmas he gave out bicycles to poor children. He was not a cartel, but he was connected to them. He was a gang leader, and he was very, very clever, and he managed everything. Then Shiny and Pinky [from the notorious Tillett family] rose under him and took over when he was extradited. But they were much worse, and the violence started, and George Street fell apart. The new generation of George Street are scary, and some are psychopaths. (2022)

The Belizean state may have aspired to exert the rule of law at the time, but clearly did not have the capacity to do so, and Southside saw a period of increased lawlessness. A researcher and UDP party member told me "we have these splinters, that's what happened. It's a *medusaizing* type of effect. A chopping off of the head and you get seven more" (2022). A retired civil servant that had spent many years intervening with gangs said:

> The error that everyone makes and still makes is cutting the gang off at-de-head. The kingpin strategy means that you don't really have leaders as such, just some incapable squabbling sprats rising up. We not really have strong leadership since when [way back]. The homicide rose and when that started it is very, very hard for the government to bring it back, but the government treat them like an underclass to be used. (2021)

A Southside community leader reflected on that period:

> Back in de day, dey [police] started killing off de heads [Generals] because dey wuz able to be identified. So, widout heads de gang situation basically jus' got outta hand, cuz de killers are now 17 and 18 years old. New leaders fight for dis position. (2016)

Sheldon "Pinky" Tillett and his brother Gerald "Shiny" Tillett Sr. of the George Street Bloods are paradigmatic of this fragmented violence: In the 2000s, they began feuding with a new rival Blood faction a block away in Taylor's Alley. Arthur Young, the leader of Taylor's Alley Gang, allegedly shot Pinky dead in 2012 at a petrol station, leading to tit-for-tat violence across the city. A week later Arthur Young was killed, possibly in an extrajudicial killing by the police.[7] Shiny took over the gang and was shot in 2016, then, his son, Gerald Tillett, who succeeded him was gunned down in 2021.[8]

Belize's long western frontier with Guatemala is lush tropical jungle. On the Belizean side, San Ignacio is the main border town and adventure tourism hot spot. From there, the road winds over the hills through the village Benque Viejo del Carmen and across the border into Melchor de Mencos. This is a well-trodden route by day-trippers from San Ignacio who visit the towering Tikal Mayan ruins in Guatemala. It is the only major border crossing and Melchor de Mencos has become a notoriously violent town in recent years (Dudley 2011). This route is likely to be a gun-running thoroughfare, but concrete evidence is hard to come by. Gang members, police, a magistrate, and a member of a drug-trafficking family did tell me that the overwhelming majority of guns come through family connections in post-conflict, weapons-liquid Guatemala. Of Southside gang members, 93 percent reported it would be "very easy" or "somewhat easy" to get a gun (Arciaga Young and King 2019, p. 30). Author Ioan Grillo's figurative description of gun flows as "the iron river" applies here.[9] The majority of guns do not come, as I had assumed, through Mexico by proxy from the United States. These dynamics set Belize apart from much of the Caribbean where the iron river flows overwhelmingly from the United States to critical nodes in the region, then guns fan out across the islands. Indeed, this is a phenomenon largely understudied and shifts the burden of responsibility for violence toward the United States and trafficking networks that flow south (Fabre et al. 2023, p. 76; Grillo 2023). Gayle and Mortis interviewed twenty-three gang members in 2010. They said that 9mm ammunition came from Guatemala, but the gangs mainly used middlemen who were non-Black Belizeans (2010, pp. 318–319). This is logical given the family links between Mayans and mestizos across the Belize/Guatemala border, and, staggeringly, that Guatemala registered the legal import of a scarcely believable 41 million rounds of ammunition in 2021 alone. This figure does not include illicit traffic. There is no pressing need to source ammunition from Mexico. Further, after a hiatus from fieldwork due to the COVID-19 pandemic, I put the question of arms and ammunition trafficking to a senior police officer in November 2021. He said "sacks" of weapons come in from Guatemala, and these have been high-powered guns since the late 2000s. As with coastal drug traffickers, gun smugglers may or may not actually be *family*, rather this word is a signifier for microlevel smuggling between trusted individuals as opposed to a large-scale organized criminal racket.

I also had the opportunity to speak to a high-ranking Guatemalan army officer, who said that there were hundreds of blind spots along the border and that the jungle is so dense after only a few steps you can no longer see where you came from. Anecdotally, I crossed over the land border twice between Melchor and San Ignacio in early 2022. I drove my seven-seat family sized SUV, filling out the requisite forms and paying the necessary taxes. Despite there being no one in front of me in the line of traffic on the way over from Guatemala, the whole bureaucratic experience took a Kafkaesque two hours, much to the chagrin of my three young daughters. Yet, in all this time, no official on either side of the border even came to look at my car, let alone search it or even cross-check that I had put the correct license plate down on the forms. The vast majority of border area is uncontrolled, yet where there were official controls, they were so lax as to be irrelevant.

The early 2000s saw the scale-up of gangs' arsenals; from old shotguns and colonial rifles to modern 9mm handguns with extended magazines, and fully automatic weapons. At Raccoon Street police station, an officer told me he had even confiscated grenades (2016). Notably, when guns enter communities, they rarely leave, staying for decades. One gun can be passed around or hired out, accumulating homicides or "ghosts" (Sanatan 2018). Street-level disputes turned into something far more lethal. Today over 80 percent of homicides in Belize are caused by firearms (UNODC 2019). As one former gang member said, in no uncertain terms, "da guns dat is out dere *is big guns*, n***a!" (2017).

The spike in the national homicide rate occurred between 1999 and 2000. Gunpolicy.org reports that most are gun deaths, and the vast majority were men (Alpers and Picard 2022). They show in 2000 there was just one female gun death to every twenty-one male deaths. This ratio was at its most unequal at 1:41 in 2003, and in Belize's most violent year on record, 2012, this ratio was 8:86, some 11 percent being women. Pitts and Inkpen studied gun trends in Belize between 2011 and 2020. They noted that firearms continued to be "at the heart of much of Belize's violence and crime [and that] the widespread circulation of guns—both licit and illicit—is a growing concern, particularly because the types of firearms circulating are increasingly sophisticated and include military style weapons" (2021, p. 212).

The changes gangs went through in this period define them today. They became characterized by high turnover, ephemeral leadership, and frequent, lethal spats. Fragmentation begot fragmentation, setting off a chain reaction leading to a kaleidoscope of gangs. The nine gang sets in the 1995 Bird's Isle negotiations became thirty by the 2000s. Gang membership snowballed from three hundred to an estimated fifteen hundred by 2015 (Haylock 2013, p. 46; Peirce 2017, p. 21). This may not seem like a significant number, but we might recall that Belize City has a population of just sixty thousand, meaning a ratio of 2.5 gang members per 100 population. Tellingly, almost half of the youth respondents (43 percent) in Gayle and Mortis's Southside survey had a family member who is affiliated with a gang (2010, p. 263).

Gang territories expanded into peri-urban swamplands such as Bac-a-Lan (Back of Land), while existing gang territories continued to subdivide, increasing the number of interfaces for potential disputes. This was described by a local expert as an "intensified ghettoization process" (2017) as rival turfs pressed closer and closer together.

In a visit to Belize in 2016, over lunch I casually asked a young Southside man who had passed through the SYSP gang intervention program to tell me which gang was dominant in his area. He drew a deep breath and said that, in fact, there were four gangs intersecting his neighborhood: PIV, *Bac-a-Lan Crips*, *Complex City Crips*, and the *Third World Bloods*. He went on to estimate that half of all young men in the area were involved with gangs. The CYDP, now called the difficult-to-remember Behavior Modification and Conflict Management Services or BMCMS, reported a bewildering assortment of thirty-six gangs (Arciaga Young and King 2019). Yet, even here, there are gangs missing, such as the North Front Street Gang, indicative of the constantly rotating gangland kaleidoscope. As soon as it is written down, it is out of date. (See Table 3.1.)

In 2018, in the Belize District (Belize City and environs) the homicide rate was 78 per one hundred thousand (Belize Crime Observatory 2020). Trauma among boys is considered the highest in the Caribbean (Gayle, Hampton, and Mortis 2016), and as Muhammad said in matter-of-fact terms, Belizean gangs are "a black thing, a youth thing, an urban thing, a poor thing, an unskilled, undereducated and unemployed thing" (Muhammad 2015).

The Gangland Kaleidoscope

Shorty, the former gang leader, stands only 5'5" tall but has a strong build. Born in 1978, he emigrated to Los Angeles with his mother as an eight-year-old,

TABLE 3.1 ACTIVE GANGS IN BELIZE CITY BY AGE AND MEMBERSHIP

Gang Name	Age			Membership	
	Youngest	Oldest	Average	Low	High
Peace in the Valley (People in Violence) Bloods	12	40	26	100	200
Southside Crips	12	40	26	90	100
Gaza New Generation Bloods	11	19	15	70	90
Ghost Town (Banak Street) Crips	11	45	28	60	70
George Street Bloods	18	45	31.5	40	50
Majestic Alley Crips	12	45	28.5	25	50
Jane Usher Bloods	12	40	26	35	45
Supal Street Bloods	12	40	26	30	40
Jungle Bloods	12	40	26	20	40
West-Molan (Taylor's Alley) Bloods	12	35	23.5	30	40
Louise Bevans Crips	14	35	24.5	30	40
Antelope Street Bloods	14	40	27	20	35
Victoria Street Bloods	12	40	26	18	35
Jump Street Crips	14	40	27	15	35
Lacroix Blvd Bloods	12	39	25.5	20	35
Back-a-Town Bloods	14	45	29.5	20	30
Back-a-Lands Crips	14	45	29.5	20	30
Kelly Street Crips	12	40	26	20	30
Kraal Road Crips	13	40	26.5	20	30
Police Street Crips	14	38	26	30	30
Conch Shell Bloods	14	35	24.5	25	30
Gill Street Bloods	13	35	24	20	30
Plum Tree Bloods	14	35	24.5	20	25
Amara Street Bloods	14	35	24.5	20	25
Kings Park Crips	18	40	29	15	20
Rocky Road Crips	17	35	26	15	20
103 New Road Bloods	12	30	21	15	20
Riverside Boys	12	20	16	15	20
Jerusalem Crips	12	45	28.5	10	15
Afghanistan Bloods	14	35	24.5	10	15
102 (Parham) Crips	18	35	26.5	10	15
Belama (Riverside Bloods)	15	35	25	10	15
Simon Lamb Street Crips	20	35	27.5	10	15
Neals Penn Road (Gaza) Bloods	15	35	25	10	15
Sunset Crips	14	35	24.5	10	15
Horse and Carriage Blood	12	35	23.5	10	15
Average	13.6	37.4	Total	938	1,365

Source: Conscious Youth Development Programme. From Arciaga Young, M., and King, D. (2019). *Community Gang Assessment, Belize*. Inter-American Development Bank. Copyright © 2019 Inter-American Development Bank. Licensed under a Creative Commons IGO 3.0 Attribution-NonCommercial-NoDerivatives (CC-IGO BY-NC-ND 3.0 IGO) license (http://creativecommons.org/licenses/by-nc-nd/3.0/igo/legalcode).

later joining the Bloods as a teenager. He was arrested and deported back to Belize in 2011 when he was 33 years old. In his own words, he became a gang leader and reference point for young men on Southside because of his U.S. credentials—his American accent, gun know-how, and firsthand experience of the iconic gangsta life. I interviewed Shorty twice. Once in Belize Central Prison in 2016, where he was beginning the second year of five for illegal firearms possession, although he was released on parole the following January. Then a second time, in 2022, at his new home on the outskirts of the capital Belmopan, as he sought to break from gang life in Belize City. When I first interviewed him, it become clear that being a gang leader on Southside could mean running just a handful of teenagers on a single block, he said, "everybody wants to be a Chief, no one wants to be an Indian." This was a significant departure from the Generals time. The tendency for gangs to divide and scale-down, and the seemingly ever-younger members, indicates the way street violence should be understood in modern-day Belize. Shorty explains these dynamics:

> SHORTY: My name is [Shorty] an' I am the Prince of the Rollin 20s. Everybody know who I am. I was in the States for 27 years, an' I grew up in the Rollin 20s. . . . I was born in Belize City, I left here in '86. My mother came and got us, all five of her children and took us to the states. When I got there, 27 years later I was deported to this country [2013]. Now when I came here, I'm under a rule where Bloods don't kill Bloods, but in this country Blood kill Bloods. So, I stay away from them. [There are] those who take this as a joke, coz it's not love no more. Crips been killing Crips, that's nothing new. But to come to a country and see someone with a two zero [tattoo] on their arm, and they shooting at another gang which is two zero, it don't add up to me . . . because gangbanging is not a gangbanging thing no more. See, I'm not a gangbanger, I'm a representative of a gang, and that's the difference in this country. Some homies fall back from this madness, but as we've seen a lotta deportees have died, coming from Los Angeles. . . .
>
> [I was deported in] 2011 April 30, I [first] went to Belize City coz I was living back at Kings Port. So, then I went to jail and decided, I'm not messin' with Belize, I'm going straight to Ladyville, for two years. People love me [in Belize City] but I won't socialize with them coz I know for a fact that they wouldn't hesitate to kill me.
>
> [Bloods didn't kill Bloods] Crips got beef with each other, but when I came here, they did it the wrong way [Bloods killing Bloods]. It was West Street and George Street against Majestic

Alley. Coz people used to go to the movie theatre, and people would get fucked up there. An' when you go there these guys would jump you, coz they got their apartments they would run out of, you feel me?

West Street and George Street was good friends, then you have a couple of people who disrespect each other in the club, an' thas when the war started. Over that. . . . It's not beef no more, it's eternal beef. It's something that's embedded in them. "You kill my cousin, I'm gonna kill your cousin." An' it's gonna keep going on and on and on, until that two groups come to an understanding, "listen you know what, enough is enough." But the hate is stay in they heart forever. I stay in my own lane. . . .

Now when I went to jail, I came to know a caliber of dude, but they're not dudes, they not men, n***az are psychopaths. . . . What I have learnt from them is that you can't trust nobody in this country. The country itself is untrustworthy. An' the youts, I don't blame them [for being violent] and that's why we have the attitude we have now as Belizeans.

They not gangs, they youts. Because the gang is organized . . . because in the same hood like Ghostown [gang] you got Mayflower and Bana [Streets], they beef, an' they from the same gang! They killin' each other, just like PIV, just like George Street. In George Street [now] they fightin' for leadership. The guy leading George Street right now, he's not qualified to lead the gang. We knew Mama Blood, coz they wuz young [new leaders] I'm older than them guys. When I came to Belize [City] in 2003 all them little n***az was *on my dick*! When I came back 2011, they killin' an runnin' shit. They never disrespect me, they jus' treated me like "hey Shorty!" . . . but if you killin' yo' own kind I don't respect you. *It's like how it is in this country, you got something for them, they gonna be your best, best, best friend*, but if you don't got something for them then they be like "n***a I gonna kill his ass tonight. That dude is dead. Coz he didn't give me no $5 of weed for free." "Why?" "Coz I felt like it. That n***a don' give me 5 dollaz o weed."

AUTHOR: That shit happens?

SHORTY: *All-the-motha'-fuckin'-time*. That guy who got shot over the bike [bicycle] was killed in San Pedro, but that move was over pussy [a woman], not the bike, they jus' put the bike in . . . in this country you can't trust nobody.

To kill somebody is to know somebody. You can have Bloods and Crips living in the same house. They brothers. So, a long time ago the war was the war [between the Bloods and Crips] you don't know notin' about it, but you hear about it. So, yo' thing is to try and get a strike now, be General, by killing someone from that area and talking about it later, and the reason why you killed that individual. That's all they got to themselves. . . . They call them General when a little kid idolize someone, an' they call them General.

You can't trust nobody. You just can't have a n***a hangin' with you, coz you don't know what a guy done. He mighta kill somebody last night, come here and hang with you, they comin' for him, and they see you. . . . If they can't find him and they saw you hangin' with him earlier they gonna hit you. That's the way that is.

AUTHOR: I would see it as a strategy to stay safe. I see you as a survivor.

SHORTY: I am a survivor. *I stay the fuck out of the limelight.* . . . Since I been here, I lost two homeboys. Got killed one week apart. One was having sex with a George Street guy's wife. He went to have a meeting with the motherfuckers, and they killed him right there. Shot him in his neck. He's so stupid, why would you go there and have a meeting with these people you can't trust. But I loved my homeboy, I wish he'd a did it differently. (2022)

A few years earlier, Shorty said:

[Gang violence] 'bout small beefs, [gang members] be like chil'ren. One beef started because someone step on someone else's shoe in a club, and now they can't even remember what the original beef was about. Like a dog in a cage, then you put another one in, and it ok. Then you throw a piece of meat in and they gonna kill each other for it. *Man a kill a man for nutin'*, for no reason, it's fucked up. . . . Now Vartas and Driver [rivals splitting PIV gang in two] hate each other. Like I said, it's a dog-eat-dog world. (2016)

Life is cheap. I was so struck by Shorty saying "Man a kill a man for nutin'" it became the title of an article (Baird 2021a). This is the "prison-world of the ghetto" described by Shabazz, citing Hill-Collins, where Black men "simply turn on one another, reflecting heightened levels of alienation and nihilism. Faced with few job possibilities, insufficient schools, drugs, and easy access to guns, Black men kill each other over seemingly inconsequential things" (2009, p. 277).

Internecine brutality produced by the social terrain. Beefs, often over unbelievably inconsequential matters, epitomize this nihilism. Aliases JK and

Messiah, a dancehall singer and rapper, respectively, former fringe gang members, said:

> JK: It not like when gangs first cum to Belize in past years. You can be on da same block an' now dey're beefin'.
>
> MESSIAH: People still say "I'm Red" or "I'm Blue," but I'm not Red to a point dat when I see a n***a dat's Blue I'm about to spray dat n***a [with bullets]. It is to an extent about territory, but it's not too much bout you movin' into my territory and teking my money. Some n***az be killin' n***az over a bitch an shit. An' den de two n***az dat was fightin over dis girl just end up havin' a bunch of n***az, dat's dey're squad, you see what I mean, an' when dey see dem n***az [punches fist into hand to indicate them being killed]. And dat goes on for years an' years an' years, until de origin of de beef is even unknown [they do not remember how it started]. (2016).

Arciaga Young and King stated that back-and-forth cycles of revenge sustained violence and that half of the locals on Southside reported someone being shot and killed every day (2019, p. 24). Incessant *beefin'* means, as one civil servant said, young people are increasingly confused about gang territories (2016). When I spoke to Vartas, leader of PIV, he wasn't even sure who the leader of the George Street Bloods was (2016). What made this statement remarkable was that George Street was his main rival across the street.

Today's gang structures pass through short cycles where they consolidate for a period under one leader before fracturing again, creating a continual series of violent spikes. For example, when Shelton *Pinky* Tillett, who headed one gang faction on George Street, was shot dead in 2012 this led to a succession battle. Then his successor, Gerald *Shiny* Tillett, was killed less than twelve months later, creating another spate of violence, and so on. A Southside resident said, in 2016, "Now Shiny's boy tekin' over and he only 16, and people already scared of him." The extent of these processes was laid bare by an exasperated senior police officer in a candid interview in his Raccoon Street office (2016):

> POLICE OFFICER: George Street has at least eight subsidiaries to it, and each have their own leader. They fight under George Street still, but not everything they do is under control of the leader of George Street. The inter-gang rivalries are the most difficult to police, you never know who is who, and because of the small geographical area in which they operate it is difficult to police them. Most of the gangs begin to fragment after the main leader die.

AUTHOR: George Street was Pinky then Shiny?
POLICE OFFICER: [Nods in agreement] So, after Shiny dead, there is a fight over who will be the next leader. Others [names three] are proclaiming to be leaders of George Street. . . . After Pinky died, George Street disputes started, and some went with Shiny and some with [another gang leader.]
AUTHOR: What's the violence about?
POLICE OFFICER: Most of them don't know what they are fighting for. It's just that they grow up in an area, and they know that this area have an issue with that area. We have also found that much of the violence is driven by hate and anger. They hate this man because of this or that. And we find that they get upset very easily. They think that the easiest way to resolve a conflict is with the use of a gun.
AUTHOR: So how organized are gangs?
POLICE OFFICER: Structurally, I don't think that they're properly organized, but they are to the extent that they can become effective [lethal]. Weapons come in from Guatemala, the same routes as marijuana. Gang members [aren't rich] like Jamaica. *Belizean gangs are poor!* [his emphasis] The money that they make from the sale of drugs, it's like day-to-day.

This was in 2016. In 2021, I spoke to another police officer who had spent years negotiating cease-fires with gangs on Southside, and he knew all the main players:

George Street now bust into five or six factions. For example, we got Gaza and GNG—George Street New Generation Gang. Jane Usher [gang] now split up too, an' di Mayflower Crips broke up. . . . George Street is fucked but in di Martins area, PIV, and Bac-a-Lan at peace, [Vartas] played a role. We used to do inter-gang mediation, but now it's intra-gang mediation and much more difficult!

He went on to explain that his job of negotiating truces between gangs had become infinitely more challenging. Not only were gangs fragmenting or creating new alliances but some "splinters" were now reconnecting again. I struggled to make sense of this chaos, gangs seemed like synapses disconnecting and reconnecting in bewildering fashion. The George Street Bloods, the biggest gang in Belizean history, seemed to have morphed into something altogether more ethereal, a brand, rather like the *Oficina de Envigado* in Medellín, which is not actually a physical office but a crime syndicate-cum-constellation of underworld groups.

One evening I spoke to a middle-aged lady on the corner of Majestic Alley. I noted in my field diary that we were within eyeshot of the downtown ferry terminal, where speedboats whisk tourists away to Caye Caulker and San Pedro beach resorts. Her husband, former Crips leader George "Junie Balls" McKenzie, was murdered in 2007. They had just killed her son who took over from him. It was a tragic and emotional scene. As a researcher, I was on ethical thin ice, so I just explained who I was and let them say what they wanted. "They killed my baby," she said, only three months ago after he took over Majestic Alley. The police had let a rival gang through so they could "get rid" of him. The other gang was from Jungle [the neighboring Pickstock Street area] . . . *yet another gang splinter* I hadn't heard of. She was taking care of her now fatherless two-year-old granddaughter who played next to us on a brightly colored plastic truck. Even though I was talking to the former leader's mother we were being watched suspiciously, and my gatekeeper, Angel, himself a former Crip from Majestic Alley, was getting nervous. After a few minutes, he motioned for us to leave, so I wrapped up the conversation and we jumped back in the van. As we drove off, he said that George Street was splitting apart yet again. It's impossible to keep up (field diary, 2016).

What this interaction brought home was the territorial intimacy of murder. The violence felt far more pressed together, condensed, than the larger cities I had previously conducted research in. A youth worker took me for a walk down George Street one afternoon in 2017 and pointed to two rival corners, or *bases*, barely ten meters apart on opposite sides of the street. Microgangs, microdisputes, and well-armed microleaders, reflecting Glebbeek and Koonings's gang-held "micro-monopolies" of the street (2015). These flash points are so scaled down that one civil servant referred to them perceptively as "interpersonal violence at a gang level" (2017).

Violence is always close to the surface in community life. After we left Majestic Alley that night, Angel made a stop off at his ex-partner's house to pay informal alimony for their young daughter. He said he was a little behind and was contrite for not paying earlier. When we pulled up in the van the children playing on the street stopped and looked curiously at what I imagined was the uncommon spectacle of a foreigner on Southside at night. When she opened the front door the demeanor of the ex-partner suggested payment was, in fact, more than a little late. He went inside and I sat in the van for what seemed an inordinate amount of time to drop off some money. When Angel returned, he looked furious. He climbed into the van and slammed the door. I assumed they had been arguing over money, but that was not the case. It turned out his eldest son, a gang member in his early twenties, had a beef with rivals and committed a shooting that day, at least injuring and potentially killing three young men. The details were not clear as this only happened a few hours earlier and Angel had not spoken to his son. He called him then and there, but his cell phone was switched off. He said he had likely "gone hidin' in Orange Walk," a rural and notoriously lawless district to the northwest, known for marijuana cultivation and as a onetime hideout for tech mogul John McAfee when he was on the run from the law.[10] Thereafter a conversation began about how his son ended up in this predicament. Angel said he had found him a job at the four-star Best Western Hotel on the Northern Highway on the outskirts of Belize City when he was a teenager, but he had dropped out to smoke weed with his *homies*. The rest was a familiar tale of a young man socialized to the streets, the shooting being the culmination of tit-for-tat beefs. He was particularly frustrated because he had made such effort to keep him on the straight and narrow but was morbidly resigned to his son's fate "Dere's no ting I can do. He will a end up gettin' shot" (2017). When I returned, in 2021, Angel confirmed his son had since been shot dead and he knew who did it.

Even after knowing him several years, Angel only spoke to me once about the personal impact gang life had on him when he was younger. As he recounted street wars he had been in, he lifted his shirt to reveal a scarcely believable patchwork of scars on his torso and arms, from knives, machetes, and bullets. He also walks with a debilitating limp. Angel would not let me buy him a beer, saying he could neither drink nor spend too much time alone with his thoughts because "dat when da demons come out" (2017). The way he first brushed off the prospect of his own son being murdered was a stark demonstration of how inhabitants faced with chronic levels of community violence manage its effects on their lives. This harks back to sociologist Daniel Pecaut's explanation of excessive violence eventually being normalized, even banal, among affected Colombian populations (1999) and reflections by anthropologists Michael Taussig (2003) and Nancy Scheper-Hughes (1993), where locals living in deadly communities must keep horrors at a psychological arm's length to be able to survive. Angel was not actively looking for his son's killer, but if he chanced upon him on the street, there would be blood.

Conclusions

By the mid-2000s, some two decades after the Bloods and Crips first appeared in Belize, unlike the progressive institutionalization of some maras in Central America, *pandillas* in Medellín, or the Primero Comando da Capital in São Paulo, Belizean gangs had broken up into a soup of smaller gangs. The George Street Bloods are paradigmatic of this change as the once major gang powerhouse under George Herbert, then the Tillett family, is now split into numerous factions: sometimes warring with each other, sometimes making new fragile alliances, but always shape-shifting.

These gangs spread across Southside but remain at the margins of cocaine transshipment despite nearly four decades of existence. While they have access to guns and ammunition, their connections to cocaine trafficking are indirect at best. This does not mean, of course, as Briscoe averred regarding the maras, that street gang members will "graduate" into organized crime, but it does show that we should not conflate multiple criminal political economies, rather we should seek to understand their nuances. This is not to say there is no blurring of boundaries or overlap at all, but the facile conflation of drug transshipment and violence needs to be understood in context, on a case-by-case basis. The Belizean homicide boom is not a direct consequence of drug transshipment, counterintuitively, elite and family-based *surf 'n' turf* drug trafficking are notably nonviolent, relatively speaking, and have been remarkably effective at keeping gangs at the margins of the trade. Gang members, such as Shorty and Vartas, who appear throughout this chapter, *would* like to have access to the cocaine transshipment bonanza, yet they are not invited in.

In sum, street gangs on Southside might be best described as *disorganized*, *weapons rich*, and *drugs poor*. This counters more widely held narratives that gangs organize then engage in violent competition over illicit street economies, driving up homicide rates, or that drug transshipment somehow objectively causes surges in violence. Becoming a transshipment country has not played an obvious or significant role in the spectacular rise in homicide in Belize in recent years, contrary to widely held assumptions in the literature (e.g., UNODC 2019).

Soaring gang violence is mediated by community-level factors tied to the social terrain. Enduring and location-specific legacies of marginalization and exclusion create chronic vulnerability, which not only generated fertile conditions for the arrival and embedding of the Bloods and Crips, discussed in Chapter 1, but also ongoing vulnerability continues to galvanize patterns of gang recruitment and formation. The hyperfragmentation of gangs across Southside since 2000 increased the interfaces for beefs and homicide levels rocketed. Worryingly, this violent street culture shows no signs of abating, bar the outlier COVID-19 pandemic years in 2020 and 2021.

The next chapter returns to the roles of masculinities and continual gang (re)formation in Belize City. Beyond the gangland kaleidoscope presented in this chapter, gangs are discussed as culturally syncretistic phenomena, "creolizing" and "Jamaicanizing" in recent years. Despite the fluid and evolving state of gangs, their violent male figureheads persist undiminished, a stubborn local hegemonic masculinity that underlies incessant violence.

4

Adaptation

The Syncretistic Gang

Gangs on Southside are culturally syncretistic and have always been a unique hybrid: Stock imported Blood and Crip identities *creolized* upon entry then *Jamaicanized* in subsequent years. Today, Belize is in a "posttransnational gang" era. Despite the gang's cultural syncretism and constant evolution, violence is a mainstay, because it is indivisible from gang practices that deliver ever-coveted male status. This is how gender plays an essential role in the continuity of violence.

The gang sits high in the gender hierarchy of the streets: all-male status, pomp, and glory, are the trump cards of recruitment that maintain the gang in perpetual motion. Even though Southside gangs slide between American gangsta, Jamaican dancehall, and local Creole identities, and, despite unpredictable fragmentation and reconnections, the hegemonic masculinity of the gang remains intact. Normatively, they continue to be seen as "successful" men as we have seen with the term "General," which has morphed from meaning gang leader to any man who commands respect, in local lexicon.

These arguments require unpacking. To do so, this chapter first delves into the meaning of cultural syncretism and the posttransnational gang, then it considers the connectedness between hegemonic masculinity, gangs, and violence, and, finally, it explains the role that masculine vulnerability, derived from chronic vulnerability, plays in the continuation of gang violence on Southside.

Let me flag an essential question: What about girls and women? This section also teases out some ideas around meanings of *feminine vulnerability* on Southside and how these connect to gangland masculinities. While men may make up the vast majority of "hard core," violent, and leadership roles in gangs, this does not mean women are somehow outside of the gang world. Rather, they are, in fact, essential figures.

Cultural Syncretism and the Posttransnational Gang

A few years ago, I published research that presented early gangs in Belize as a straightforward copy of the Bloods and Crips (Baird 2021a, 2021b). With hindsight, that observation lacked a shade of analysis. In 2021, after a break forced by the COVID-19 pandemic, I returned to Belize and sat down with my old friend and youth worker, Jabbar. He had read one of the articles and agreed with the overall premise but explained that the Bloods and Crips that first appeared on Southside were not a carbon copy of their U.S. cousins. How so? While Belizean gangs *did* imitate U.S. gangs, they adopted and creolized their cultural cues, practices, and behaviors. Almost inevitably with the passage of time, as these imported identities were not historically and locally rooted, they faded in a way Belizean *creoleness* never would. The moment any transnational gang connects with a new social terrain, it is subject to syncretistic transformation and the forces of localism. Upon being received in host communities, transnational gangs are immediately "becoming" something else, something different, something *posttransnational*. These transformations cannot occur in isolation from wider society, rather, they are part of it. Making history.

At Krem Television, radio, and recording studios on Southside, in 2016, I spent a morning interviewing the two young musicians mentioned in the previous chapter. Messiah was cut from the same cloth as U.S. gangsta rap and JK was a singer heavily influenced by Jamaican dancehall, who spoke with a soft Creole lilt. Both had grown up on Southside and spent their formative years hustling to make ends meet, drifting in and out of gangs. They were emerging faces in the small but vibrant Belizean music scene, cutting YouTube videos, and playing at street parties and music events. They were verging on celebrity around town, and their social media numbers were on the rise. I have been following them both on Instagram since our first meeting, and it is warming to know that they have gone on to become successful, even travelling overseas to perform. Nonetheless, at that time, they still hung with gangs, and their street hustle never felt far from the surface. JK had recently been involved in a shoot-out, but he said the police let him off the hook because they knew he was trying to get out of gang life and into music. The next morning, I messaged Messiah on WhatsApp to ask if he could set up a meeting with some gang members. He came back with a message saying, verbatim:

> Yo! We're right over here chillin' n***a. Let me see if I could fuckin' get dem n***az together probably for Tursday. I'll see, I'm not sure I could do it. We'll see wud'up. An 2.56 d if everyting come tru, I'm gonna holla at'chyou an' den we'll scoop you up an' den you jus' put gas in the car, an' I'll tek you over dere.

It is hard to convey the blend of accents on the page, but Messiah, a born-and-bred Creole Southsider used U.S. gangsta lexicon—*here chillin' n***a, I'm gonna holla at'chyou*—part of an acquired rapper persona, with a slight Creole inflection. It was striking the way he performed foreign identity so fluidly and with such ease then would instantaneously flick to thick Creole to address JK. Within one sentence alone, Messiah said "police dem chancy mothafuckas." *police dem chancy* in Creole, meaning the police are corrupt, and *mothafuckas* in an accent straight from the LA streets. JK's identity, conversely, had no discernible U.S. influence whatsoever. I was bamboozled. He came across as a Belizean Creole, Jamaican patois, dancehall singing amalgam. Admittedly, identifying the subtle differences between Creole and patois is challenging for non-Caribbean foreigners, but JK's lyrics were littered with both Jamaican and Belizean references. I know this because during our interview he would break into song when I asked him about his music, part pride in his work, but, intuitively, it felt like a status performance to a foreigner asking him questions, which was understandable.

Many Belizeans "speak American" with foreigners, that is, less Creole so outsiders can understand. "English" is actually associated with Creole English, so requesting clearer English counterintuitively results in more Creole. The majority of Creoles I spoke to could switch between American and Creole English with ease, however, some young men and gang members—such as Vartas—did not speak American English. This was about class and lack of education; they were *very* street. The idiomatic switching reminded me of the leader of the opposition (as of 2024) Mr. Moses "Shyne" Barrow; the stark contrast between his New York City accent on U.S. talk shows on YouTube, and his interviews in Belize on Channel 5 News where his Creole flows. Like any bilingual, the dexterity is impressive. Belizeans are a culturally syncretistic nation, seamlessly so—the word *creole* itself means mixed descent—and not just absorbing U.S. and Jamaican influences but also within the country. While it is rare for Creoles to speak Spanish, the Indigenous population is often bi- or trilingual. When interviewing a community police officer of Mayan origin, our conversation switched between Spanish and English multiple times. It is hardly surprising, then, that Southside gangs are culturally syncretistic. They are, after all, Belizean.

As noted in the Introduction to this book, a significant number of Belizeans live overseas, mainly in the United States, particularly adults in their twenties and thirties. Bolland observed in the 1990s that this "substantially reduced" the Creole and Garifuna communities at the time (1997, p. 271). It is not surprising that influences from the United States are so strong, but Jamaica, a short distance across the Caribbean Sea, has always been seen as a big brother. National broadcaster, Nuri Muhammad, said when I interviewed him in 2016:

> Jamaica has always been our partner in culture, so all the way back to the reggae time . . . going as far back as Harry Belafonte, has always been our brother in culture. The American culture has also been there by virtue of the fact that we mimicked their culture because so many of us lived there . . . the clothes we wear, the styles we licked up. . . . it was even pre-Hattie [hurricane in 1961]. The American [culture] is worldwide, but it is even more so in the Caribbean, particularly with Belize . . . because we are on the mainland we've always been travelling up into Texas.

Importantly, prior to the 1980s, very few Belizeans had a television set, and numerous Belizeans spoke of the power of cultural transfer from the United States during "the TV era."

> Many young Belizean Creoles are increasingly influenced by African American and Afro-Caribbean cultures. Not only is Belize a complex and changing multi-ethnic mosaic, but many individual Belizeans, perhaps even the majority, are in many respects multicultural. What, then, does "ethnicity" mean in Belize? (Bolland 1997, p. 272)

Elsewhere, in rural Belize, Melissa Beske referred to a "Hybridized, Creolized, and Mestizoized" society, where interlocking peoples have historically been "characterized by mixtures and contradictions" (2016, p. 64). Jabbar, combined cultural and migratory influences:

> Belize is also at a state of war, of cultural war, bombarded by all kinds of nonsense from Jamaica and America . . . the culture, the hip-hop, the dancehall, the TV, the glitz and the glamour. And we are a third-

world developing country, and we are so close to America that most of our parents have left here to go and live the American Dream, and have basically abandoned us.... This has been a continual thing since 1961. (2021)

Mr. T, a former gang member now social worker who has worked with young people across two decades, described gangs on Southside as "copy-cats. Copied Bloods and Crips. Copied the Jamaicans" (2021). Gang transnationalism in Belize has been a process of local adaptation. This is an empirical inflection per Nayak's reasoning, that flows of global culture produce hybrid youth identities, including youths at risk (quoted in Johns 2014, p. 301). Creole youths absorbed and interpreted foreign gang culture as a tool to help them negotiate the harsh realities of everyday life. As one national academic put it, "It's always been a mix with the Caribbean. Belizeans don't have identity. It comes back to that. They adapt everything.... The Maya and Garifuna do have identity, not so much the Creoles" (2022).

Syncretistic gang identities have been detailed in other contexts: Mendoza-Denton (2008) notes the evolution of linguistic differentiation between English- and Spanish-speaking Latina gangs in California, and Brotherton and Barrios (2004) have charted the profound change of Latin King and Queen gangs from violent gang to social movement in New York City. Muhammad (2015, pp. 16–17) states:

> Gangs are both foreign and local in origin at the same time. Foreign in the sense that media images of the gangster in the 1980s and 1990s were the Black youth of Los Angeles.... Whilst these images were foreign in style, there were socio-economic and historical conditions for our own crop of gang activity.

Southside was never a tabula rasa; as with cultural transfer, one does not simply override the other. Even though the gangs imitated Bloods and Crips, they were always shaped by the Creole culture they were inserted into. Typical of Belizean cultural syncretism, the early Blood and Crip leaders were called "Generals," a term that actually comes from Jamaican not U.S. gang culture. Warnecke-Berger notes that American-based Bloods and Crips make extensive use of signs to exemplify their differences, for example, hand signals and language, "yet these were never entirely adapted in Belize" (2017, p. 213). Belizean Bloods and Crips almost exclusively sold marijuana. By contrast, U.S. Bloods and Crips were "slinging dope," hard drugs, a difference personified by Shorty who only sold marijuana in Belize, but, when he was gangbanging in the United States, he sold cocaine, crack, and angel dust.

One Belizean academic was relieved that hard drugs were not common in gang life, "That's a good thing about them" he said. I asked, "What if they started using crystal meth or something similar?" He replied, "Then Belize would be fucked, it would be fuckin' over man, fuckin' over" (2021).

Mr. T recalled that the splintering of Blood and Crip duopoly in the city and the loss of the dominant General figure, helped push the *colors* identity into the past (2021). From about 2005 onward, he identified a strong uptick in Jamaican cultural influence in street gangs. Muhammad described this as a hardened Jamaican gang culture "born in the ghetto and nurtured in the prisons, [that] has spread to the nation through poetry, songs and dance hall music" (2015, p. 42). Mr. T concurred that Jamaican gang culture brought a new "brutalism of violence . . . in the last eight to ten years it's become a children's war and families have been shot up," creating what he called "a ripple effect" of retaliatory violence.

Jamaican tropes were absorbed by the next generation, like JK, who was twenty-eight in 2016. I asked him where his cultural cues came from. He struggled to "speak American" but tried for my benefit:

> LA go firs,' den it change to da new modern set up. . . . Ya know da youts dey change a lot, dey wearin' different clothes, ya know da Jamaica mix. . . . So dey still wear some American clothes, but dey 'ave a Jamaican mix, Jamaican stylin' ya know?

In the 2000s, gangs intertwined cultural cues from Jamaican musicians such as Vybz Kartel from Gaza, and Mavado from Gully, ganglands in Kingston, spread through the country's musical outputs. Young Southsiders "like Vybz Kartel above all, who has bad lyrics," according to Mr. T. This notorious Kingstonian dancehall star, whose lyrics glorify gang violence in stereotypical fashion, is serving a life term for multiple gang-linked murders.

In 2016, I spoke with three young men in their late teens, two years after they had been through the SYSP gang intervention project. They showed me social media posts on their phones by gang members they knew. Alias Rahim said modern gangs "copy Vybz Kartel from Kingston, dey copy dis culture [points at gang members posing in music videos]. You can . . . spot a gangsta straight away by deir pulled down trousers an' de way dey dress." Alias Tiger, a teenager on the fringes of gang life said to me:

> TIGER: People look up ta George Street, as de main gang coz dey get de name Gaza from de gang in Jamaica.
> AUTHOR: So, a George Street gang [splinter] just took the name Gaza from Jamaica?

TIGER: Gaza! Dey just tek da name from Jamaica! Dey just call de gang Gaza. So, everybody look up to Gaza as de main gang. . . . Dey got de most gang members, dey're de biggest gang down dere, dey got more weapons.

A young journalist brought up on Southside said, "Vybz Kartel is a big influence, areas like Gaza and Gully. Gaza is a gang over here now. *Shottas*, that movie [about Jamaican gangs] was a big influence over here, [we] are very influenceable" (2022). With poetic symmetry, *Shottas* from Jamaica influenced gangs in Belize the way the movie *Colors* from the United States did two decades earlier.

The critical difference between U.S. and Jamaican gang influences is that no Belizean gang members learned their trade in Kingston or Montego Bay to be then deported to Belize City. Nor did Jamaican gangs seek to franchise into Belize. The Jamaican influence of the 2000s was purely discursive, aided by the advent of social media. Mr. T remembered when he was a young gang member before the internet, they would be watching MTV and gangsta rap videos nonstop. He went on to say that, while some cultural traits and brutality of Jamaican gang life had been appropriated, Belizean beefs were still an immature "spite game" and gangs only aspired to be more organized criminals like Jamaican gangs. "The difference between us and Jamaicans is that it's just a façade, we are pretending to be like them, but scratch beneath the surface and we are not" (2021).

Present-day gangs still bear remnants of U.S. gangsta culture, most notably in red and blue clothing, and imported Dickies trousers, but, rather like the youthful Queen's head on the banknotes, it has lost significance. A young journalist told me how his friend "was murdered by one of his own best friends on George Street. They don't care about Bloods and Crips, it's now all about 'what relationships benefit them for the bottom line'" (2022). Or, as Vartas, the leader of PIV, said frankly, "Bloods and Crips don' matter no more" (2016).

Belizean gangs are syncretistic. Rather like Hinduism absorbing Gods from other faiths, they have taken on overseas street cultures. Admittedly, this takes a little sociological imagination, yet these tendencies, combined with their incessant splintering, have given rise to a more violent and unpredictable gangland milieu of posttransnational gangs. This differentiates Southside gangs from neighboring maras that have tended toward organization as they evolve, as discussed in the previous chapter (Bergmann 2020; Sullivan 2006; van der Borgh and Savenije 2019): two different pathways to violence.

Although Belizean gangs are in a constant state of flux, two features have changed little: the gang's elevated position in the gender hierarchy and the chronic vulnerability of the social terrain in which they are situated. Here the terrain (structure) and subject (agent) are thrust into a dialectic, where gang power satiates masculine vulnerability. This process is proposed here as an explainer of violence.

Gendering Vulnerability

Masculine Vulnerability

The Introduction to this book revised the academic literature on gangs and masculinities, demonstrating that, while no single condition determines gang emergence, young men in contexts of urban exclusion are a consistent feature. Further, this literature has shown that, although not disconnected from the wider world, hegemonic masculinities are contextually situated; they are legitimated and constituted in the social terrain. If chronic violence only occurs in contexts of chronic vulnerability, from a gendered perspective, "masculine vulnerability" is fundamental for violence. I would be so bold as to say that masculine vulnerability *causes* of chronic violence. This may feel prescriptive, but it is pitched as a provocation to be tested and debated. Clearly, not all vulnerable males break bad and become killers. In fact, most young men do not become gang members in contexts of constraint. Despite this, the argument offers a novel conceptual connection between gender, class, and violence.

The manpower for gangs, a gender-appropriate term, is marginalized youth. To be glib, there is no such thing as the middle-class women's street gang. Still, this is not a masculinist *Boy's Own*–reading of gang life. Contemporary research incorporates multiple masculinities and women's relational roles, attributing rather than denying female agency, in the production of violence. Individuals have many masks. We should not be surprised by the rapist-murderer-extortionist gang member who loves his mother, wife, and children or the perceived "mother-monster-whore" (Sjoberg and Gentry 2007) amalgams, born of vulnerability and myriad pressures.

If masculine vulnerability exists, so, too, must "feminine" and other layers of vulnerability. How might vulnerabilities differ, and Why is it relevant? By asking these questions, the aim is to widen the conversation about the role gender plays in lasting gang violence, while differentiating the risks young women and men face in places like Southside. This will generate more questions than the analysis provided here can answer, but that, in itself, is progress.

Hierarchy is crucial to hegemonic masculinity, locating "real men" at the top and subordinating women, femininities, and nonhegemonic versions of masculinity—think "softer," feminized, homosexual, and nonwarrior types. This requires continual legitimation, from across the community, cultural consent, and the delegitimation of alternatives (Connell 2016; Messerschmidt 2018). Gang "legitimation" experiences have been seen across the Caribbean (see, e.g., Blake 2013; Jaffe 2013). There has been some debate over the extent to which marginalized Black and Brown men, particularly in the Global South, can actually embody hegemonic masculinities, yet the gang male should not be dissociated from global hegemonic ideals, rather he should be understood to be a connected local inflection that maintains the underlying principle: the legitimation of unequal gender relations (Messerschmidt 2018, p. 48).

This is exemplified in Connell's (2016) discussion that cites numerous studies, many from the Global South, which have proved masculinities to be adaptive and transhistorical, from colonial and postcolonial through neoliberalization to the present. "Adaptation" helps explain how gangs maintain their position in the local gender hierarchy, despite the severe structural turbulence of the gangland kaleidoscope. This adaptation pivots around the use or threat of violence, which aligns with Bourdieu's (2001) model of *Masculine Domination* "reproduced" through social practice.

The emergence of the Bloods and Crips on Southside heralded the reconfiguration of street life, tying patterns of masculinity to gangsta culture, with discernible hegemonic traits. Jewkes et al. (2015) identify multiple hegemonic projects locally, which supports the idea of gang transnationalism being established as a model of localized hegemonic masculinity. In Belize, this model founded a lasting set of gang practices that fit the bill in terms of Connell's descriptors of hegemonic masculinity, albeit in a pronounced and contextually adapted way, particularly regarding performance: the aesthetics of language, the pose, the cars, or gold chains, and the symbolic shotta notoriety and fear, sexual access to women, street parties, drinking, and drug taking. This can be understood as significant "masculine capital," which I have written about extensively (Baird 2012, 2018a), flaunted to an audience in the ghetto to acquire meaning (Fraser 2013, Sandberg 2008, and Shammas and Sandberg 2016 have written about gang capital but not from a specific gender perspective). These displays of capital are always a specific localism, yet simultaneously global, given the undoubted common ground between gangs the world over, in terms of a shared street-level masculinity.

Southside Belize City was not devoid of its own variant of hegemonic masculinity when the Bloods and Crips arrived; rather, local historically rooted masculinities were present at the time—for example, the Base Boys with their street corner reputation for dealing marijuana and disco punch ups. Modern contextually constructed male hegemonic orders resonate with the past, as they are adaptations or, partially at least, reproductions. Equally, Matthew Bishop, Dylan Kerrigan, and I (2022) found that certain postcolonial masculinities in poor parts of the Port of Spain acted as catalysts for contemporary gang identities:

> While steelband gangs, followed by Bad Johns and then Bad Men, were notorious, they have been supplanted by more violent contemporary gangs with colloquially known Alpha or Zesser leaders, whose violence has been made lethal by the interdiction of firearms, competitive gang territorialization, and institutionalization [one expert we interviewed said]. "Before it was cutlasses, knives, bottles, but no less brutal. Now it's guns. Since 2000, guns have really come on the scene, so that changes the whole thing. A lot of the guys too, they're just young—16, 17, 18, you know. I did foolish things when I was that age too—it's just that now we have guns in the mix. . . . So, in that regard I just see it as an extension of an inter-generational acceptance of violence." (p. 646)

Hegemonic orders are most easily identified by looking at gang leadership figures. The original Base Boys were succeeded by "Generals," the first generation of Blood and Crip gang bosses, who in turn gave way to new generations of leaders, now called *Big Men*, *Boss Men*, *Shottas*, *Killer Men*, *Strike Men*, and *Big Sprats*. The Generals were the prototype of the modern armed gangsta. Weaponization in the 1990s meant power, allowing Generals to extend their influence and illegal moneymaking activities to support an increasingly flashy lifestyle. Furthermore, acting as go-betweens for political party clientelism allowed them to reinforce their status as self-declared "community leaders." The consolidation of the influential General identity package, an eye-catching set of gangsta behaviors and practices, took less than a decade. Alias Tiger said:

> TIGER: Mi father was a member of a gang, but he ded. Mi brother was a member of Bac-a-town gang, but Ghost Town [gang] end up kill him, like tree year ago.
> AUTHOR: Why they kill him, what was the beef about?
> TIGER: Mi brother was [laughs self-consciously], mi brother was deir killer-man. He was the strike-man for Bac-a-town, an' Ghost Town wan revenge . . .
> AUTHOR: Why do they fight?

TIGER: Dey fight for respec' an' ting. Coz mostly ting happen when dey got a party on. When all da gang members meet up, and ting just start to flick-up [flareup]. Deir beef done start simple. Simple ting cause beef down here. Dey teef [steal] a bike down dere, small tings! Den dey come up into bigger problems, ya know? (2016)

Young gang members' narratives discussed identities consistently linked to domination, status challenges, and the rejection of nonhegemonic traits. Vartas said, "Everybody wanna be a man, you da man if you kill somebody, if you don't do it, ya pussy" (2016). Haylock's research with male youth offenders corroborates this: "Everybody wants to be known as the 'big man' out on the streets. We want everyone to think we are 'bad' enough, being a 'killer, murderer, or a prisoner' is respected" (2013, p. 31). Messiah agreed in his typically evocative language, "There's n***az who have respect from the streets and n***az know, 'don't fuck wid dat n***a coz he will shoot the fuck out of you'" (2016).

Poverty promotes masculine vulnerability to the trappings of the gang space. The absence of licit or dignified pathways to manhood supports the reification of the gang world. Gang identity is accessible, a rare opportunity to establish self-esteem in the face of structural humiliation. Moura et al. recently concluded that gender-segregated cultures reinforce patriarchal power (2022); the gang as a male socialization space is not necessarily indicative of a wider segregation, but it is a men-only subculture whose patriarchal power reverberates across the community.

One gang member was taking part in an apprenticeship program at the Institute for Technical and Vocational Education and Training in the Northside of the city, with a view to finding a way out of the gang. "In a gang area you get respec' if you a Bad Man. . . . You gotta be in politics or a gang or in de GSU [police anti-gang unit] coz dey de tough guys." The alignment of gangs with politicians and police tells us of the men jostling for position in a *field* of gendered competition, on the streets of Southside (after Bourdieu 1977). In the minds of young men on Southside, they are variants of "tough guy" success, legitimated as "the most honored way of being a man [requiring] all other men to be subordinate to it" (Connell and Messerschmidt 2005, p. 832) despite their widespread violence and corruption. Violence and corruption do not undermine this legitimacy, rather, perversely, they enhance it because they deliver status, money, and power. In contexts of desperation, the morality of the *means* is easily offset by the *ends*. One retired government worker told me:

Kids are now much more traumatized. The gangs are competitors [as employers], they provide status and money that kids can't otherwise get. And they are also dictators, they use violence to obtain and hang on to it. We can't romanticize them. They also behave like the politicians by telling kids to rob BZ$100,000, then they pay them with chicken and fries and a coke, or they give them only BZ$20. (2022)

Gayle and Mortis's (2010) study on Belize City households showed that only 20 percent were single parent, 10 percent being single father, which is markedly lower than the Caribbean average. "Compared to many other countries in the Caribbean and even some developed and transient countries, Belize has a solid nuclear family base on which to develop" (p. 82). This is encouraging, but we should note an important disjunction: Mrs. N, former manager of a gang-prevention program on Southside, underlined the vulnerability of the young boys she worked with who were almost all from struggling single-mother households. Although this is not survey data based on large numbers, it adds credence to my experiences in Medellín, where I observed that two households can be markedly different even if they are next-door neighbors. And, while it is not always the case, the boys in Medellín tended to join gangs if they came from households that were clearly struggling. Often such households were single-mother households with few revenue streams to draw from. For clarity, this is not an argument for incentivizing absent fathers to return as a solution to "deviancy." Conversely, pushing fathers that are negative influences back into the home increases the probability that the children will end up in conflict with the law. That said, Mrs. N went on to say, with no positive older males in the home, "the only men that talk to these boys are gangs on the streets, who they look up to and idolize" (2016).

During one of the interviews I conducted with Mr. T, he picked up his cell phone and said, "watch this," and called a young man on Southside. With the phone on speaker, the young man answered, "Yes, General?" even though Mr. T is no gang leader. It is indicative of the ontological power of gangs over the meaning of masculinity that "General" has seeped into local language as a term of respect. Yet clearly, "respect" can be problematic. Jabbar said:

> Boys tink dat being rude and acting like a gang member is how you get respec' off someone. Dere is no longer manhood. We have overgrown adolescents, right? Dere's no male role model. Actually, da role model dat most of our young males seem to be gravitating towards are gangsters. Back in da day, when you went to jail you got scorned. Now, you get stripes, street credibility, so street credibility has taken over masculinity. (2016)

A journalist I spoke to who grew up on George Street said former Generals, Shiny and Pinky, ran the area about a block from his school, so he had to humor them, and many of his school friends were in the gang. Even though he never joined, he admitted that "it was hard not to admire George Street [gang]" (2022). Pinky was killed before I had a chance to try and interview him, but another academic I know did and described him as the only gang member he had met in Belize who he believed was truly psychopathic (2022).

Not all boys on Southside grow up and join gangs; in fact, while all community members have to engage with them to some extent, only a minority become "hardcore" gang members (see Muhammad 2015). However, only a small number of hard-core gunmen are needed to have a significant impact on local communities, such is the terror that lethal violence provokes. Despite a relatively small hard-core, sufficient numbers go through the "ganging process," a gendered rite of passage that molds "badness" to facilitate gang continuity (Baird 2018a). Jabbar refers to the "transition" to new generations:

> Like, right now de leader of George Street is a guy dey call [anonymized], because he's unknown, he's a young fellow, and he's more ruthless coz he knows what happened to his seniors [murdered gang leaders]. So, da killers are more ruthless now. Dey are new, dey are young, and da transition is faster. Some are 13 years old. I saw a young guy who I know is a shotta, and he is not more than 11 years old. So basically, what we have in Belize is child soldiering. (2016)

As fate would have it, in keeping with the village feel to the city, the young man Jabbar referred to was arrested and wound up in Wagner's youth facility at Belize Central Prison, where I interviewed him in 2021. He was eighteen years old and a typical GNC (George Street Next Generation) player. He chose the pseudonym "Irving" after his favorite basketball player in an example of the "let's choose your nickname" icebreaker I have been using for years when interviewing gang members (Baird 2009, 2018b, 2019). The "transition" to new generations has been speeding up since the homicide boom in 2000. In part, because they are killed off more quickly and new blood rises up, as Irving said, "da killers are more ruthless now . . . dey are young." He killed his first person when he was fifteen years old. Certainly, the GNC leadership is far younger than the previous Generals, and Irving had nothing in common with George Herbert who led George Street until he was extradited in 2002. Vartas is the last gang leader resembling a General left in the city, and he was born in 1980, a middle-aged man who felt like the last of a dying breed. Irving's generation is the future.

Irving's narrative that follows is arresting. Covering loss, trauma, violence, and hopelessness. The way that he replicated the violence of his murdered father and uncle, both gang leaders, was conveyed with a sense of inevitability. I interviewed him in the computer room at Wagner's youth detention facility in the main prison, a quiet space a friend working at the prison had organized. It felt awkward that my friend sat at the back of the room like a chaperone for most of the interview. When I asked him why later, he said he was concerned that I may be physically attacked, even though Irving called me "Sir" repeatedly like a nervous tick during the interview. I sensed Irving's understandable trepidation; he had an alien middle-aged white man asking him personal questions not long after he had murdered someone. He cast a broken figure. "He is ultra-aggressive," my friend advised, "like a puppy Pit-bull. You can play wid him, den he turn roun' an' bite you. Dat's when you see his demon come out." He also said that "dere is no hope for him now," that if he goes back to his neighborhood, he will be forced to rejoin the gang, mainly for protection as so many want him dead. Irving had already killed three, maybe four, people. "These kids use it as a badge of honor," my friend continued. Plus, his family name was infamous, and not just on the streets of Southside. I had heard people talk about this family across Belize. They would kill him for the homicides his father and uncle had committed, even though those two were long since murdered themselves. It reminded me of the comments of a community leader I met in Medellín over a decade earlier, *el pasado no perdona* (the past never forgives).

Even though Irving was in his teens when he was arrested, his historical family ties to gang leadership and the "stripes" he earned killing people meant he was fast-tracked while still a child. I asked my friend about Irving's post-juvenile sentencing process. He was not sure but expected him to be moved to the adjacent men's prison in the coming months.

> IRVING: Growing up wasn't really good, Sir. It was good when I was going to primary school an everyting because my mom used to provide for me, an' she work hard for it. An' my father he's an old gangbanger, he was in [gang name anonymized]. He was a very good Dad, Sir, but before I come here, he and I was going tru a lickle conflict, Sir. Coz, you have a lot of splitting of de [gang], Sir, an' I was dis side he was dat side, Sir.
>
> AUTHOR: So, when [gang name] split, you were hanging with one side, and he was hanging with the other side?!
>
> IRVING: Yes Sir, I was living wid my grandmother den Sir.
>
> AUTHOR: How did you join [the gang]?
>
> IRVING: Sir, when I was hanging around wid my older cousin who passed away a couple of months ago, General [anonymized, notorious gang leader]. Me and him was like close, close to each other, from small, growing up to dis age, Sir. We fought, be bad, we

can do whatever we want. Nobody can tell us what to do, nutin'. Den, I grow up wid a dat mentality and I said, I left school, den I start beefin' other peoples from different gangs. Den, I got to fourteen, fifteen and I found a new ting to do an I start robbin' people, Sir.

AUTHOR: Why did you join the gang?

IRVING: Well, I was kind a frightened, Sir, coz my father he a killed a lotta people, Sir. He from [gang name] and other people from different gangs know him, Sir [they wanted to kill him]. I fear about my father a lot, Sir, I have my father's features and everyting, Sir.

AUTHOR: You look like him?

IRVING: Sir [nods yes]. So, if I go round da block next to school maybe people try and hurt me, Sir. Main ting is I a stop caring about life and start gangbanging, den dey killed my grandmother, Sir. I was thirteen den, Sir.

AUTHOR: Why was that a key moment when they killed your grandmother?

IRVING: Well, when dey kill her, I dunno Sir, well it just took half of me, Sir. Coz my grandmother she showed us noting but love, Sir, she spoiled us, took good, good care of me, Sir. She was de mother of my mother, Sir.

AUTHOR: What about your relationship with your mother, what was that like?

IRVING: She used to beat me, Sir, and tell me not to hang around wid dose guys. One day I got tired of it, Sir, an' I run away for about a couple of months.

AUTHOR: Two months?!

IRVING: 'Bout two months an' a half, Sir. [I was] 14, Sir. I go wid one of my father's old colleagues [in the gang]. He took care of me, everyting, Sir, he treat me like a son, Sir. He still livin' dere right now, Sir.

AUTHOR: Was he outside of the gang or inside of the gang?

IRVING: Inside of de gang, Sir. He makes me what I am right now, Sir, he told me what's right from wrong and what you should and shouldn't do. First, he told me to go to school, den I told him my dream was to become one of dem [gang leader], Sir, but he told me it wasn't right. I didn't know much about de gang den, Sir, I was just a kid, I was tekin' it for granted, I wanted to be a gangbanger an' to kill people, Sir.

There are a number of key moments for the intergenerational passing of the baton to the "new generation" in Irving's case. His home was fractured, and he was in conflict with his mother who beat him. This led to him moving in with, not his father, who by then was in a rival gang, but his father's friend. This man was a senior gang figure, and Irving was in his formative years. Although he tried to persuade young Irving not to join the gang, initially, this was not deterrent enough. Understandable. Irving's family were "gang royalty," said my friend.

> AUTHOR: Do gangs nowadays behave in different ways to the old times, like when we had [I name some former Generals]?
> IRVING: Dose were my uncles, Sir.
> AUTHOR: Oh! Has it changed?
> IRVING: Well, none o dem can tell me "do dat, o do dat, o go rob dat man," Sir. Dey know I'm my own mentality, Sir. When I was fifteen, I got my own piece, Sir, a Glock G80, a small black gun, Sir. Den, I start robbin' stores and stuff, Sir.
>
> We never rob our own neighborhood, Sir. Like sometimes I wear a blue shirt [Crips color, as a disguise] and go to de street and rob someone, tek his tings, his jewelry, his monies an' ting den go back to [his gang territory] wid different clothes on. So dey say "ah it was dat gang, it was blue [a Crip gang, not his gang]."
>
> When I was fourteen an' I went to live wid [a General, his father's old friend] he taught me a lot, Sir. He taught me dat if you want to be a gang member you have to be street smart and you have to look smart.
> AUTHOR: What did he teach you, what does that mean?
> IRVING: How to deal wid da police. Da police tell us we evil monsters, Sir, because when I kill my first person, I was fifteen an' a half.
> AUTHOR: That's really young . . .
> IRVING: Sir [nods in agreement].
> AUTHOR: Tell me about that.
> IRVING: Sir, I was smokin' [marijuana], den de police come and dey say you not supposed to be smoking. So den I dash it [threw it away]. Dey hit me an' kicked me off my foot [knocked him down], jump [kicked] on de ground. And den I was ready wid my own piece den. Den I told my uncle I tired of de police, dey always hitting me, searching me, tek me to da police station.
>
> So, I tell my uncle next ting I best go kill someone [out of sheer frustration] an' my uncle say "dat's not how fi dey" [that's not how it's done]. I was ignorant, I wasn't tinkin', I jus' walk [and shot a rival gang member dead in a different neighborhood]. So, from den I was just supposed to come to jail [after he was caught for murder], coz I wasn't tinkin'. I say I kill him out a frustration Sir, coz, coz, dat's what da police cause.

ADAM: So, the police made you really angry and you shot this other guy?
IRVING: Sir [nods].
ADAM: But did you have beef wid dis other guy?
IRVING: Sir [nods]. She [grandmother] died from gun violence.
AUTHOR: But how did that push you into the gang?
IRVING: Sir, because, she was innocent, Sir. It was all big mistake, it was a mix-up sir, coz a gang boss was messing around wid a gun behind her head, Sir, it went off, and de guy dat shot her, he was killed himself, Sir [he was murdered for killing the grandmother]. I was thirteen, Sir, from den my heart was jus' cold, Sir. My mum and my dad was tryin' to hide it from me, Sir, and one day before de funeral I was using her [mother's] phone, and I went into de gallery, and I see de picture [of the grandmother who had been shot in the head]. All blood, Sir, and I start crying.

Irving also explained that he shot two other people in a rage when he saw the photos of his grandmother's gunshot to the head on the cell phone. While there are beefs and gang rivalries, this violence was caused spontaneously by a highly traumatized boy. The murders he committed were not directly attributable to orchestrated gang warfare over turf.

AUTHOR: What's the difference between your generation and the old generation?
IRVING: Well, when Shiny was livin' everyone listen to each other, Sir, now dey don't listen to we [us]. Dey don't worry about colors anymore, Sir, coz I a member of di next generation. No one can tell me I can't wear a blue shirt, Sir.
ADAM: How did you end up in here?
IRVING: Sir, because I killed my friend's cousin, Sir, I was angry, Sir, I didn't want to do it because dere was a girl there, but I'm right here [ready to pull the trigger] so I can't go back [feels he has to shoot him despite the girl being there, which he had not expected].
ADAM: How did the police catch you?
IRVING: Because I shot di girl [by mistake] and the next round I miss [he failed to kill his male target], so he told the police. He knows me for over two or tree years.
AUTHOR: Where do the guns and ammunitions come from?
IRVING: I don't really know sir. Coz, I get my firs' gun from my uncle, sir, and de second gun I teef [steal] from my father, Sir. De bigger

heads [gang leaders] dey do dere own ting, Sir. We, de younger generation, when we rob, we a buy weed an' we sell, Sir, we sell weed, Sir.

AUTHOR: When you are younger generation do you have a General or a boss?

IRVING: Sir, we no need no boss sir! "New Generation" we donna need a no boss, Sir. If Lil' Shiny [next generation gang leader] was still livin' he was gonna be my boss. His father was a boss so everybody respec' him [son of Shiny, former General]. Everyone respec' me too, coz dey say I'm young but I walk around an' I shoot people, kill people an' ting...

What stands out in Irving's case was his immersion in gang life from birth. In my field diary the evening after the interview, I wrote, "these kids have no chance," recalling Victor Gaviria's film set in 1990 Medellín, *Rodgrigo D, No Futuro*. A film where the young protagonist is stripped of choices in life, pushing him to make kamikaze decisions that precipitated his demise. Irving's gang world immersion is reflected in his coming-of-age comments, such as getting his first gun, what Angel calls becoming "da Big Man," a performative "badness." While he is a victim, cutting a brutalized figure, he was also a feared and dangerous young man, notoriety he had secured as a child.

In contexts of constraint the gang becomes a vessel or, as I jotted down in my field diary eccentrically, "in darkness, the gang is light" (2021). As an escape for struggling young men, this is, in a nutshell, how masculine vulnerability fuels gang membership. Despite the specter of violence, death and permanent injury, the gang is an attractive *project* for poor young men. The gang project finds legitimation, consent, and complicity among the local population, derived from its accumulation of social capital relative to the exclusion of the social terrain. Muhammad said "a cyclical drama is being played out" in the ghetto (2015, p. 139). Mine is a gendered reading of this cyclical drama.

Masculine vulnerability is complex, being both subjective and context specific, between agency and structure. Although we cannot predict individual reactions and trajectories precisely, as a whole, settings of chronic vulnerability fuel gang membership. Of course, there are numerous other stories of struggle and survival in tough neighborhoods that do not involve colluding with gangs. This struggle, in Southside parlance taken from U.S. streets, is *grindin'*. Similar words have emerged across the world. In Colombia, they call it *rebusque*, in Mumbai *jugaad*. It is, in effect, a term to encapsulate the daily bread existence of the poor; a take-your-chances approach for those who walk out of their homes in the morning not sure how, or if, they will put food on the table that evening.

The grind is more than just a struggle to put food on the table, it also translates as hard work. Empathizing with the grind from a gendered perspective casts an explanatory light on lives on Southside. I have heard gang members say that grindin' is synonymous with hustling, getting out on the corner early morning and selling weed. This I expected. However, JK and Messiah surprised me. One meeting with them reminded me of Philippe Bourgois's ethnography *In Search of Respect: Selling Crack in El Barrio* (1995), a struggle for esteem, dignity, and identity. They had flirted with gangs when younger and still hung out with them, and JK had even taken part in a drive-by shooting. They were victims of structural violence, but no angels. It was clear from speaking to them that they had shifted away from what John Pitts (2008) described as the "relative riches" of gang life and had gone some way to compensating for the loss of masculine capital the gang provided with the status their music celebrity afforded them. Social media and technology has meant that a number of young people on Southside have begun producing their own music videos using phone cameras and basic software programs. One viral hit was a phrase quoted earlier from Messiah, "Police Dem Chancy,"[1] a scaled-down Creole version of N.W.A.'s seminal "Fuck Tha Police" from Los Angeles in 1988. Messiah's imported rap and JK's dancehall identities enhanced their community standing and made them something more than your "average" Creole Southsider, leveraging that Belizean "cultural vulnerability" and tendency to admire the foreign described in chapter 1. For Messiah and JK, the cultural transfer and syncretistic incorporation of highly regarded foreign identities became a way of resisting the pernicious effects of exclusion and the threat of emasculation through each one's publicly displayed musical aesthetic, an assertion of a syncretistic Americanized *and* Jamaicanized Creole masculinity.

Our interview had its fair share of masculine braggadocio, which both informs and distorts the research process, something I have critiqued in the past as "macho research" (Baird 2018b, 2020b), and recently gender positionality and gang research has been questioned in detail by Méndez and Van Damme (2024). We were more relaxed after the interview as we chatted informally when leaving the recording studio, and a less performative, more confessional, conversation emerged. At the time, neither JK or Messiah were cutting it financially and were working side jobs to support their children. "We grindin'" Messiah sighed. Being an aspiring musician in the best of circumstances is tough, let alone south of the creek in Belize City. It was then I noticed JK's state-of-the-art smartphone. How could he afford it? I wondered out loud. He said a wealthy older lady had "given" it to him. When times were tough, which they always were, they operated as gigolos on the side. JK was coy, yet Messiah made a veiled attempt to cover his shame, bragging that "rich bitches" in Belize "wanna get with famous n***az." I did not press the issue, but it was a rare insight into male sex work. Certainly, sex work broadly understood, and what might be called "the sexual politics of the street," is entirely unresearched in Belize. Stories of male politicians and their "mistresses" turn the soap-operatic rumor mill.[2] Time and again I heard comments about sexual relationships between the wives or daughters of politicians or powerful businesspeople and male gang members. One Belizean researcher, a member of a political party for over twenty years, told me:

> *You know women and gangsters!* [that gang leaders attract numerous sexual partners]. Some of the wives [of politicians] and their daughters get caught up with gangsters. I am not talking about rumors. *I am telling you I know.* These ladies were with *heads* of gangs. [A former politician's] vehicle was rolled into the water because of a lover. It was actually a gang member, the cousin of the [lover] who did it, she instructed him to take the vehicle. Then he [the politician] beat up his wife, [then] a girlfriend, and [then] another one,[3] and got kicked out as leader of the opposition. Belize is a village. You have to be careful. (2022)

As if to reinforce this last comment, when we left the café where the interview took place, we bumped into some people she knew. I noticed she felt the need to point out to them she was in a work meeting with me and not on a "date." As we walked off, she said, "Everyone knows everyone here."

We are fortunate to have an in-depth study conducted by Gayle et al. (2010, 2016) on Southside with a focus on male youth exclusion. Young men suffer lower academic achievement than women, drop out of school more regularly, and face different types of stigmatization than young women. Boys also face a range of domestic abuse, including high levels of sexual violence and rape, but, most tellingly, they are much more susceptible to incarceration, murder, permanent injury, and disability than their female counterparts. If we remember the statistics in the previous chapter, female victims account for a small percentage of murders. Suicide is also higher among males. One missionary described her frustration at trying to connect young Southside men to social services, because the mainly female civil servants she encountered held them in disdain, "red-taped" their efforts, or simply ignored requests, in a way they did not for young women. She remarked that any young man from Southside who looked a little "street" was rejected out of hand. An academic at the University of Belize, who was brought up and still lives on Southside, said the educational gender gap was glaring and widening every year. She lamented that so few men made it to university and that well-educated women simply could not find the partners they were looking for. Anecdotally, the homeless people I saw around town who clearly had drinking or substance abuse problems, were all men, bar none. Viscerally, it felt like an accumulation of lost generations of men. There is something about public destitution in Belize City that is male, but this is not a masculinist reading of the phenomenon, rather it is a disaggregated one. Gender influences how each individual mitigates or offsets precarity, and we can trace these processes empirically by studying men's and women's decision-making under contextual duress. One might ask, If men hit the streets, where do women end up, and How do their survival strategies differ?

Young men can join a gang to survive or offset feelings of worthlessness, or they may pursue other strategies. JK's and Messiah's grindin' was a fascinating take on this process. Yes, they were formerly fringe gang members but had managed to transition out. The masculine capital they secured in the gang was replaced symbolically by nascent musician celebrity and materially through a grindin' mixed economy that included sex work. Selling sex to survive highlighted their vulnerability but is far more common among girls and women on Southside, which we come to later in this chapter.

Gang practices demand displays of violence and toughness, shaping the internal norms of the group. I have described these processes in sociological terms as the "strategic essentialization" of masculinity, a type of "brutalist meritocracy" within the gang (Baird 2018a). The capacity for lethal violence plays a dominant role in organizing the gang hierarchy. There are rarely leaders who have not killed. Irving, discussed earlier, knew this implicitly. Aspirational boys absorb these normative expectations. Power means to wield a gun, create fear, control the rank and file, use violence "when necessary," and a host of similar practices and performances of *ganghood*. These identities are not solely constructed among the gang membership but also relationally vis-à-vis other members of the community, where the gang tops the gender hierarchy, symbolizing a local hegemonic masculinity that so appeals to children living in squalor.

Childhood

In 2011, I designed the SYSP gang intervention pilot for the UNDP, which was funded by the Central American Regional Security Initiative (CARSI) at the U.S. Embassy. The next chapter focuses on interventions, but there is a takeaway from the SYSP program to use here that helps us understand vulnerability.

When the program started, one staff member, alias Mrs. N, described the difficulties she encountered getting the young men taking part to concentrate in the workshops on offer: schoolwork support, vocational training, job placements, et cetera. Mrs. N quickly realized it was because they were hungry. Key to the functioning of the project was diverting a tranche of the budget into a "feeding program," essentially a soup kitchen. When designing the project, I had completely underestimated the widespread malnutrition of children on Southside. Later, a Belizean academic told me that "people are scavenging for food daily"; and a young man who had been through SYSP said he often went hungry and as a result could not stay awake in school classes. Gayle and Mortis state in their report:

> Among the poor families, parents try desperately to ensure that their children get food to go to school in the mornings and can buy at least one healthy meal before returning home. . . . 1 in 5 children expresses food concerns . . . 6% are near starving or about to collapse, which has in fact happened at schools as found in the study. . . . The biggest single problem identified by 51 of the 59 schools [surveyed] is chronic hunger. (2010, pp. 90, 122)

A decade later the United Nations Belize (2021) found that nutrition remained a significant issue: "Children in homes with upwards of more than four (4) siblings experience hardships owing to food and nutrition shortages. Those from low-income households and who live on Southside Belize City are likely to be underweight and . . . tend to experience wasting" (p. 70). For a middle-income country, these revelations are an indictment of wealth distribution. Mrs. N continued:

> What we are dealing with is that the whole family structure has gone. A lot of parents are young parents that don't have the skills, and they don't have any knowledge to pass on to their children. So these children grow up and they have no sense of identity, they don't have no sense of belonging, they don't know who they are. They don't have much exposure knowing that they have role models they can look up to, the absence of the father figure at home, and so they look at other things for those needs. *Their needs is literally not being met!* An' I say that because I am thinking of the young man we mediated on Friday. An' you know what he says? *He would prefer to go to jail than go back and live with his mother!* And he told us "you can lock me up, but I am going right back to the gang leaders house when I get out."

What stood out in my conversations with Mrs. N was the sheer rage omnipresent among young people. A number of Belizeans I spoke to would talk about "demons." At first, I thought this just meant losing their temper, but, after listening to a number of accounts, I understood it was a reference to trauma. The demon *was* trauma, and, when it surfaced, it could create a number of reactions, from anger and violent outbursts to nervous breakdowns and depression. I was slow to realize this. I only became aware after speaking to Angel several times over the years. His demons would come out when he was alone or drinking, so he kept himself busy and had become teetotal. His demons were multiple. Memories of people he had murdered haunted him. Then one day he said, as we sat on a shoreside bench by the colorful "Belize" sign tourist attraction, "My son dey kill him like two years ago." He had a new demon. "If I see that person walking there [who killed his son] I don't know what I would do. I look for something." He points at a rock on the ground, indicating he would smash their skull in (2021).

Mrs. N connected the anger and violence of young men in the SYSP to widespread sexual abuse. This tallied with Gayle and Mortis's (2010) survey of households across Southside concluding that "conflict in the home" and "child abuse" was "extreme" (pp. 70–73).

> These young people are angry and so you have all this rage boiling up inside of them. And *a lot* has happened to them. And I look back and there was a young man on the program and he was *so angry*. And you know what happened to him? He was raped repeatedly, and [he] was going to shoot his uncle.

Mrs. N persuaded the young man in question to go to the police instead, and, with the support of SYSP, there was a prosecution, although the uncle was only sentenced to two years "so [the young man] was still really, really angry." Prosecution for abuse is exceedingly rare. One unpublished report shown to me by a Belizean academic found that, astoundingly, only five out of more than two thousand sexual and violent crimes against girls had been punished. A 0.25 percent conviction rate. "There is no justice in Belize for sexual crimes against girls, and investigations have been blocked and derailed with bribery," he said, adding that the report he showed me had been suppressed because it would be damning for politicians, the police, and the judiciary (2017).

I spoke with three women, one middle-aged mother (Mrs. B) and daughter (Miss C), who was seventeen at the time, and a schoolteacher working on Southside (Mrs. A, although present, did not make any comments in the particular section of conversation that follows). We talked about the difficulties children faced on Southside. The interventions of Mrs. B and Miss C were telling because they not only lived on Southside but had fostered three children from households with gang ties. Fostering is not regulated. There is an unofficial Belizean way, where concerned citizens, mainly women, house and care for children in need. Mrs. B, Mrs. N, and the "Researcher" who appear in this book, all took a number of children into their homes for extended periods, often years.

> MRS. B: Kids are oftentimes groomed at home [into gang culture]. Our two foster children were already groomed, and they were five and six.
> MISS C: I was giving the example of [names six-year-old foster brother] when he first came to live with us.
> MRS. B: His idea of being a man was to go out and kill people.
> AUTHOR: And he was six?
> MRS. B: Yes. He was that violent. At six, he could have pulled the trigger and killed someone, even at six. He was hanging out with his brother who was seventeen. He had so much pent-up aggression. Now he's twelve, he's made a huge turnaround. We also [fostered] two of his biological sisters. But *they take a lot longer, harder,* to turn around.
> MISS C: Yeah, it's weird. If you take a guy out of a gang and put him in a better house [it takes less time to rehabilitate him than a girl.]
> MRS. B: At the risk of sounding sexist, the boys are taught by gang culture to be tough, to be hard, to be macho, that's already the masculine slant. The girls are taught to be nothing.
> AUTHOR: What do you mean?
> MRS. B: The girls have no self-esteem. They're trained to have no self-esteem from the time they're small. The mothers will coddle a baby boy, but not so much a baby girl. See, *both* are marginalized, but in *different* ways. The boys are marginalized because they are given no responsibility. They're expected to be rough and tumble . . . but the girls, the only thing they're expected to do is to work and do housework, and they are not rewarded or even praised for that. So, they are nothing.
>
> Girls that are nurtured into this role know they're garbage, there is no good in them. The only good is what you can do for someone else. So daily, daily, daily, you have to tell them they're good because, they're great, that they do their homework, maintain personal hygiene . . .
>
> So, for the boys it's like a switch. Changing from violence, this roughness, hardness, to "oh, I'm good because I can get good grades and because I'm nice to people and because I appreciate who I am." It's a smaller flick of a switch. Girls have to be *totally reprogrammed.*
> MISS C: By the time he [the six-year-old fostered boy] was eight, he was like a completely different person.

MRS. B: We fostered [names girl] when she had just had her fifth birthday. Nobody knew it was her birthday. We had missed it and she had come to us just days after her birthday. Her birthday went by with nobody even telling her. She wouldn't speak, she wouldn't even speak to her brother, she would just look at him and he would speak for her. He would ask her if she wanted this or that, and her brother would tell us what she wanted. She was five. She thought she was two, wanted me to hold her to my breast, as her foster mother, because she was that traumatized, and that delayed.

Her birth was not registered until she was four years old. We're not sure that the date we celebrate her birthday *is* her actual birthday, and although our kid's personal stories might be a little extreme, they're not unusual.

MISS C: Back to the self-harm; there's a lot of ear twisting.
AUTHOR: What?
MISS C: They [girls] pull their earlobes down and twisting them around, so they get red, red, red, and really, really, loose, and thin.
MRS. B: I've seen a lotta girls do that.
MISS C: They also like, twist their wrists.
AUTHOR: What?
MISS C: [mimics wringing and twisting of wrists]
MRS. B: There's a lotta small incidents of . . .
AUTHOR: Like body language that you can pick out that indicates trauma?
MISS C: Or like this [demonstrates], twisting your fingers, bending them. It's what we would call fidgeting, but it's beyond fidgeting, they are hurting themselves.
MRS. B: We've also seen a lot of teenagers sucking their thumbs.
AUTHOR: Oh . . .

Mr. T was unerringly honest about the plight of many children growing up on Southside:

We should tear down the ghettos and start again. Nothing will ever change until the living conditions change. These kids live in a room with a piss-bucket in the corner with their siblings and mum. The mum's c**t is getting abused by some man right in front of them. Then he gets up and pisses in the bucket in the corner right by them. They see this. And the mum is on the bed, high [on drugs]. So, then they see this guy pissing in front of them who just fucked their mum. This is true, happens to a lot of them. They have told me. (2021)

One counselor told me a powerful story of a volatile young man in Wagner's juvenile prison (2021). He was constantly "in the hole" for fighting. He would get out after a fourteen-day stint, start another fight, and go straight back in. One day, the counselor sat him down in his office, gave him chips and a soda, and put a music channel on the wall-mounted television. He then asked him about the fights and if he knew he would go back in the hole? He said he liked the solitude, being away from the noise, being somewhere people would leave him alone. The counselor countered, "No, something else is going on." The counselor told me, "Then the kid looks me in the eye, shows his demon [so the counselor would back off]. So, I show him my father demon back [to hold his authority], and the kid says, 'you don' know what I went thru. How would [you] behave if you had a dick up your ass at seven years old?'" The young man had never told anyone before. The counselor replied, "'You know what brother; you are the strongest person I know. You are stronger than me, because I would not have lived through it to tell the tale. *You must deal with your spirits!*' The kid got out of jail and never been back, and the kid's other counselors could not believe the change and asked me how I did it. . . . It was miraculous, a turning point for him." It was an emotional interview. The counselor said, "I have never told this to anyone," reminding me of Kimberly Theidon's observation that good ethnographers are "traffickers of secrets" (quoted in Baird 2018b). But it was just one case out of hundreds, probably thousands, on Southside.

A great many Southside children can be described as extremely vulnerable. In the absence of basic needs and the presence of multiple forms of abuse and abandonment, often leading to mental scars, rage, developmental setbacks, low self-esteem, self-harm, and suicide, understandably their demons are numerous. This is the gangland backdrop.

Feminine Vulnerability

Rates of rape and other sexual violence in the Caribbean are among the highest in the world, and higher than in Latin America (UNDP 2012). A schoolteacher, Mrs. A, explained how common sexual violence toward girls and women was at home, "There's a lot of inter-family rape. A lot of the time girls would be raped by their uncle or father" (2016). It reminded me of a conversation with a taxi driver in 2017 who said that he could sleep with a lot of young women because "dey are hungry," offering them a free lift and BZ$30 (US$15) for sex. I held a focus group with five young women, from fifteen to seventeen years old, students of Mrs. A, who estimated that 50 percent of their peers had sex for money or gifts (2016). Gayle and Mortis (2010) observed:

In 7 schools teachers have to deal with girls (and one boy) who sell their bodies in order to survive. "They have sugar daddies and they keep in contact even during classes. They hide the phones in their underwear so we cannot access it. When the phone rings they rush to the bathroom and then you will see them disappear to provide the service. What can we do?" Surprisingly this problem is not restricted to secondary schools. Teachers spoke of students as young as 13 years old who rely on the sale of their bodies to survive from Standard 5 in primary school. (p. 122)

A social worker who supported SYSP said that girls often become pregnant by the time they are fourteen. "What it is, is dat you have *a lot* of young people having children and they can't take care of themselves, so how you gonna take care of a baby?" (2017). Mrs. A, Mrs. B, and Miss C, discussed the risks girls face further:

> MRS. A: Most of them [girls] do it [have sex] for the money. Most of the time they don't have anything to eat so men take advantage of them. That is very common, this is a way they get by.
> AUTHOR: How many girls of secondary school age, say twelve to eighteen, do you think would be forced to engage in that sort of thing, out of one hundred?
> MRS. A: I'd say like, 80 to 85.
> MISS C: I would say the majority because they go to school and they don't have the means to pay their way through school, so that is a means to get by. They either do that or they get raped when they're younger. I would say about 50% are raped. I live on Southside and rape happens every single day. . . . It starts from twelve, thirteen.
> MRS. A: When I was eight, I was wearing a tight t-shirt and shorts [around Southside] and I was asked "how much?" by a middle-aged man.
> MISS C: I've met girls who've been raped way younger. I met a girl who was raped when she was four.
> MRS. B: I know girls who have been raped and threatened with their life if they report it, even if they just tell somebody they know.

While all children on Southside face high levels of sexual abuse, as they become teenagers, girls and young women are disproportionately affected by sexual violence and more likely to sell sex as a survival strategy. In Medellín, women are susceptible to sexual violence when partying with gang members (Baird 2015a). Gayle and Mortis (2010) observe in Belize City that "girls most commonly serve as girlfriends or perform sexual acts with promoted [gang] soldiers.... These practices have devastating impact on girls and young women who live in gang-impacted communities because it erodes their self-esteem" (p. 266). However, sexual violence toward women by gangs is not *aberrant* behavior, it actually reflects pervasive sexual abuse in the wider community. Gayle and Mortis surveyed fifty-nine schools and found teachers dealing with sexually abused children as a day-to-day occurrence, mainly connected to domestic incidents or girls exchanging sex for money to cover their basic needs, including hunger (pp. 122–123). The stories of sexual violence I heard most frequently were of the domestic rape of children by male family, stepfathers, or "friends" of the family. Further, we cannot make a blanket statement that gang members are simply misogynists, yet gang socialization spaces expose women to elevated risks.

Gang members tended to have children with multiple women, but this is a community norm. Most siblings in households are half-siblings, often many years apart in age. When I visited a handful of gang and former gang members at home, none lived with their children or female partners; their intimate relationships were characterized by instability. They were all estranged, often bitterly so. The dynamics of the single-mother household has contributed to the veneration of "the mother" by sons. Decades ago, Colombian journalist Alonso Salazar published interviews with gang members in his (1990) book *No Nacimos Pa'Semilla* (*Born to Die in Medellín*), writing famously that "you only have one mother, your father could be any son-of-a-bitch," a turn of phrase that has now become common in the city's poor neighborhoods. This is a signpost to the conflicting relationships gang members often have with women: venerate mothers, denigrate young women they have sex with.

Mrs. A said, "Girls want to be part of the group, drinking, smoking, having sex, but there are not many good sturdy relationships on Southside. Most of them do it for the money, so instead of having one sexual partner or boyfriend, they have another to get money from" (2016). The transactional dynamics of "sex for money" reflects young women's desperation. In terms of "options" available to young women, full or hard-core membership with the gang is not open to women to accumulate capital in the same way it is open to men. *Pleasing* as Miss C puts it euphemistically in the following dialogue, is the most common way a young woman can access the benefits of the gang world. Like men, this may simply be a survival strategy; they may see the gang space in ambitious terms as the best way to accumulate money, status, and power. In other words, the gang's *masculine capital*—both material and symbolic—can transfer to women, becoming *feminine capital*.

> MISS C: There aren't many women in the gangs, but there are a lot of women associated with the gangs, because they have a boyfriend in the gang. I don't know, except for like the *Pleasers*.

AUTHOR: The what?

MISS C: Pleasers. That's the only thing I can think of. It's sexual.

AUTHOR: What's the difference between a Pleaser and a girlfriend?

MISS C: It's a different thing. She hangs out with the gang, "that's that girl who's always hanging out with the gang, the guys." [She sleeps with them] for protection, for money, shoes, phone, tablet . . .

[Gang leaders] have a common law wife, they have a mistress, they have a girlfriend, and they have "baby mamas." They get [money] and they feel protected, but it's false protection . . .

AUTHOR: Because they are vulnerable? Do you think they are vulnerable to sexual violence from gang members?

MRS. B: Absolutely.

MISS C: Oh yes.

MRS. A: Yeah.

MRS. B: And that starts at a young age. We know girls who are twelve years old who are passed around [gang-raped or "trained"].

MISS C: If you say no, it still happen anyway.

AUTHOR: A Pleaser, is she showing what we call "agency," is she showing some will to hang out with the gang?

MRS. A: Yeah, dating them. You know, it's not the girl's fault what she wears and how she acts, but yet there's some decision making there. I think we've done a disservice to young women, [so] they don't have to take responsibility for the way they carry themselves, dress themselves. It doesn't mean "she wants rape," but it *still sends a message, it still sends a message.* They then see them as meat.

AUTHOR: And they want protection and material things from the gang at the same time.

Mrs. A's final remarks, that the way a girl dresses "sends a message," feels like victim blaming, but she is wondering out loud how to keep girls safe. In these circumstances, boys and girls take safety into their own hands and carry weapons.

MISS C: The younger boys carry [pencil] sharpener blades [and] if women have a weapon, it's normally a small blade.

MRS. A: A surgical blade.

MISS C: Coz I know a girl who is not in the gang but got attacked by other girls with razor blades. An' got cut up, cut up, cut up!

MRS. A: And people love to watch that. Girls fighting, its entertainment, on their phones, YouTube videos. Sometimes they fight over the males, sometimes off of vanity, because they envy the way [others] dress.

MISS C: There's a *lot of vanity* here.
MRS. B: People worship vanity *a lot*.
MISS C: Even tho' the girls don't have self-confidence, they still have vanity.

When I talked to female friends and colleagues there was a depressing sense of inevitability that if a girl is not a victim of sexual abuse in the home she will face it on the streets, or at some stage will be pressed into exchanging sex for money to survive, for a job, for a promotion, or similar. Turning back to the focus group:

STUDENT 1: There's plenty sexual violence on the streets too . . . could be linked to drink or drugs, or you out on the street, and it jus' happen.
STUDENT 2: A lot of the time girls specifically want a boyfriend that's in the gang to gain protection . . . but they get things in return. I join it because I get what I want, you get what you want [sex]. [Girls get] bought clothes, they get defended, they use gang members to sort their problems out.
MRS. A: This generation of [young] women are in this cycle of "this is what I can get, this is all I can get," so the girls are just using the gang members for money and protection and for gifts and for all of that. They are mentally stuck in that position of "there's nothing better."
STUDENT 4: We frightened to walk from one gang territory to the next. When dey kill dey have no mercy. They don' care who dey gonna kill. Harassment [catcalling] is jus' normal if you walkin' around. I feel dat a lot of de time, dat, dat happens, dey can see the vulnerability in you, so they push themselves further. Da police also [harass us].
MRS. A: Well, a lot of the times, girls are just very vulnerable. Well, this whole generation, they just corrupted. . . . They drugs, they partying, sex, everything, pornography, pictures, they just beyond. They are desperate.
STUDENT 3: Well, on George Street at night my mum wouldn't let me and my sister walk on our own . . . to go to the store or something. But if all three of us sisters go, it's ok, but it's not so safe.
AUTHOR: I heard that young women may sleep with several gang members in one night. Is that true?
STUDENT 4: Yes, dey train them. Dey run a train. Dey are young, 16.
MRS. A: In my mind they don't really know what they are doing. It's just been happening to them since they were small, small, small,

but they never report it, coz it's more problems than anything right? And there quite a few of the police that are involved too.

When I asked gang members about the mothers of their children, there was a lot of hand-wringing, teeth-sucking, and use of the invectives "hoes," "bitches," and "whores" associated with gangsta rap lyrics (see Weitzer and Kubrin 2009 in Messerschmidt 2018, p. 59). Shorty said:

> Besides my other whores, I had this beautiful woman . . . [goes on to talk about teenage girlfriend. He was thirty-three at the time]. The bitches who love gangstas only love the dude for the stuff he's doin' on the streets. . . . They all want the same, they only like him because of his name, then they always fuck their best friends. Now [names Vartas] and [another gang leader] hate each other. They were best friends and now they fightin' over a girl. [Vartas] shot one friend dead because he fucked his girlfriend.
>
> Yeah, we train them. I've seen ten gangbangers do one woman. Some are forced, some wanna do it to show that they are down, it shows they love them. . . . The dudes don't really hang out with the home girls, they hang out in their own groups, they are separated. Women don't hold guns . . . but I know one who killed two people, because I taught her how to be a real, real, real home girl (2016).
>
> Here [in Belize] we respect girls more than in LA. In Belize we speak nicely to them. You can put your hand on their pussy and touch them and shit, they don't mind. (2022)

Jabbar talked about female agency and what women seek from gang spaces:

> Women don't want no punk for a lover, man. Dey want a hard-core gangster who represents security and stability, coz den nobody come and mess wid her, coz her man gonna be there to protect her. If a man not working, then [they say] he has to gwan rob somebody to bring [them] baby food and Pampers. So dat's the kind of man dey want.
>
> If the women were to decide, I don't want no gangster man no more, I want a respectable man for my children, there would be no more gang problem. In Hattieville prison, women who are actually married go there to look for a gangster boyfriend! Yeah bwoy, I serious. Seriously, don't take these women in this country lightly *at all*! Dey play their cards tight! Belize is serious! [sucks teeth] (2021)

Gender relations in gang settings on Southside are characterized by an asymmetry of power. Hume and Wilding (2015) have argued that the extreme nature of rape suffered by some women engaged with gangs "highlights the role of loyal and submissive femininities in reinforcing dominant masculinities." Further, Aguilar Umaña and Rikkers (2012) said that in these settings their bodies become sites of domination, reproduction, and pleasure (p. 15), subject to the *libido dominandi*, the male desire to dominate (Bourdieu 2001). Unfettered sexual access to women is part and parcel of the hegemonic masculinity of the streets, whereas playing a role in childcare, for example, does not push gang members up the gender hierarchy. Mrs. A said, "They don't have to take care of kids, they have to show their virility. Being a man is fathering children, but not being a father, to a lot of young men." It is harder to display childcare; it cannot be paraded around the neighborhood like a girlfriend, motorbike, or new sneakers, and it does not invite people to drink beers and smoke weed on the corner.

It is difficult to gauge women's agency and relations of power in these spaces. Women are not *always* subjugated; relationships are intricate, and we should not deny their agency. But, this is agency amid chronic vulnerability. I asked Mrs. B, "Is the absence of self-worth connected to them, you know, turning into 'Pleasers' for gang members, and if they don't value their own bodies, it makes it easier to fall into those traps?" She replied, "That' right. You can't just say, 'oh, you should have pride in yourself.' That's *totally* foreign." The tragic irony is that many young women engage with gangs to assuage their vulnerability, yet, when they do, their risk of victimization increases.

The exchange of capital is sociologically dynamic. Women provide gangs with masculine capital, and, in return, symbolic and material capital transfers to women. They party, and derive status, money, and goods through gang association. If sexual access to women were withdrawn, the gang's hegemonic position would suffer. In that sense, as perverse as it may seem, women's agency and participation are key to gang making. *Women are simultaneously powerful and vulnerable in gang spaces*. We should be careful not to blame women, to blasély claim that they are "responsible" for promoting gangs, but it is important to flag the power that women have to *make men*. It is an insight that raises important questions about we how might better intervene with gangs to reduce harm.

Conclusions: The Nihilism of the Ghetto

The emergence of the Bloods and Crips in Belize City established gang practices: the aesthetics of language and pose, the gold chains, the clothes, and the symbolic shotta notoriety, fear, sexual access to women, wild parties, drinking and drug taking, and, of course, a propensity to use violence. These have been described as masculine capitals, the gang persona capturing ontological ground in terms of local meanings of masculinity. This position, at or near the top of the gender hierarchy, is absolutely fundamental to gang continuity. Belizean gangs are culturally syncretistic, readily adopting American, Jamaican, or other "brands," but these are ephemeral. We have seen how Blood and Crip identities faded with time as a posttransnational gang type emerged. Despite identity changes, the gang's position atop the gender hierarchy is nonnegotiable and immovable. A recent report stated that 73 percent of gang members interviewed felt the gang brought them significant "respect" (Arciaga Young and King 2019, p. 86). Young members have to prove themselves with lethal violence. Shorty said that younger generations "get pushed into it and are given guns and told to do hits by older men" (2016). As one government official said, gangs "are an important social organism in the human ecology of Southside. That's why people join gangs. It's like a factory" (2017).

While the provision of welfare and covering basic needs on Southside is beyond question, specific interventions to tackle gangs would do well to consider ways to reduce the "attractiveness" of gangs by targeting or counterbalancing their capitals. They might do this directly, by finding ways of persuading young men and women to avoid gang members, or indirectly, by creating competing *routes to capital* that appeal in a gender-disaggregated way. It is undeniably hard to compete with the draw of the gang, but these opportunities must cater for young people's intelligence, ambition and generate dignity. We would do well to learn from JK and Messiah who used music and hustle to provided them with enough masculine capital to escape gang life. Unfortunately, Southside's history has been marked by the failure to create these opportunities, which I discuss in the next chapter. We are now witnessing our third generation of gang members. Violence continues unabated. The nihilism of the ghetto.

5

INTERVENTIONS

The Challenges Ahead

I was once told by Jenny Pearce, an experienced and widely respected professor, that as an academic researching vulnerable people, I must never lose sight of working for change for those involved. Needless to say, maybe, but as the pressures of family and finance accrue in the middle years of an academic career, focus is pulled, inevitably, toward climbing the career ladder, that entails myriad publishing, fundraising, teaching, and administrative pressures. This chapter is a deliberative effort to analyze why Southside lags behind the rest of the nation on every conceivable development indicator. It has not been easy to write; not only because of the seeming intractability of exclusion or the challenges of reducing runaway violence after the fuse has been lit but because it is fundamentally about holding power accountable. It will make uncomfortable reading for Belizean institutions, politicians, and even members of the international community, but it is not a mud-slinging exercise; rather, it is the opposite, a solution-finding one.

Let me add two qualifications: This chapter seeks to address systemic issues beyond the culpability of one single party or another; further, the majority of the research in this book occurred before the 2020 PUP administration found its stride and is not intended to present a detailed critique of current government policy. The PUP has made plans to tackle poverty and specifically discusses vulnerability with their *Blu #planbelize* manifesto, in 2020,[1] and, on January 24, 2023, the *Plan Belize Mid-term Development Strategy, 2022–2026* was launched.[2] Considering the impact of the global COVID-19 pandemic, the PUP understandably made a stuttering start upon its election in 2020. The opinion of a Belizean journalist was that it is difficult to turn the political and institutional equivalent of an oil-tanker around, and "solving a problem like Belize City is a good [difficult] question" (2023). There was cautious optimism and policies for welfare provision on Southside, including social housing. He continued, saying recipients were "incredibly grateful, so there is something to be said about the programs they are implementing and there does seem to be some focus on the poor" (2023).

Unpacking the causes of violence in Belize raises many ethical questions, hypocrisy even, at the heart of gang responses. The dominant discourse on gangs in Belize is based around the decay of social values and moral outrage around violence, continually framed by politicians, state institutions, and the media as unacceptable and unjustifiable. It is hard to disagree with this sentiment, and it has become politically obligatory to finger point and rail against the perpetrators of homicide. Yet, amid the public noise around gangs, there is scant moral outrage from the ruling class about decades of state failure to help Southsiders meet their basic needs and to create political inclusion and economic opportunities. This failure perpetuates chronic vulnerability, the very condition necessary for the gang violence causing such outcry. The way the debate on gangs is controlled in Belize reflects Foucault's (2000) framing of dominant discourse as a clear manifestation of asymmetrical power in society. This asymmetry scuppers the possibility of a more profound and honest reflection about state failure and institutional incompetence. This means that discourse on gangs has become a constituent part of the longstanding subordination of Southside communities by obfuscating the failures of development. I sat down one afternoon and had a long conversation about political representation with a community police officer who had spent a decade working the streets. His appraisal was as succinct as it was damning: "They are not about empowering their people, they are about keeping them dependent, they give them nothing" (2022). As they say in Belize, "fullbelly tell empty-belly what to do." And thus it ever was since the founding of slave barracks on Southside two centuries ago.

In communities like Martin's, Mahogany Extension, Bac-a-Lan, and Port Layola, infrastructure is the responsibility of the poor. Families squeeze into one room to sleep at night, there is no toilet, just a slop bucket or outdoors. Street lighting is scant, so, after dark, locals use their phone torches to find their way around or across the "London Bridges" plank walkways.[3] I avoided hurricane season for my field trips, so during the times I have been to Southside it has been relatively dry, the marshland forgiving. "The frightening thing is that people consistently use garbage to fill in the morass . . . the stench from chemicals in the garbage burns the eyes. [People] live in a morass and dump around them with garbage. Such pictures give the impression that people are on their own and there is little or no sense of parameters for social and physical action" (Gayle and Mortis 2010, p. 133).

In 2017, I met an African migrant who had lived in Belize City for decades. He used a lot of proverbs and metaphors to explain the political dynamics on Southside. As he talked, I struggled to untangle his messages, but one comment stuck in my mind, that funding spent on Southside was like "pouring salt in the river." It eventually washes away without a trace. Development agencies will be familiar with this dynamic: the struggle for transparency and accountability so that monies reach beneficiaries, rather than being absorbed by overheads, salaries, and related project costs, or simply being siphoned off through corruption and kickbacks. The sad reality is that very little has changed on Southside in the forty years since independence. Demons are the outcome of this misery.

At a conference in Mexico City, in 2022, I was questioned about my positionality as a Western scholar critically appraising societies in the Global South.[4] Without delving into the vibrant decolonizing debates raised by the likes of Denzin, Lincoln, and Smith (2008), although the title, *From South Central to Southside*, pivots toward the American academic market for pragmatic reasons, it is written, above all, with Belizean readers in mind.

When visiting Southside communities, I was surprised by the number of locals who told me they were waiting for me to publish this book. Many actively asked me to tell their story, some even demanded to be named, wanting their complaint to be aired. This highlighted a sense of voicelessness and impunity that not just Southsiders, but Belizeans outside the elite as a whole, felt about the plight of their society. International academics, bar those that can be counted on one hand, have taken zero interest in issues of crime and violence in Belize, and the most vulnerable on Southside languish in a realm somewhere beyond forgotten. There are many, many voices still unheard.

We must know our history, lest, as the axiom goes, we are condemned to repeat it. A principal difficulty observed by Gayle and Mortis (2010) is that Belize lacks "critical skill sets in human resources" (p. 129). The political dynamics that hamper progress on Southside were expressed to me as I gathered information on the ground, in no uncertain terms, by many who worked within state institutions. I quickly realized, when I spoke to national experts, that they needed to be completely anonymous. This was not because they feared some violent backlash from gangs, or even the police, but because they feared a very *Belizean* type of political persecution: where individuals and their families are frozen out of work, contracts, placements, and promotion by powerful individuals within, or connected to, political parties. In Belize, you upset a politician at your peril, especially if you work at a state institution because they can take away your livelihood. There were two interviews with expert women that stand out in my memory: both seasoned professionals that had worked for decades on child and youth issues in the city. Despite their position of authority, they were terrified of a certain politician's wife, alias Shirley, who appears later in this chapter and who had a significant influence on Southside, running an expansive youth intervention program. As a result, they turned down an invitation to speak at an academic conference I had organized at the University of Belize with the UNDP in Belmopan, on masculinities and gang violence in 2018.[5] They feared Shirley would show up and criticize their "competing" intervention work. Regardless of not being invited, Shirley did show up, commandeered the microphone, and proceeded to berate a panel of Belizean experts, sucking the oxygen out of the room in scenes I have never witnessed before at an academic event.

If you speak up against corruption, you not only lose your job, you lose your employability. This means civil servants walk on eggshells daily. A UDP-loyal civil servant who lost her job when the PUP came into power, in 2020, said "politicians make or break you in this country." This was brought home to me in conversation with an individual I knew who went from acting director of an institution to being sent out to build chicken coops overnight, for challenging their notoriously corrupt yet politically connected boss. He was forced out, not only of the institution but of all possible state employment while the PUP is in power and has been since forced to relocate with his family from Belize City to a town on the south coast.

And the poor on Southside? They are politically impotent, there is scarce civil society organization, and no meaningful political participation. Residents are hostage to parties and institutions that rarely help them. To lean on Spivak (1988), they are *subaltern*. Colloquially, fieldslaves.

I replied at the conference in Mexico City that we have to be mindful of who the research benefits, that young people themselves on Southside have no seat at the table, no say, and that they embody the very meaning of exclusion from politics, economy, and mainstream society. In terms of helping the vulnerable make a change, this book intends to provoke debate within Belize, among Belizeans, about solutions. The conceptual focus on chronic vulnerability is a speaking truth-to-power exercise leveled at elites, and a gauntlet laid down to dominant discourse that frames gangs as "the problem." They are not. They are a symptom of the real problem, which is the historical and continual failure of the people on Southside.

In terms of identifying "interventions," the reader will require a little patience when reading the first two sections of this chapter, "Downfallness" and "The Partial Rule of Law." Yet these are an essential foregrounding for why interventions are failing. "Downfallness" was a morose word plucked out of the air by Shorty as he tried to articulate how systemic marginalization makes people give up all hope of change. "The Partial Rule of Law," applied to the poor, not the rich, illustrates how marginalization is "baked in" to the psyche of lower-class Creoles. Downfallness and the partiality of state apparatus hamstring interventions meant to ameliorate gang troubles while propelling vulnerability forward. With these dynamics in mind, the rest of the chapter considers "Current Interventions" in finer detail, looks at the challenges of contemporary "Negotiations" with gangs, and shows how predatory politics, where "If They Could, They Would Steal It All," means the targets of interventions rarely benefit. Lessons are then drawn from the SYSP. As I designed this program, I admit there may be some positive bias toward the outcomes of the project. But, as I show the reader, it is no hagiography, rather I lean on the project as a gateway for analysis. Finally, the chapter turns to the role of the "International Community," who, despite the desperate humanitarian needs on Southside, are nowhere be seen.

As a methodological addendum, even though I have been working on and off in Belize for years, have both UN and academic credentials, and could rightly be considered an "insider," the international community demonstrated a general recalcitrance to my overtures. Maybe because so little was being done on Southside? Interviews were hard to come by or effectively blocked. I asked one whom I had met years earlier for a thirty-minute meeting in Belmopan, the capital, in 2022. They replied, "I am not available for three months," then did not reply to later requests for a Zoom call. The interviews I did secure, bar one that was excellent, were poor quality. One interview in Belmopan was remarkable in that it was over half an hour long, yet somehow the respondent provided me with no useful information whatsoever.

"Downfallness"

At the end of 2021, I asked a senior police officer at the Raccoon Street Station how many gangs and gang members there were. He called the female member of the staff in charge of statistics into his office, who listed 861 gang members and 27 gangs. In fairness, gangs notoriously—academically at least—defy definition, from loose youth groups on the streets to more organized forms of crime. Perhaps even more challenging is distinguishing between the hardcore gangbangers and the affiliate hangers-on. Mr. T described the inevitability of his socialization into the gang and the "big difference" between a gangbanger and the gang affiliates.

> MR. T: Yeah, you know . . . I started arming myself when I was like 16 years old. Umm, it was tough at dat time, I mean literally, das

why I could deal wid these boys now [working with gang-involved youth]. I was *not* a young man who grow up in poverty, but I was in a poverty-stricken neighborhood. . . . My friends were not as fortunate. But one ting in a neighborhood like that, you end up with friends you can't let go of because of the nature of the community, so you grow up with them. . . . So I had the need to defend myself as well. So, although I wasn't a gangbanger, I was what we term now as "gang affiliated." It's a *big* difference.

AUTHOR: So explain that difference?

MR. T: So, you have the actual gangbangers, are the guys who are married to the streets. These are the ones you find with poor parental support, poverty, and the innate generational inheritance of *di gang culture*, within their homes. You find that more in Majestic, George Street, ah, Ghost Town. Grandfathers an' . . .

AUTHOR: Like layers of history.

MR. T: Those groups [gangbangers] are just a handful. It's their affiliates that makes the gang big. (2021)

A missionary working on Southside since 2018 estimated that there were closer to fifteen hundred gang members in some fifty gangs in 2022. With this, or the police estimate, it is a substantial number when we consider Belize City has around sixty thousand people, and Southside approximately thirty-five thousand. That would make about five gang members per one hundred of the population. Although these are very rough figures, it goes without saying that gangs permeate day-to-day life.

One Belizean academic, alias Mara, who was brought up and lives on Southside, said she will not let her "dark-skinned younger brothers go out to buy groceries on George Street after dark" because it is too dangerous (2021). She went on to say that "bouts of rage [are] very common, people have very, very short fuses here [because] there is strong cloud of hopelessness." The recent economic implosion as the tourism industry collapsed during the COVID-19 pandemic and rising food and gasoline prices have compounded problems for the worst off. Mara told me a depressing anecdote about the poor who used to buy shrink-wrapped packs of eight hotdogs for BZ$2, but now the small convenience stores dotted along the streets sell individual hotdogs from the packs as "people simply do not have BZ$2." It seemed ordained, as we looked up during this conversation about starvation from our table in the coffee shop, to see several overweight tourists pass by on a "land-train" heading back toward the cruise ship.

Not long after that meeting Jabbar sent me a WhatsApp message. "Bro, we just had our first massacre in Belize." It felt inevitable. These issues are all connected.

MR. T: I will tell you this as a grass-roots Belizean man, and I am not ashamed to say this. Belize is way behind time, we're so backwards. But what is happening now is a direct result of something historic, [oppression] that was never recorded. With all of this violent crime that is happening, how come we didn't have any civil war? How come no politicians are getting killed?

AUTHOR: Like I always ask, where's the revolution? These kids are angry. But they are like a snake eating its own tail. Why are they not rebelling against the power structures in the country?

Here the snake eating its tail was a misattribution because Ouroboros is actually a positive symbol of eternal life. What I was trying to explain was that communities living under constraint often turn their frustrations inward, whereas outward-facing and organized ways of holding power to account are rarely seen on Southside. Gangs are symptomatic of structural asymmetry, a male class rebellion (Baird and Rodgers 2015). Yet this energy is used against each other, an internecine conflict that Muhammad calls fratricide (2015). Similarly, Connell observed that rebellious masculinities tend toward self-destruction (2005b). The absence of change is frustrating for everyone working for progress on Southside, so where, indeed, is the revolution? Or, at least, where is civil society, organizing and pressing for transparency, accountability, and change?

A decade ago, after spending a number of years conducting gang research in Medellín, I flew to Kingston to carry out brief UNDP consultancy on youth inclusion (Baird 2015b). A notable difference between the two cities was the vibrancy of civil society. In Medellín, activism had led to the successful election of independent mayoral candidates, academic Sergio Fajardo in 2004 and later journalist Alonso Salazar in 2008. It was the first time in the city's history that anyone outside of elite-controlled parties had won. Two major triumphs that marked a turning point for state-led investment in poor areas of the city and urban renewal for peace about which much has since been written (e.g., Doyle 2019; Maclean 2015; Naef 2018). Kingston's civil society organizations felt a long way off. I asked why? A University of the West Indies professor I was with at the time said in a sardonic tone "after fifty years we're still waiting for civil society to rise up!" The more elaborate answer was related to the machinations of garrison politics in the poorer parts of Kingston West and downtown (see Edmonds 2016; Evans and Jaffe 2020). Clientelism and intimidation stifled civil society organization that might hold politicians accountable. Belize has less intimidation but has suffered the same plight.

The contemporary dynamics of political control in Belize City were unpacked by one expert who made it clear they wished to be totally anonymous (2021):

EXPERT: They did a lot of buying of votes, they continue to buy votes, they do that a lot. What stands out is that the UDP took control of Southside for the last four or five elections. Mesopotamia, Collet, Queen's Square, that's their stronghold. There are elements of tribalism and definitely garrison. Dean Barrow has a garrison, [Said] Musa has a garrison, Patrick Faber has a garrison, the Finnegans are Mesopotamia.

AUTHOR: How would you define garrison politics?

EXPERT: Well, I gave you the example of [anonymized politician], he bought all those long barracks and give it to people so that he has control of those individuals through the property. That's one example. "I own you." They control their lives, and they control them mentally with that same collective identity, they are then part of that group [party].

Although the UDP emerged in opposition to the PUP, it developed a garrison power base that has been nothing short of a remarkable electoral bloc. Collet, Queen's Park, and Mesopotamia are safe seats passed dynastically between what one respondent called the "Creole Royalty." Three-term prime minister Dean Barrow's sister, Denise, known as "Sista B," holds Queen's Park; his son, Moses "Shyne" Barrow, holds Mesopotamia; and the same surnames are always found at the UDP top table.

We might assume that gangs exert a street-level quasi-political power, but gang governance today is weak. I spoke to one middle-aged UDP member who lamented that "boys don't respect gang structure anymore, they just want a gun. . . . They steal, they lie, and are out of control" (2016). What sets Belize City apart from some other contexts in the region is that, even in the halcyon days of the 1990s Blood and Crip Generals, gangs never bossed politicians, and politicians always used gangs as tools. One Southsider said:

Gangs are not self-sufficient, they are run by these politicians. They even employ them as drivers, and whatever. Someone has to do the nasty job and that's where the gangs come in. The politicians control gangs, those guys can't be on their own. They are not well organized, they don't have capital.

Shorty confirmed that gangs are mobilized at election time:

Well, the gangs be used for BZ$50–75 a vote. That's when they you're best friends for a period of time [in the run up to elections]. So, when they need that vote they have this money to give these individuals.

But as soon as they get that vote, they [disappear] that's what I'm sayin'.

The gangs do influence the vote the majority of the time. So, the politicians give say $20,000 to an influential person and say "go get me votes." But they [gang leaders] keep most of it for themselves, and just give out 50–60 dollars for a vote. So, the people, they don't think about the future, they just think about "what we gonna get now?"

Jabbar agreed with what Shorty said that most direct payments do not "go down the ranks" to lower gang members. He went on to say that gang leaders receive regular money from politicians, more akin to a payroll, that swells at election time, adding that patronage works in complex ways. If the gang member helps the politician to secure votes, then their families and children get benefits such as letters supporting them to join the police, work contracts, or jobs in government or at state institutions. Conversely, noncompliant citizens are frozen out, an overbearingly powerful combination to subject the poorest in society to.

Gangs, like the wider Southside population, have been subjugated by the political machine, they do not rebel against their "masters." This much was clear when I first met Shirley in 2016. With one swift phone call, she had Vartas, the most powerful gang leader in the city, sitting in her office answering my questions.

Another time I met Vartas on Southside, he complained that he had spent the past few days digging a drainage ditch around his house in preparation for the hurricane season, that the government never helped, and he was expecting to get flooded anyway. His house was ramshackle but sat on a decent plot of land; however, it was a few feet below the level of the drainage ditch, and I suspected he was correct about the imminent flooding. "We on our own," he said (2021). Why was Vartas, long-term leader of the biggest gang in Belize, carrying out manual labor in the searing Belizean sun? Surely, with his long-standing relationship with politicians, Shirley being his conduit to UDP power holders, he could have pressured them to put in basic infrastructure where he lived? This raised questions about power, evoking the late David Harvey's work where "The Right to the City" is "confined to a small political and economic elite who are in a position to shape cities . . . after their own desires" (2013). I brought this up with Mr. T.

> AUTHOR: The politicians use "bait and switch," that "if you vote for me, I'll help you out," but they never do. From what I'm listening to over the last two days, it's a politics of control and manipulation. And there is something going on there which is, a lack of educa-

tion, resources, which stops any, like, critical consciousness, right? I think if you went in there and started preaching critical consciousness, something bad would happen to you, I don't think the political power structures would like that.

MR. T: Like I said, at the end of the day, you don't disrespect and "go up against the master," that's the first rule, *no matter what!* "See that other slave beside you, take it out on him!" That's what you're supposed to be thinking about.

AUTHOR: Like a present-day translation [of master and slave dynamics]. (2021)

A Belizean academic (2021) told me that these dynamics are socialized into the lower classes in innumerable ways, notably throughout the educational system, which Gayle and Mortis say is still colonial and has never been modernized (2010, pp. 107–109). The academic said, "Education here is about a culture of obedience. Our students are *so* disempowered that they have accepted that they cannot change anything. You cannot get anymore disempowered than that. The political system *is* subjugation" (2021). Mr. T continued with his analysis:

It's quite easy. Political clientelism a was model created to keep people dependent on the political directorate, and it's hard to disassociate it with slavery and colonialism. At the end of the day, it is about stratification, and when we speak about that, we know that we have to keep these people poor and dependent. [Belize is] a young independent nation, for forty years, but the political parties have never sat round a table and said, "what are we gonna do for [poor] people."

Jabbar spoke bitterly. "Politicians not motivated to change, they love it just the way it is . . . gangs have always been involved [with politicians], they get jobs due to political connections, you are rewarded for loyalty. The system is deliberately not being allowed to work so [the politicians] can keep control," finishing with a flourish, "*We have gangs in suits, gangs in the hoods!*" (2021). Alias Renata, a retired youth worker, said:

Gang responses by politicians are about the aesthetics of political point scoring, they want something photographic that looks good, they want points. There is no real investment on Southside. The mentality is one of abandonment, deep classism. They don't think you should spend or invest in poor people, they are just there to be used to secure their seat. This a very colonial trope of "stay in your lane" to the fieldslaves. They are in effect an underclass. . . . Politicians want them for the mileage they can get out of them, then after a year or less they disappear, then the locals get angry and frustrated. They political system uses them.

[Southside] is not there to be helped. For example, "let's put them in an aircon bus to go there" and the response is "what?! These kids from Southside! No way, put them in a pick-up!" But if they were kids from St Catherin's, Northside, they'd say "ok." Or on programs, they don't give them bacon and eggs, give them rice and peas.

A decade earlier Shoman (2011) wrote that poor youths in the city are "denied opportunities [and] are objects of negligence and discrimination" (pp. 388–389). Young people on Southside are acutely aware of this abandonment. There is no social contract. State institutions flex their authority by making citizens bow, and wait, and hope, a tactic familiar to readers of Javier Auyero's book *Patients of the State: The Politics of Waiting in Argentina* (2012).

These experiences feed the demons. Young men on the SYSP project would often "flick up" into rage over trivial issues. Gayle and Mortis (2010) said in their report, "The 274 youth involved in the study went to great lengths to express how much the social structures have failed them. . . . Consequently, many of them have been abused in various ways as they have no protective frame, neither from family nor state" (p. 279). Shorty described the impact of this:

> We like some bulls, soon as you brand us, we gonna kick. There's a lotta people in this country that allow themselves to become killers, gunmen. And I don't blame them because it's a struggle. The government themselves have put them in that position, where they have to do what they have to do to survive, to eat. They have kids, they mother don't work, social don't pay nothin'. I've witnessed brothers get up in the morning and they don't have a dime, they go out there beggin' for a 75 cents cigarette. *It's a downfall to its own downfallness* [his emphasis]. Because of the greed, those who on top, only wanna keep stayin' on top. Those on the bottom will remain there if they don't make up their mind and do somthin'.

Belizeans I spoke to that worked with or within state institutions delivering programs on Southside ordinarily referred to institutional corruption and "kickback culture." Jabbar described this as a systemic practice, "Contracts and basically anything where money is spent, they get kickbacks . . . 'if you want to work in a call center, I want a kickback.' *Any* contract requires a kickback. . . . They keep you dependent on them. Ministers decide who goes into police as you needed a letter of recommendation [in 2021, there were three thousand applicants for just two hundred places in the BPD.]⁶ You get sent back if you don't have political support.... When you are not for sale [politically] you get fucked, like me" (2021). Jabbar was referring to how he was forced from his job for complaining about corruption.

Politicians use locally adjusted, culturally relevant, clientelist and patronage mechanisms:

> RESEARCHER: They use [politics] as a control measure. When these poor people gets linked with a political party, that gives them a collective identity that they would otherwise not have. They don't have anything, so I think this is what these political parties have been doing for years. Some of the barracks in Majestic [Alley] belong to [names dynastic political family]. People work very hard to maintain political dynasties for the money, political patronage.
> AUTHOR: How are the people controlled?
> RESEARCHER: They pay for a piece of land, school fees . . . give them jobs within government, contracts . . .
> AUTHOR: [Interjects] Patronage?
> RESEARCHER: Yes! It's clientelism! Jobs in the police, jobs in teaching, jobs in the BDF [Belizean Defense Force]. But I have seen the army deny the political people because the army believes in structure. So a lot of time the politicians clash with the military.

In 2022, I spent an afternoon in Belmopan with Shorty as he sold weed out of his living room to a steady trickle of customers. I asked him about politics.

> SHORTY: Well, I vote for this guy [names politician] because he promised to fix my roof. You see my roof? *M-o-t-h-e-r-fucker!* He hasn't fixed it [both laugh]. I'm telling you, these people is vindictive, evil, and they don't have no love in their heart for the Belizean people. Coz when you get in a higher position, yo' thing is to stay there, coz one fall, you gone. An' they will ridicule you, criticize you, demote you, and probably try to lock you up, talk bad about you, scandal you. This is what this country has to offer. It's a struggle, it's like a crab in a bucket, it whoever get to the top, pull me back in.
>
> But the thing they [gangs] doin,' they doin' it the wrong way. . . . I'm saying we can overthrow this government. I'm not saying no bad vendetta I'm jus' saying with the votes, we can overcome. Our parents' parents, our parents' parents' parents, can overcome. But no, they don't do that, they wanna kill each other and don't have nothin' to eat.

AUTHOR: I'm glad you brought this up. I've been thinking, where's the revolution?

SHORTY: Coz they don't have that fuckin' spark. It was never born in them. They didn't reach different levels in life. They sit here with this corn and crop shit. They never went somewhere where they learn what the fuckin dynamics of life is. The race thing. The poverty thing. You ain't went nowhere, you jus' been in yo' country . . . but you ain't went and travelled and learned things, in college, you know. People don't understand what's going on in this country.

As Shorty grasped to articulate "a downfall of the downfallness," a picture was painted of a depressingly *lumpenproletariat* Southside, which can never be politicized into action. Even gang leader Vartas cut the figure of *lumpengangsta* next to Shirley. I asked Shorty what he thought of the flashy new leader of the opposition, Moses "Shyne" Barrow, ex-rapper in the United States and friend to stars such as P. Diddy (Sean Combs), JLo (Jennifer Lopez) and DJ Khaled (Khaled Mohammed Khaled). He replied, "I never speak to him. I don't need his help, I don't need nothin'." Politicians are masters you go to cap in hand. You never go against the master. This is baked into the Creole psyche, a colonial legacy that has facilitated the rise of predatory politics on Southside today.

The Partial Rule of Law

Despite frequently made and wide-ranging recommendations, in the past forty years, for improving institutions, precious little has been implemented. Recommendations have actually led to oversight mechanisms being put in place, including, inter alia: oversight powers for the National Assembly over the executive branch, recommendations for strengthening the independence of the judiciary, a Contractor General to monitor government tenders, the creation of an Ombudsman's office, a Public Accounts Committee, a Governance Improvement Commission, a Finance Audit Reform Act, and a Customs Act to stop ministers from indiscriminately granting duty exemptions. Yet, Bolland (1997) stated that "economic and leadership issues, including questions of management and corruption, still predominate Belizean politics" (p. 280), and, fourteen years later, Shoman (2011) demonstrated that little had changed: "Several key bodies established to improve transparency and accountability did not function effectively. The Contractor General, Ombudsman, Integrity Commission and Public Accounts Committee in particular, were under-resourced and rendered ineffective because members of the executive routinely by-passed, manipulated or ignored them" (p. 324).

More recent scholarship by Gayle, Hampton, and Mortis (2016), Warnecke-Berger (2019), and Ferrell and Wainwright (2022) confirm these problems persevere. Shoman (2011) noted:

> At one time the Finance Minister himself Fonseca in 2004 was forced to resign for cooking the books, yet faced no trial or investigation. . . . No corruption charges have ever been proved against any politician . . . both UDP governments wracked with charges of corruption and maladministration against several of their ministers, as were all previous PUP governments. By 1998, the perception was that corruption in public life had become pervasive. People were cynical about politicians and public officials, believing that several ministers had been abusing their office for personal enrichment and using their positions to break laws with impunity. (pp. 323, 326)

To test this, I asked the administrators of Belize Central Prison, in 2021, how many politicians have been in jail for corruption, drug trafficking, or any other criminal activity. The blunt reply came "None. Ever." In 2012, Fowler and Bunck wrote:

> Rather than adhering to a rule-of-law ideal, the Belizean legal system has continually overlooked the transgressions of elites. Citizens of influence have infrequently been arrested and even more rarely prosecuted, convicted, and sentenced to prison terms. (pp. 79–80)

The U.S. State Department uses mechanisms for "designation" known as the "Magnitsky" and "Engel" lists.[7] These deny individuals implicated in corruption or human rights abuses, and sometimes their immediate families, visas to the United States, and can block financial transactions in, or passing through, the United States that involve a designated person. The significance of the lists is also symbolic and damning, and not just for the individuals concerned; the lists indicate that a country refuses to prosecute their politically and economically powerful. In 2022, former Belizean minister John Birchman was designated on the Engel list for "significant involvement in corruption."[8] Under the current national regime, it is nearly impossible for Birchman to end up in Belize Central Prison. Similarly, Belizeans have spoken to me in resigned tones about Jasmine Hartin, former partner of the son of British Belizean billionaire Michael Ashcroft, who was charged with the manslaughter of police superintendent Henry Jemmott in May 2021. She admits to shooting him dead, but accidentally, on a pier in San Pedro. When I asked about the chances of her going to jail, the response was incredulity. Later on June 1, 2023, Hartin was ordered to pay a BZ$75,000 fine and carry out 300 hours of community service by the Belize high court. It surprised no one that she received zero jailtime.⁹

If the rule of law is partial so is economic opportunity. Shoman (2011) wrote that in the late 1980s and early 1990s the economy was booming due to privatization and foreign investment (p. 320), but Southsiders did not benefit. Beyond the historical failure of trickle-down economics across the globe, this was an expression of what marginality means: Southsiders kept at an arm's length from productive society, excluded from the means of production and new technology, the depiction of Castells's "fourth world" (2000). As Durkheim (1895/2007) said a century and a half ago, mentioned in the Introduction to this book, deviancy is a challenge to the normalized repressiveness of the state, as succinct an explainer as any, for gang violence on Southside.

Shorty sold BZ$20 bags of weed out of his living room as we drank beer and ate chicken and rice. Having spent time with him, an ex-con with limited skills and training, living in poverty, he clearly has few other options. One Southsider told me, "You either join in or you suffer" (2022). I was informed by an individual, in 2022, that a small group of ranking gang members regularly travel to the northern Chetumal border with Mexico to collect duffel bags full of marijuana, the coveted Mexican "kush" supplied by the Cartel Jalisco Nueva Generación, throw them unceremoniously into the back of a pickup truck, and drive back to the city. Done in a casual way, "Belizean style," one would assume not only because of the cartel's control of the police but also because of the decriminalization of the personal possession of small amounts of marijuana back in Belize. Although dealing is still illegal there is generally less tension around sales than there was when I was first visited the country in 2011. It certainly felt that way hanging out with Shorty.

More broadly, policing remains a challenge. Crooks (2010) and Gayle (Gayle, Hampton, and Mortis 2016; Gayle and Mortis 2010) have written about this extensively. I was told by police at the Raccoon Street Station that only 70 percent of police officers finished their primary school education. One officer in Gayle and Mortis's (2010) report is quoted as saying, "Police come from poor backgrounds. We have hustling in our blood" (p. 138). Gayle and Mortis continue "In terms of social behaviour, many beat their partners in public, drink heavily, and operate like gangs. In Belize they are known for torturing youth to point out the marijuana seller so they can extort him; and they often use their position to brutalize youth who compete with them for women or resources" (p. 136). Many police, like other Belizeans, smoke marijuana, and many come from Southside. Some have worked for gang leaders as bodyguards and facilitated drug deals. In rare cases, the police have been accused of being contract killers, although I have never been able to substantiate this beyond hearsay. One researcher who had spent decades working on

Southside told me point-blank, "Some of these [police officers] get paid to do hits. The police and gangs are so intertwined and mixed up" (2022). It is also telling that some 90 percent of complaints to the Ombudsman are about the police. One officer was quoted as saying, "The corruption in the Department runs from the hill to the sea" (Gayle and Mortis 2010, p. 138).

Gayle and Mortis (2010) spoke to twenty-three gang members who underlined the "endless extortion by dozens of police, especially when it come to our little weed business" (p. 320). He noted that "three of the seven police officers were discussed as drug dealers" by gang members, who would steal weed off gangs and sell it themselves (p. 320). Shorty spoke to me at length about his run-ins with the police in the capital Belmopan after fleeing the violence of Belize City.

> SHORTY: The police used to tax [extort] me. This is a police fuckin' city. They fuck with you.... Business [selling marijuana] is never bad, it's just bad when the police come coz they want to extort.
> Well, the majority of [guns] come from Guatemala. But the police got guns [seized from gangs] that they reissue out to the public, they sell them [back to gangs], then they go back and get it. It's a recycle.
> AUTHOR: It just seems like the police be taxing all the time?
> SHORTY: That's all they do. Every day. Every minute. Every second. Dem some chancy [corrupt] motherfuckers here! That's why I got my camera now [CCTV outside his home], so dem motherfuckers don't come. Coz last time they broke my back door, I had to get a new back door, that's BZ$280 for that door to get it put on. An' I just got my bathroom remodeled and they just broke all my tiles in there, so I have to get it all done over.... They come in my house when I wasn't there. My neighbors call an' tell me the police is in my house [looking for drugs and money]. I'm Shorty and I'm a high-risk person [ex-con, deportee and former gang member]. They know who I am. (2022)

The police did not find Shorty's cash or stash of weed, and I did not ask him where he hid it. He complained bitterly about the costs of police harassment. After all, Shorty was financially supporting a child in another town in Belize and also caring for his uncle with special needs who sat with us. He was not wealthy by any stretch of the imagination. In perhaps the greatest irony I came across in ten years of fieldwork visits to Belize, Shorty had installed CCTV on his premises *to protect himself from the police*. It worked; they do not kick his door in anymore.

Policing Southside is an undoubtedly daunting task, plus the force has tremendously limited human and other resources. But it is a system where the poor police, police the poor. The application of the law among fieldslaves was never intended for the elites. As Jabbar said, if you are "appointed politically you are immune from arrest and accountability. 'If I give you my blessing, you can do what you want'" (2021).

The rule of law, understood as policing, judicial process, incarceration, and beyond, is consistently subject to political manipulation. Even police officers themselves are victimized by being threatened by powerful politicians to release certain gang members they are affiliated with. Gayle and Mortis (2010) state, "It is very clear that some politicians who have symbiotic links with gangs and grassroots criminals enjoy the weaknesses of the [judicial] system.... On occasions as soon as one of their 'people' is caught they begin calling the magistrate" (p. 139). They continue, citing a police officer:

> Belize is small and that put a lot of pressure on a lot of politicians to get all sorts of funny favors done. Do you know how many serious criminals I have arrested and the MP call and say that one is related to Mr. So and So, and I must let him go, or I have no job tomorrow. (p. 144)

A police officer negotiating with gangs to reduce violent beefs told me that there is only a 6 percent conviction rate for murders so "everybody in Belize has a gun because people want satisfaction [revenge]" (2021). Even when arrests are made, the judicial process often suffers interference. "[A police officer] was demoralized by a politician. He arrested this bwoy [*sic*] three times and the same politician tell him to let him go" (Gayle and Mortis 2010, p. 145). This is a telling insight into the balance of power between the elites and the state institutions, particularly those staffed by the lower class, such as the police force.

This is the heart of the matter. The partial rule of law is a function of class; it has become a normative, assumed discourse, where higher classes are above the law. Conversely, it dictates that poor, particularly dark-skinned Creole men, are met with the full force of the law. There is something particularly insidious about the poor disciplining the poor. Bourdieu and Wacquant's (2004) notion of "symbolic violence" springs to mind, where harmful practices by a group or individual are carried out against themselves in a less than conscious manner because of social pressure. This discourse is buoyed by public calls to crack down on gangs, that conveniently ignore the gaping inequity in the rule of law. This inequity is never clearer than when walking past inmates in Belize Central Prison who are overwhelmingly impoverished Black and Brown men—after reading Daren McGarvey's (2022) recent work on class in my home country of the United Kingdom, this resembles "class war" far more than it does justice. Just ask the men in the prison.

Current Interventions

The idea here is not to present an exhaustive analysis of gang interventions to date. That would be a book in itself considering the continual institutional responses to gangs since the early 1990s; further it would be a challenge to compile given the general absence of monitoring and evaluation of these interventions, which is still a problem today. Neither will this chapter conclude with a list of actionable recommendations. These lists have been put forward repeatedly by, inter alia: the Crooks report (2010); Gayle et al. (2010, 2016); a number of IDB reports, the latest of which, at the time of writing, were by Peirce (2017) and Arciaga Young and King (2019); the broad Community Action for Public Safety (CAPS) I and II funded by the IDB; and a host of piecemeal recommendations emerging from smaller intervention projects, such as those from SYSP, which I put forward myself. Numerous intervention programs and institutions have been set up to either target gangs or overlap services for vulnerable youths in active gang areas, for example, CYDP, Restore Belize, and Youth for the Future, to name but three. With the change in government to the PUP, in 2020, Restore Belize became operationally defunct, as a UDP initiative it was immediately struck down. The CYDP was kept but changed its name to BMCMS, and the Leadership Intervention Unit (LIU) has emerged connecting individuals from the BMCMS with others across institutions, including the police on Raccoon Street. The LIU has a Facebook presence, but it is unclear what its quasi-governmental, nongovernmental, or legal status is.

What Belize has in abundance, then, are recommendations for gang interventions, at-risk youths, and violence reduction. The recommendations by Arciaga Young and King (2019), Peirce (2017), and Gayle et al. (2010; 2016) overlap in agreement substantially, putting forward well-argued and achievable targets, which not only are logical but have achieved evidence-based success in other countries. The question is not, What new recommendations can we come up with? Rather, Why are current recommendations failing or not being implemented?

Negotiations

Since Bird's Isle in 1995, negotiations have been a most consistent feature of governmental interventions, spearheaded by the then CYDP, and staffed by civil servants and what are ostensibly community police. They have since developed long-term relationships with gang members, the renamed BMCMS were able to take me deep into Southside to meet Vartas. The BMCMS aims to reduce gang tensions, responding to flare-ups, to avoid retaliation and escalation. These are street-level truces, akin to what is often referred to as "violence interruption" after the world-famous Chicago designed *Ceasefire* program.

In Belize City today, there is still a confusing range of interlocution with gangs. Officers from BMCMS may be in discussions with gang leaders one day to diffuse a violent beef, then the following day the Gi3 anti-gang unit of the police could storm their houses. In 2018, 181 suspected gang members[10] were rounded up and put in jail for a month. Even Gi3 activities feel unpredictable, driven by personalities rather than strategy, and there is negligible coordination with the BMCMS. It is not unusual for the police commissioner to change his mind between pursuing negotiations or pursuing mano dura tactics. Recently, we have seen the latter[11] leading to clashes between the Gi3 and gangs in Bac-a-Lan.[12] In the background to these goings-on, politicians linked to gangs still maintain a dialogue with them for their own ends.

Historically, a number of negotiations were green-lit by former prime minister Dean Barrow. This led to several gang truces during his twelve years in office between 2008 and 2020, ranging from quick firefighting interventions to more structured approaches offering gang members exit strategies through stipends and work placements. One notable truce brokered by the CYDP at the time, lasted over a year, between 2011 and 2012, until project funding ran out, in many ways, mimicking the successes and failures of the original Bird's Isle negotiations in 1995. I was told by one person involved that money was distributed during the truce as a type of gang-member payroll, which kept them pacified for a while but was ultimately not sustainable. Another told me that putting gang members on a "stipend" to motivate them to reduce violence was the easy part, finding jobs and persuading them to take those jobs and leave the gang proved far more difficult (2021).

The truce-building process itself is laden with challenges, first and foremost is a lack of institutional capacity. When I visited the newly branded BMCMS, in 2021, the first discussion I had with them was about how to capture the historical memory of gang intervention experiences. Nothing had been written down, and, when the PUP came to power, the former director with thirty years' experience was unceremoniously removed taking their knowledge with them. The rough idea was to develop a gang manual, a type of "living document" that would be continually reviewed, but the office was in flux with an acting director, and it never came to pass. As the primary gang intervention office, the lack of resources was telling. I noted in my field diary:

Their office is dilapidated as hell. Doesn't even have a sign out front, or a street number. [My contact] sent me a WhatsApp, "it's between the UDP HQ and the Transport Office. It's a green building." It was falling to pieces. The reception was a young lady at a plastic picnic table sat on a plastic chair. They have no money to do anything.... Restore Belize was UDP so now it's dead, even though their nice office downtown is still there! The LIU's presence is only on Facebook as far as I can tell, it's not yet organized, has no official budget, and is looking at setting it up as NGO. These are people working within state institutions, supposedly with state budget. It's unbelievable they feel that to get anything done they have to do it outside of their institution.

The BMCMS had one solitary vehicle, a pickup truck, which was only available during weekdays as the acting director used it to drive home and lived out of town. Another vehicle had, allegedly, been taken away from the BMCMS by the prime minister's office "to give to one of his secretaries," I was told in resigned tones. Although I was not able to independently verify this, I had no reason to doubt them, and there was clearly just one vehicle left available on the lot. This conversation arose as I was trying to coordinate a ride along with the BMCMS into gang territory. Given that most violence flares at night, normally on weekends, they lacked the capacity for rapid response. It turned out that the BMCMS interventions tended to happen in the days after violence flared, massively undermining its ability to prevent retaliation.

Scholars have earnestly begun to explore the potential of negotiated approaches in delivering sustainable reductions in gang violence (e.g., Felab-Brown 2020; Muggah and O'Donnell 2015; Schuberth 2016; Wennmann 2014), but precious few include empirical data with the protagonists of the negotiations themselves: gang members. Negotiations are notoriously politicized and fragile, and some researchers have largely written them off (e.g., Kan 2014; Maguire 2013). In short, dialogue with gangs is never easy, even with serious political and economic backing. This I know from experience having worked with gang members in Medellín on a demobilization program in 2007 and 2008. Said program was very well structured, funded, politically backed, and even had a legal framework, yet the majority of gang members still did not make it out (Baird 2011; Rozema 2008). Ecuador's experience is the regional standard bearer for successful negotiations with gang members that took place a decade ago (see Brotherton and Gude 2020), yet persistent urban exclusion in Esmeralda and Guayaquil, and the shifting sands of transnational drug trafficking, has led to renewed armed violence in recent years.

Mr. T explained the perennial problem, that intervention programs "can't replace the gang's drug income" (2021). His comments brought to mind a conversation I had with a sicario and mid-ranking gang member one night in Medellín, who told me he would only leave the gang for a job as a bank manager, because it was of equivalent status to his position in the gang (Baird 2018a). That he was a semiliterate, alcoholic, drug-addicted, and traumatized young man, who had murdered dozens of people, presents the challenges in stark relief.

Those I spoke to were totally unmotivated, saying that the vast majority of money destined for poor neighborhoods was always siphoned off by "kickback culture." BMCMS work is challenging at the best of times. A gang member told me, frankly, "Truces don't work. The kids don't shoot each other for a week, and then they go back to it" (2022). Another police officer explained that they struggled because gangs made vanishingly short-term alliances and betrayed each other, "There's a lot of snake game." Throwing up their hands, they continued, "De government before [UDP] pay gangs to be quiet, but dey use da money to buy guns!"

As I interviewed one officer at BMCMS, we were joined by another two, making an ad hoc focus group about gang responses:

OFFICER 1: You need to add different spices to de pot depending on each situation. We have to be responsive to de needs of each individual or situation on any given day.... You cannot be intimidated when you go, gang members can sense fear. (Non-BMCMS) police are afraid of gang members, which is why dey go in wid guns. We are on de streets, we are in deir lives.
OFFICER 2: Confidentiality [is] paramount.
OFFICER 3: We are less police and have many responsibilities. We are counsellors, social workers, police, we are hybrid police officers, yout' development officers.
OFFICER 2: You have to be real [with gang members.]
OFFICER 1: De mediation is just to stop de bleeding, so dat "wrap around services" can get in and other tings can be done. Problem is dat dey are not ... people getting frustrated!
OFFICER 2: It's difficult as people are really pissed off and dere's really not much we can do from dis little office.
OFFICER 1: Survival skills kick in, of course dey sell drugs ... but [Belizean institutions] are fishing wid artificial bait, but *we are false ass motherfuckers*! You can't go into dese communities empty handed. Dey tink dey'll get someting, dey don't, dey get tired. Government come in last year and notin' happen, dey do notin'!
OFFICER 2: Curfew [due to COVID-19 set at 9 P.M.] stops gang members making a living [selling marijuana at night]. Schools closed,

kids have no Wi-Fi at home, so what dey gonna do? Crime and robbery has increased a lot.

There were many committed individuals doing their best to reduce violence despite institutional limitations. I admired the officers I met at BMCMS; they did not simply see gang members as the enemy. They all had a keen social analysis of crime, violence, and society. When I was chatting with one officer at the plastic reception desk, two boys came through the door. The officer I was with knew them from the neighborhoods they worked. It turned out the boys hadn't eaten all day, so the officer, using their own cash, treated them to lunch. It was not a performance for the foreign researcher. They cared. This reflects Gayle's experiences with schoolteachers, obliged to engage in a wide remit of student care, often paying for them to eat as they would turn up to school with malnutrition-related illnesses. During interviews, the teachers, including men they point out, would regularly break down in tears (Gayle and Mortis 2010, p. 121).

As the focus group conversation wound down, a vehicle became available, and we prepared to head into Southside to meet Vartas. There are not many foreigners who come into Southside asking questions. I was sometimes asked if I was a reporter with *Vice News*, who have been twice in recent years.[13] Locals told me that I was being checked out because *Vice News* reporters were suspected as DEA or CIA informants, though it was never clear why. Remarkably, I often get asked if I know British actor and broadcaster, Ross Kemp, who filmed an episode of *On Gangs* in Belize over a decade ago.[14] Some gang members are *still* unhappy with the depiction and who he chose to interview. However, I suspect this is less about Kemp's analysis and more that they missed out on "international fame."

Here is my field diary entry slightly edited for clarity from that afternoon.

> Went to Vartas' place today, near the swamp on the edge of the city. The BMCMS took me out in the 4x4 Mazda pick-up. Had to hang around for a while, chatting to the ranking officer before we left. Anyway, we drove round and round the [anonymized] gang area for ages looking for Vartas. They eventually just called him on his mobile phone, which made me wonder why they didn't just do that in the first place, and we met at his house. We weren't invited in, we chatted outside.
>
> The house was run-down. It seemed strange as this guy was the last General in the whole city, yet he lived like this. He had done a lot of the renovations himself, he explained. I took note of his steel Rolex Explorer II with a too-loosely fitted bracelet, and wondered if it used

to belong to an American tourist who weighed a few pounds more than him. The cognitive dissonance of a Rolex-toting gang leader living in poverty.

Vartas pot-bellied body was covered in scars, he looked haggard, the effects of years of drugs, weed, and booze. He had come close to death, having been shot in the back. I was told gleefully by a rival gang member that he can no longer get an erection because of his injury, and that Vartas killed someone for sleeping with his girlfriend—or at least, these were the rumors.

He looked red-eye stoned and was drinking a bottle of Belikin beer, wearing a cheap white vest with a gold chain and baggy Dickies shorts that reached below the knee. He had a burner and a smart phone which he was constantly checking. It was pretty obvious why he had a burner, and ironic he was using it in front of the police. He's thirty-five now, he looked older, and his eldest son in 17. He doesn't want his son to join the gang, he's very good at football he said, and has trials to go and play overseas. He said he had 15 or 17 kids, he wasn't sure, and right on cue, his three-year-old son wandered out to say "hi." I mentioned I had a three-year-old too, a feeble attempt at bonding I blurted out because of nerves.

Vartas said the rules on the street are "three strikes and you're out." That's how he runs his gang and controls petty crime in the neighborhood. He'll kill you if you continue to steal or step out of line, rules agreed with gang leaders in neighboring areas. He wants better future for his son and was looking to get a house out of town to escape. That was his plan, but after so many years leading the gang, it just didn't feel likely. His said that his uncle and cousin were murdered for things *he* did and said that it should've been him instead. He seemed most angry about rule breaking by rival gangs; killing family is against the rules. He said he will pay his debts if he fucks up "I understan' dat I can get kill fa whatta I do."

Normally gang members foreground their victimhood, evoking the witticism "the only reason you haven't found out a criminal is a victim, is because you haven't spoken to them yet." But Vartas was candid, speaking in resigned tones. He said openly that he sells drugs, and that although he has calmed down with age, is still the local sheriff and hands out punishment when he has to. On the other hand, he said a lot of people had come to him because COVID-19 meant people have extra health and funeral bills to deal with.

As we were talking, it was interesting to observe the balance of power between a hardened gang leader and the community police officers. It was always a delicate, edgy situation, but the police officers were the ones looking tense, doing the humoring, not Vartas. He openly explained that he controls who gets killed, between swigs of beer, that his gang keeps the murder rate down, as the police officers nodded along in agreement. It was a real window into the rule of the jungle. He says he is fair in his judgement, so who am I to judge? Maybe in the Southside context he is fair.

Vartas's discourse was convincing up to a point, the point where it was clear he would never relinquish power. He was attempting to cast himself as a benevolent dictator. But he himself is trapped by the gang system he has played a leading role in maintaining, his history generating a long list of people who want to kill him. When he talked about leaving, you could sense the strain he was under, the pressure was real, shaping his options; maintain power to protect himself or flee far away. Gangland fight or flight.

Vartas was clearly an important interlocutor for the police, perhaps their most important. The police later told me that the area was at "peace" because Vartas was the one who kept it. This explained their softly-softly approach; they were suggesting politely, not telling Vartas what to do, anathema to different police units, namely the Gi3. They clearly had no *authority* over him, as this was his territory. I did not ask directly, but that afternoon conveyed an understanding that not only were they happy to have a General keep the peace but acquiescing to it was part of their job. I was left wondering about the pros and cons of the police subservience in that situation, without coming to any clear conclusion in my mind. Such are the dilemmas of negotiating violence reduction with gangs.

That afternoon, Vartas agreed to a life history interview with me at some later date, just before our interview was interrupted by one of his runners telling us that his son had just crashed his new car. We taxied Vartas in the police pickup a few blocks to where the crash happened. It turned out to be his son's fault, and the car was scratched down all four side panels. The air turned tense. Vartas, furious, struck his son with a full-force slap to the face that staggered him. The police had backed off letting this play out, and I hung back by the pickup. Seeing Vartas flick a switch and show his demon was chilling, and seeing the police so apprehensive made me uneasy. I never ended up doing the life history interview with him after all.

"If They Could, They Would Steal It All"

It is hard to reconcile the dilapidated areas of Southside around the swamp with the fact that Belize is a middle-income country with US$4,420 annual income per capita in 2021.[15] This is perhaps not what the country's founders had in mind when they named it after the Mayan word *baliz*, meaning muddy waters. Research funding to go to Belize was hard to come by. I stretched out a series of small grants to cover five field trips over the years and funded a handful of visits myself, leaving me personally out of pocket to the tune of US$10,000. One of the consistent problems I encountered trying to secure research funding was the ineligibility of Belize as a research site for some streams of overseas development funding in the United Kingdom, because of its middle-income status. It is likely that Belize also suffers stereotyping as a foreign paradise; even some of my colleagues would scoff at my "research trips to the Caribbean." However, Belize's Gini coefficient places it sixth in the world for wide-open inequality.[16]

Inequality has a corrosive impact on homes, families, and individuals located at the bottom. How this connects to social violence was discussed by two social and youth workers, Mrs. D and Mrs. N in 2016, who were connected to the SYSP project:

> MRS. D: One of de tings is dat *we are not listening to dem* [poor young people]. You know what dey want? Dey want eat, dey want food, dey want consistency knowing dat, dat meal is dere. And he tol' us [one young man at SYSP], dese gang members make sure dat he eats every day. Dey want somewhere to rest deir head. He end up sleeping on de floor. Do you know how many children his mum have? *Twelve!* De basic tings dey want. Dey just want to know who dey are. You can't show me a paper dat says "my name is John" because dere's no paper [birth certificate] dat exist.
> AUTHOR: But why is it violent?
> MRS. N: Because all dese needs are not being met. Dese young people are angry. I tink de multiple failures to develop, tek care of, protect Southside, leads to dis anger. I tink [what we need to do] it's meeting the needs of dese young people. *We have to listen to dem.*
> AUTHOR: And d'you think that if we meet the needs of these young men, it will stop them joining gangs?
> MRS. D: *It will* [she insists.]
> MRS. N: It's not just dat material ting. Dey want you to help dem deal wit dat pain, dat hurt dat dey have. I mean I have tree children dat I am fostering right now, and when I got dem, dere is so many tings dat has happened to dem. Yes, I bought dem nice clothes, I did dis, I did dat, but dat inner need dat is still inside . . . when we start opening dat [trauma] I mean, I don't even know if I could handle dat, I couldn't go thru dat. I have a little girl who is now

twelve, as' she was raped and molested by her father. An' I got her when she was eight, so imagine what she's went thru an' dat happen to her.

MRS. D: One o da tings when working wid dese young people, you cannot jus' work wid dem in isolation. It has to be de holistic approach where you have to work wid da family an' de community . . . you have to connect to de family to know what de needs are. We try to connect dem to government programs where da family get assistance. An' it do help, because listen to me, dey used to deir sons selling weed all day and bringing money home, and if the mother isn't working, you teking away deir income. And so, dis is what we mean, we look at what deir needs are. So, we went to different ministries an' we look to deir financial assistance so dey can get food. So, they say den dat dey don't have their parents fight dem [parents pushing them to sell marijuana] because dose needs are den met. So, we went thru an organization for women, an' dat is how we were able to get jobs [for the mothers]. We would say to the mothers, "listen, don't let your child go! We will show you how to provide for your family." *It can be done.*

MRS. N: You can't judge dese people [poor mothers] We need dis program [SYSP] for young women too.

Belize lacks financial resources and well-trained people, but that is also a convenient discourse that obfuscates the "legendary rapaciousness of officialdom," to borrow a phrase from Peter Evans's description of predatory states (1995, p. 43). In a review of Evans's book, Campbell observed that predatory states "lack the bureaucratic institutions (e.g., corporate coherence, meritocratic recruitment, professionalism, esprit de corps) necessary to ensure political elites have sufficient autonomy to resist corruption and capture by actors whose rent-seeking behavior [derails] the state's efforts to promote development and formulate policy in the national interest" (Campbell 1998, p. 103). Mrs. N and Mrs. D, in the previous dialogue, were desperate to get services to the most vulnerable, but while they had their hands full with the SYSP project, they simultaneously had to spend inordinate amounts of time lobbying state institutions to get them to respond to the needs of the young men on the program. *Chasing the state*, in fact, took over as their main task. They had some success, but they ascribed this to the fact that they were only seconded to the SYSP program, while still officially contracted as civil servants to some of the state institutions responsible. This meant they had leverage, "pulling some strings" to make things happen.

It cannot be overstated how difficult it is for poor young people from Southside to access services. A 2021 report by United Nations Belize stated:

> Social exclusion in Belize is manifested through the existence of structural, social, political, and economic policies and practices that exempt some populations from accessing services and engaging in opportunities that allow them to exercise their basic rights. At the same time, some populations have limited engagement in civic and political spaces through which they can interact with the government to have their voices and concerns heard and acted upon. (p. 69)

The fact that so many are malnourished is a clear indication they cannot access the most basic welfare. To move away from the more diplomatic style of the United Nations, one lady, alias Molly, had worked across Southside in recent years trying to connect poor young men, including those wishing to leave gangs, to public services. She sent me anonymized files in a WhatsApp message (2022), saying:

> This report covers all the data of all the people I have referred to GOB [Government of Belize], Church, and NGOs for support and how many were helped, and some details about referrals. From here forward I will have a case report on each person I am working with including dates of referral, who was contacted, and the result. As you can see the results from referrals have been really bad for the past 2 years.

Of approximately fourteen hundred young men Molly connected to support services between 2019 and 2021, only seven have received help. That is a 0.5 percent hit rate. I asked her why the responses were so staggeringly low, and she reeled off a number of barriers: government website platforms not being fit for purpose, "bad secretaries" simply not doing their jobs or who were disorganized, undertrained, and underfunded, in addition to a generalized disdain, in particular from female staff, toward poor dark-skinned Creole males, stigmatized as gang members undeserving of help. Molly also mentioned "emotional barriers" as young men had "asked for help twenty times and not gotten it." They were ground down by continual rejection so resisted reapplication for support when she approached them. Many were illiterate or semi-literate and struggled to repeatedly fill out forms. Molly also referred to "physical barriers" for young men, where traveling to a government office or state institution would mean traversing various gang territories. They cannot walk there and have no means of transport as "they cannot afford the bus fare." Registering online was impossible for many who had "no phone, no internet, no understanding of technology.... They only access Facebook, nothing else, and have to borrow devices." Southsiders access to the state is blocked by the state itself, that is, bureaucracy as a tool of abandonment. They are ignored, rejected, discriminated against, and rendered impotent "chasing the state."

A civil servant who had spent thirty years attempting to reduce gang violence was candid in their condemnation of political practice:

> The UDP was in power for 14 years, now the PUP are in, so what they are doing is paying back their loyal backers and those that financed them. Those who financed their campaign get paid back first . . . then people on Southside *might* get some. (2022)

This is not lost on gangs. Their leaders have access to information about government misuse of funds through their affiliations with politicians and also because it is very difficult to keep secrets in the village-like city. The retired employee continued:

> Gang leaders know that 90% of program funding goes to jobs for cronies and staff and cars . . . and 10% to actual beneficiaries of programs. [Gang leaders] have exact contract details of salaries and start dates of [anonymized institutional program] staff, cars, overheads. Gangs know everything, someone filters information. They know the game. So again, they say "they usin' us! Staff and cronies make a killing off us!" They know how useless [the program is] but [the program director] is [prime minister] Briceño's boy, so he is untouchable. These people are political appointees, they are just in it for political point scoring.
>
> They [gang members] know they are getting nothing out of the deal. The [program] car went to Briceño's PR person, so now they can't even respond to violence. That is how little of a shit they give for Southside.
>
> I don't know what to do but we have to play it different. The problem is that the system won't allow you to do it.

They went on to say that there is also widespread distrust between institutions. On one occasion a large national telecom company stepped in to say that they would sponsor a significant number of apprenticeships for at-risk young people on Southside, but they point-blank *refused* to give the money to the state institution and insisted that it had to go through the civil servant's personal bank account, whom they trusted. As this was not possible, the telecom company "refused to fund it because they knew the money would just get stolen [if they gave it to the state institution]."

> If you fundraise and put money into an institution, they "red tape" it making it impossible for you to get the money for what you raised it for! Then they just siphon it off. About 20% of funding goes to proj-

ects, just to give a *veneer* [the impression] of doing something, the rest is siphoned off using a range of strategies. So, good people basically just stop looking for funding as they know the majority just goes to corrupt officials.

There was a BZ$300 electrical job to be done on one project, but the Director said "no" and hired this guy for BZ$1000. You know that that electrician gets BZ$300 and the boss pockets BZ$700. It's normal practice.

Maybe 20–25% of funding actually reaches projects, the only reason they do this is that they have to show they are doing something. *If they could, they would steal it all* [emphasizes]. Ministers have control and discretion over what is signed off so they can pretty much do what they like. There is no financial code basically, they make the rules to suit themselves.

[One institution] owes money to the [an international development bank] for gang interventions. The money was legally earmarked for Violence Interruption *CURE* work, then government said "COVID-19! So we need to borrow it," then the money never appears again. Apparently [the bank] are furious.

Everyone wants to be in politics just to be grabbing [money]. We have to take politics out and not be robbed by politics. Our problems are politically based so things will never get better, politics is very dirty, clientelism is just the tip of the iceberg.

Failing state institutions and political practices are indivisible. The upshot is that what little money there is to reduce vulnerabilities across Southside rarely gets there. As one member of the international community said to me in plain terms "gang members not confused about what is on offer from the state" (2022).

Southside Youth Success Program

As mentioned in the Introduction to this book, I first came to Belize in 2011 at the behest of the UNDP. They had invited me as a consultant to help them write a pitch for funding to the U.S. Embassy, and the SYSP was born, running from 2012 to 2014. It was the first masculinities-focused gang intervention project launched to target young men who were either in gangs or at high risk of joining them, such as, siblings of gang members, those already in conflict with the law, school dropouts, or hangers-on at the fringes of gangs.

I interviewed a number of graduates from the program in 2016. Mentoring based on "Men's Talk" delivered at a drop-in center on Southside encouraged them to find positive pathways to manhood and to reject the gang. This was further bolstered by weekly male "motivational speakers" who covered topics such as "Not Choosing the Path of a Gangster," "Losing a Loved One as a Result of Gang Rivalry," "Sexual Exploitation," and "Changing the Course of Your Life" (UNDP 2014). The program evaluation itself showed that the masculinities focus added dynamism because it gave young men the tools to critique the gang as a site of male "success." During the project, 89 of the 106 participants gained work, a paid apprenticeship, or went back into full-time education, and a number of graduations and ceremonies were celebrated on television[17] (UNDP 2014).

Looking back, I had actually set up the project to tackle *masculine vulnerability*, although at the time I had not yet conceptualized it as such. When I unofficially reviewed the project, interviewing the managers, male mentors, and young men, I was eager to hear about the centrality of masculinities in steering youths away from the bright lights of the gang. After all, casting humility aside for a moment, the masculinities approach of SYSP was, in many ways, pioneering. Analyzing my interviews, I found that "Men's Talk," mentoring, and other elements of the project designed to encourage positive, nonviolent, and nongang masculinities were useful, but given the absolute poverty that a lot of participants faced, they were seen as secondary, a luxury even. You cannot inspire people when they are hungry.

Mrs. N and Mrs. D explained (2016):

MRS. N: We had to do a "feeding program" in the morning. We helped the boys cook and prepare their own food. Some of them would go for a whole day without a meal. So, we had a feeding program.

A key component of this program, was that 85% of the young men didn't have a Social Security card or a form of ID. They weren't even registered at birth! You couldn't get them into any [welfare] program because for every program now you need to have a Social Security number. So, *I have to spend days quarrelling with those people up there!* [in the government offices] [One young man] was going by "Sanchez" but he was not Sanchez. He was never registered, that was just the name of the person who was fostering him.

MRS. D: A lot of personal issues came out when trying to find these young men's identities, because some of the parents were cooperative, and some weren't so cooperative.

MRS. N: Some had registered to get ID through a UNICEF program, but it is a [bureaucratic nightmare to get ID from Belizean authorities] so most young kids you see on the streets don't have any registered ID.

MRS. D: There was this one family, this one lady have seven children and none of them had been registered. You have to go to hospitals around the country and dig up old birth records and then register them later! That is a project in itself! It is social work. I have to go to Dangriga [in southern Belize] and ask old people about who was born when . . .

MRS. N: Without ID you cannot work in the formal sector, so they [easy pickings for gangs]. *Many of the young men cried when they got their ID.* A social work component needs to be added to the program.

Because it's very important that these young men have a sense of identity and some kind of education. I mean, can you imagine a mother having seven children and none of them are registered at birth? And none of them are productive citizens. Up to the time we work with them, they were all in a tenement yard, on the street, smoking weed. Somebody give dem a little job for the day. Nobody cared to say "let me go and finish high school. Let me be da one in this family to try an' get an education." You are not motivated like dat. But it starts coz I trying to go to school and I don't have a birth record or a baptism record like dat, to be registered for preschool. An' dey put dey in a school and dey jus' goin' tru da system.

MRS. N: When we had the first parents meeting [about the back-to-school strategy] only two parents showed up. . . . So, [Mrs. D] went out into the communities and found these parents to tell them it's a legal obligation, and [their children] have a right [to be in school]. Then after that the parents' meetings were packed.

MRS. D: You have to *take yourself to these people's houses and talk with them.* The personal touch is very important when you are working a program like this.

MRS. N: It shows people that you care, and many frustrations start disappearing when you start caring.

MRS. D: We had to start doing karate, swimming, running and physical stuff every Friday. Fitness!

MRS. N: [We had] an exercise program, and a "drop-in" centre, and then a scholarship program, which was basically jus' giving them somewhere to do their homework. And we did community service on the job training.

MRS. D: Some of the more senior kids actually began to mentor the more junior ones.

MRS. N: We had a special needs boy came and was not talking, but after a while he began to talk. . . . The other boys took care of him whenever they went out. They look out for him.

MRS. D: We asked them to do it because we wanted a brotherhood, like big brothers, and so they *really* looked after that young man.

MRS. N: For community work we did painting [people's houses], a soup kitchen, helping old people.... One boy was in the program, doing really well, on a paid apprenticeship, but his dad died, and things went downhill, and he's now in a gang.

MRS. D: [We found jobs for some as] bus conductors, but the problem is that they can't go to different areas [of the city] due to gang rivalry.... I would [doorstep] businesses to get jobs for them, because nobody's going to take in these bad boys for work. They got jobs in the post office, sorting mail, and we set them up with a male mentor at the post office.

MRS. N: And in the supermarket, and in kitchens. The majority went back to school, or are in jobs, apprenticeships, but some are undecided.

They are so confined to their neighborhoods.... Many hadn't been to the post office, Supreme Court, around the city. We also did sessions with police, US Embassy, on a tour of the BDF [Belizean Defense Force] barracks.... We took them out to the countryside to do things, and the UNDP bought them top-of-the-line boots, good quality boots. They were *so* happy. We bought the boots with a little bit of room, so they have a little growing space.

MRS. D: We managed to get one out of the gang and he is now a soldier, but he still can't come out of his neighborhood sometimes because the rival gangs still see him as an enemy gang member, even if he is wearing his soldier's uniform.

Mentoring was only effective when coupled with *tangible* alternative pathways for youths, for instance, steps to move back into education or to gain paid employment. In other words, visualized pathways to manhood made viable. Preventing gang membership by combating boys' vulnerability head on, beginning with a full stomach and ending with a life opportunity.

AUTHOR: How about the "Men's Talk" spaces?

MRS. N: It was very important. They received the message much better because it was coming from a male. They all come from single parent homes, so they only hear from women ... when the men came in it was *real talk* and they shared, I mean, really, really, really, open.

MRS. D: We even took the second cohort into Belize Central Prison to get them to speak to the men inmates.

Men's Talk, male mentoring, and visits to the prison helped mitigate the lure of the gang, but the first step was to meet a basic needs threshold, followed by reassurances that the program would connect them to genuine opportunities. These young men were brutally pragmatic because they had to be. Ideally, of course, the Belizean welfare state would function to the extent that programs such as SYSP, BMCMS, teachers, and impromptu foster parents do not have to pick up the slack. Not only do well-meaning individuals chase the state; they replace it.

The SYSP experience profoundly informed my ideas around masculine and feminine vulnerability. It was a small pilot project focused on masculinities, but other specific projects are required that focus on girls and young women who coalesce around the gang space. This could reduce their vulnerability to sexual violence, for example. Interestingly, the UNDP did establish a small SYSP-influenced project in San Pedro, northern Belize, focusing on young women, with a "young woman's talking circle." While I did not have time to visit this project, one illustrative takeaway was that, while the young men on the SYSP needed feeding, the young women in San Pedro required childcare support to be able to participate.

The SYSP program wound down as a pilot in 2014. I was told by several sources that it was due to receive funding to continue and build up from the pilot. "A bank, I don't know if it was the World Bank, or the Caribbean [Development] Bank or whoever, but the money was there to cover the continuation of SYSP, for US$1 million to expand its reach over Southside. I remember coz I was there, and it was *a lot* of money and I think it was for five years" (Anonymous 2016). Rumors swirled about why the funding to SYSP was blocked, which I never got to the bottom of, yet an Apprenticeship Program emerged soon after adopting many ideas similar to the SYSP. One civil servant told me frankly that "SYSP ideas were stolen by [names lady married to a powerful individual in the UDP] and put into the Apprenticeship Program so they could get the credit [for the ideas]" (2021). Maybe so, but in the Belizean political context, and taking a phlegmatic view, that some of the ideas from the SYSP were carried on should be taken as a victory.

International Community

What is notable about the international community is their absence on Southside. When I visited in 2021 and 2022, I could not track down a single individual from an international organization running a project there. Yes, there have been small projects implemented on a piecemeal or pilot basis, such as SYSP, and many of these are funded by CARSI. Given that basic needs are not met, programs providing shelter, basic health services, or soup kitchens, not wildly complex undertakings, would have a huge impact. Surely a low-hanging fruit, an open goal, for the international community to back?

In 2022, I was interviewed by a United Nations department working at the Caribbean regional level. We swapped information and analysis, noting that there used to be at least some presence of NGOs and grassroots organizations on Southside, but, in recent years, due to a lack of local and international funding, they had all but disappeared. There are no organizations to act as checks and balances on government, and neighborly support, the social fabric, has corroded as violence has risen. Funding and capacity-building civil society organizations (CSOs) seemed like an obvious first step, however, we also noted a reduction in the enthusiasm to support initiatives on Southside. CSOs tend to be reactive and pivot to whatever issue is receiving funding in a given period. In 2022, these were environmental and ecological initiatives. I inquired about this with the national representative of a major development bank, looking for funding for initiatives on Southside to support Molly, the missionary cited earlier. We were told that there was no funding for security initiatives, rather they were focusing exclusively on the environment, ecology, and sustainability along the coastline, and that if we could somehow organize Southside youths around those topics, then they would welcome a proposal. Yet, complex ecological initiatives out of town are simply not tenable for young people in contexts of urban exclusion. We all knew this. Molly voiced her frustration in no uncertain terms, berating the bank representative, creating a very tense atmosphere. Clearly, she was exasperated with trying and failing to get things done. We left disappointed, and I suspected the bank representative would not take any more of our calls.

One individual working for a large international organization detailed the challenges of collaborating with Belize (2023). They said in no uncertain terms that the institutions as a whole were very difficult to partner with and that during the period the UDP was in power there was widespread frustration that nothing could be done. They put this down to the Belizean authorities lacking openness, stating that the international community would like to take on a more active role. They noted that the national institutional structures were simply not there, nor were the human resources, to implement greater international cooperation and that dovetailing or alignment between national needs and international support and priorities had still not been established under the PUP. This, in addition to corruption, and what they described as institutional low self-esteem, meant there were precious few opportunities to support, although there was optimism that things would improve with the PUP.

A handful of community "Hubs" were set up in 2020, funded by the U.S. government until 2023, by national nonprofit the Love Foundation, the charitable arm of a large private multimedia company, under the project title "Empowering Communities to Empower Themselves."[18] I contacted the director of Love Foundation to organize a visit to the Hubs, but they were reluctant to take me, although I never found out why. Nevertheless, I visited several Hubs independently and ran into a group of missionaries-cum-doctors who were planning to provide medical services in some parts of Southside, which was admirable but indicative of contributions being led by the goodwill of a few individuals rather than a well-funded project run by the international community.

The Hubs themselves were managed by former gang members trying to stay out of trouble and make some honest money from microfinanced initiatives. They also incorporated and supported the wider community. They were humble; small plots of land turned into allotments. One I saw in Majestic Alley had rudimentary plastic greenhouses, but, unfortunately, nothing substantial was growing and nobody was out working the patch. Depressingly, it already seemed doomed to failure. Another at the southern end of Southside fared better. It was a decent space, with a vegetable garden beginning to grow and a BBQ takeaway service planned. Several former gang members milled around and gave the impression that they were trying to make it work. The other Hub I saw portside was further developed, although the carwash and mechanic shop was rudimentary, there was an impressive brand new drinking-water purification system about to open for businesses. As an indication of how challenging it is to work with former gang-affiliated individuals on Southside, the month after I visited the portside project, one of the young men I had spoken to was shot dead in a gang-related beef.

In 2021, I spent the afternoon at the Hub in the southern end of Southside. There were a handful of men there, some ex-convicts, but, notably, they were all former gang members actively looking for a new future. Most were quite old, late twenties to late thirties, had children, and were gradually aging out of gang life. They were noticeably poor, indigent even, wearing worn-out plastic slider sandals. When we sat down to talk, they smoked Mexican "kush" marijuana fresh from the Chetumal border. One nursed a cheap bottle of Red Top liquor. They had tended the allotment in the morning, so they said, and were just putting their feet up to hang out in the afternoon. They were not yet making any money at the Hub, the allotment did not even provide enough to feed one of them, and they were waiting on microfinancing for a couple of barrel BBQs to smoke chicken. It felt like a retired gang members social club more than anything, somewhere to go, smoke weed and drink, that wasn't a prone street corner. One talked about the allotment; the rest were disinterested. Later, in the afternoon, they hooked together some plastic carts into a kiddie's train that was pulled along the streets with children in it. There was no optimism among the men I spoke to that they would be able to scrape by on a living made there any time soon, and I left with the defeatist thought,

"Well, it's better than nothing," but one individual there seemed driven. We have been in touch via WhatsApp since then, which took us both by surprise, as we connected over a conversation about cooking times and internal meat temperatures for smoked chicken. As of 2023, however, the BBQs had yet to arrive.

This is not meant as a critique of the Hubs, and I am not intimately familiar with the *Love Foundation*, but at least they are trying to do something. What this flags are the undeniable difficulties of working with this demographic on Southside. Former gang members often have criminal records, addiction problems, trauma related "demons," low literacy, are used to "easy money" from selling weed in the evenings, spend most of their time hanging out, and so on. If we recall, Mr. T commented that programs "can't replace a gang's drug income."

While SYSP and Hubs change some individual lives, the historical failure of the state to provide any semblance of social security means they have little chance of a wholesale reshaping of community-wide chronic vulnerability. Southside suffers a form of double jeopardy: abandoned by the state and abandoned by the international community.

My international interviewees were far too diplomatic to say so directly, but there was a clear lack of trust in Belizean institutions given widespread corruption. Shoman (2011, pp. 325–326) said that this was the reason international funding had dried up over a decade ago. A Belizean civil servant who I have known for a number of years was frank (2022):

> CIVIL SERVANT: They [international community] used to finance things on Southside.
> AUTHOR: But I haven't seen much now . . .
> CIVIL SERVANT: No, well, *they stop*! [laughing incredulously]
> AUTHOR: . . . what?
> CIVIL SERVANT: The international community know how corrupt we are, and the US Embassy knows that drug trafficking penetrates deep into politics and institutions. I'm not sure about how much of an idea they have of exactly who is involved. They approached me once to be an informant. Personally, I know [names well-known senior police officer] and [names well-known senior politician]. They are both in the game [drug trafficking].

A Belizean academic reflected (2022):

> Southside hasn't changed that much in forty years, and it *has* to be about politics. . . . We really have leadership bankruptcy. We have pov-

erty, inequality, and gangs. Those are *hard* problems to eliminate. [We don't have the institutional stability] to research, respond, or design responses to mitigate the negative consequences of all those issues.

This is an extremely challenging milieu for the cooperation of the international community, which has standards on transparency and accountability. Perhaps the most damning indictment I heard was from Jabbar, who said "state institutions and politicians *actually prefer not to manage money from the US Embassy* because they have to be accountable" [his emphasis] (2021). In 2008 the IDB said, "The lack of transparency and alleged misuse of public funds for private interests is probably the single most important governance issue. . . . It is clear how severe the institutional problems were." The World Bank stopped lending to Belize in 2004 because of "increasing financial and fiduciary risks," and the IDB ventured further, "it is safe to say that fraud and impropriety is widespread throughout the public service [and there are a] lack of regulations to prevent conflict of interests." The upshot is, as Molly said, "the international community no longer knows what to do on Southside, or they got tired, so they just do green economy initiatives which are not in the city" (2022).

Conclusions

Interventions on Southside have so far failed to provide for minimum basic needs. The failure of gang interventions is paradigmatic of the failures of politics. Predatory politics were birthed as the dynamics of a racialized class-based colonial history, the marginalization of fieldslaves baked-in to the "stay in your lane" and "don't go up against the master" Creole psyche. "A downfall to downfallness," said Shorty. "Our students are *so* disempowered that they have accepted that they cannot change anything. You cannot get anymore disempowered than that," said my academic friend as our interview morphed into a therapy session.

Power asymmetry manifests in the partial rule of law in Belizean society. A dense network of social and political ties allows elites to unendingly consolidate their interests over the promotion of a developmental state. This state capture means institutions are realms dominated by ministers and party interests, with no semblance of a separation of powers, the predatory state consolidated. The results have been catastrophic, as Belize's Gini Index lays bare. Mrs. N and Mrs. D were dragging the welfare state, kicking and screaming, into Southside. Or, like teachers and the community police, they put their hands in their own pockets to pay. *Chasing the state* or *replacing the state* is a damning indictment.

Within this milieu, innovative gender-based programs that encourage positive, nonviolent, nongang masculinities can be powerful but will always play second fiddle to an empty stomach for those taking part. But as we showed on the SYSP, responses to the two must go together. What prevents gang membership is combating boys' vulnerability head on, then presenting viable pathways to adulthood that have masculine appeal, that is, those that offer them a semblance of dignity.

Conclusion

Reconfiguration

These conclusions underscore the book's key findings, demonstrating how "chronic vulnerability" underpinned Belize's homicide boom and continues to sustain high levels of violence today. This is not an argument to say chronic vulnerability is the singular cause of lethal violence, as the influx of guns into the city in the 1990s also played a defining role, but it is an argument to say *we cannot have chronic violence without chronic vulnerability*. If this sounds unbending, bear in mind, it is a provocation that asks, Where do we have chronic violence without chronic vulnerability? This is the pillar for the theory of change expanded on in this chapter.

There are three reminders to make about chronic vulnerability. First, the notion hypothesizes that, if repression, broadly conceived in social, economic, and political terms, is turned back, chronic violence will subsequently recede. "Chronic violence" (after Pearce 2007), across time, space, and intensity, is demonstrated empirically by the never-ending cycle of violence on Southside. "Chronic vulnerability" is defined as intense impoverishment or exclusion that is historically accumulated and persistent in the same location or communities.

Ideally, and further research will tell, chronic vulnerability will be applied as a framework for understanding other violent contexts. To do so, the use of relevant and varied analytical intersections are key. These may be the classic intersections of race, class, and gender, or beyond, limited only by our intellectual imagination. If the reader has diligently come this far, they will have noted well-plowed issues of history, Belize's colonial legacy, the way independence politics were malformed, and how these created the conditions for gang violence to flourish.

Second, as a concept it helps us picture the landscape behind the rise of violence rather than pinpointing the details in the foreground. It aims to help us organize our thoughts about why such brutal levels of violence emerge and are sustained, and, consequently, seeks to promote social change by stimulating ideas and impetus that create new ways of combating violence. The blunt message is this: reduce chronic vulnerability, reduce violence. Focus on changing the landscape.

Third, chronic vulnerability should be seen as a *discourse challenge* to gang interventions dominated by heavy-handed punitive responses. Belize Central Prison is packed with gang members, yet, here we are, Southside is no less violent. Following crime with punishment is part and parcel of the rule of law. When the rule of law is partial, as it is in Belize, cracking down on gangs is highly visible, therefore politically useful, and distracts the public gaze from the political and institutional deficits that mean vulnerability, poverty, and inequality are not tackled effectively. In that sense, promoting a moral panic around gangs is a form of national gaslighting. Chronic vulnerability challenges this discourse, pressing power holders, the elites, to focus their efforts on breaking the continuity of exclusion and poverty on Southside. This will take a change in perception, a reconfiguration. From seeing poor young Black and Brown men in gangs as the protagonists of violence, to seeing vulnerability as the protagonist of violence instead.

Be under no illusions. Reducing poverty and extending the welfare state into Southside is a mammoth task, given the current institutional capacities, and is a generational and less visible process that will not pay immediate political dividends. It will require substantial political courage and investment, but generating opportunities is the only way violence will sustainably be reduced.

Chapter Summary and Key Findings

Chapter 1 conceptualized the Blood and Crip arrival as a form of "transnational masculinity," a class-based one that makes logical connections between men in comparative settings of urban exclusion. This put forward the idea of a comparative *masculine vulnerability* between South Central Los Angeles and Southside Belize City, demonstrating the conditionality of chronic vulnerability and masculinity for both transnational gang emergence and transitions to extreme social violence. Beyond gender, the intersectional analysis in the chapter highlighted the crucial characteristics of race and ethnicity, language, age, and class in this process. Transnational gang "successes" depend on these characteristics being shared between source and host communities. This is significant in helping us understand how fragility leads to conflict and violence in geographically distanced yet comparable settings, which is a central concern of major international development institutions, in particular, the OECD, World Bank, and United Nations (World Bank Group and United Nations 2018, OECD 2020, World Bank Group 2020).[1] In this case, the "social terrains" where gangs relocate as a transnational phenomenon and homicide booms occur are consistent, that is, the poor Southsides of this world, not the wealthy Northsides.

Chapter 2 looked at the history of Southside, postindependence political clientelism and patronage tied to elitism that prevented the creation of a developmental state, in addition to police shortcomings, rapid incarceration, and a general failure to deliver meaningful economic progress. This was presented as an ongoing sociohistorical process, anchored in a racialized colonial past, which profoundly shapes lives in the present, flagging the indivisibility of historical through contemporary processes of subjugation. The most disenfranchised in Belizean society currently—apart from sections of the rural poor (UNDP 2021)—are the Creole descendants of fieldslaves. The continued plight of Southside is tied to the structural inequalities laid down by the development of racial capitalism inherited from the colonial encounter (see Warren et al. 2021).

The chapter showed contradictory government-state responses as gangs arose on Southside in the 1980s. At times, gangs were collaborated with as clients of political party interests to deliver votes or seen as interlocuters of negotiated truces to reduce crime and violence; at other times, they were targeted with the full force of the law and indiscriminate mass incarceration. Party clientelism and police brutalization and extortion were coupled with a resounding failure to deliver meaningful economic opportunities. The chapter demonstrated that transhistorical processes of subjugation create the social terrains that gang populations are drawn from, as the rage of the poor turns inward.

Chapter 3 proposed the counterintuitive explanation that *disorganized violence* fueled the homicide boom at the turn of the millennium. Gangs developed incrementally in Belize City, in the 1980s and 1990s, leading to a steady rather than dramatic increase in violence on the streets. During the 1990s, the institution-like control of George Street Blood and Majestic Alley Crip franchises, led by powerful Generals, kept a lid on homicide rates. These rates spiked dramatically, in 1999 and 2000, as kingpin policing strategies corroded the gang leadership structures stoking internecine conflicts within the two main Blood and Crip groups, leading to further fragmentation and a loss of the old order. Not organized violence, but *disorganized violence*.

This experience diverges from most narratives on gangs in the region, where violence increases as they become more organized around territorially competitive drug and extortion markets. In Belize City, although gangs sell marijuana locally, they remain at the margins of organized crime, exemplified by their exclusion from hermetic, and lucrative, transnational cocaine trafficking networks.

Chapter 4 argued that the original Blood and Crip model of masculinity was reimagined, *Creolized*, by young Belizean men from the moment it arrived, later absorbing influences from gang culture in Jamaica. This process has created culturally blended posttransnational gang identities that are unique to Belize. Although gangs are highly disorganized and culturally syncretistic, they seamlessly reproduce violent masculine practices. Empirically, this is evident in new generations of gang leaders such as Vartas, who never relinquish their masculine hegemony atop the local gender hierarchy. Gang identities are sites of opportunity, elevated status, and aspirational manhood that satiate the *masculine vulnerability* of young men living in excluded contexts.

Chronic vulnerability was divided into masculine and feminine vulnerabilities, where gender defines how an individual strategizes and interacts with the gang world. Feminine vulnerabilities were exemplified in the chapter through depictions of sexual violence against young women in the home, community, and, with the menace of "train" rape, gang spaces. Conversely, boys and men, beyond being vulnerable to the lure of gangland masculinity, face clear risks of being murdered, permanently injured, or ending up in jail if they join a gang. Gendered vulnerabilities shape the way women and men strategize and grind to survive and the way they search for dignity, esteem, and status. We should never underestimate how gender, amid chronic vulnerability, profoundly defines options and tactics.

Chapter 5 was highly critical of the role of postindependence politics in Belize, yet this was a concerted effort to identify systemic issues that have led to the continuity of chronic vulnerability. The failures of gang interventions are indivisible from the wider failures of state. Contemporary predatory politics were birthed from racialized class-based colonial history, leading to the continued marginalization of the descendants of fieldslaves and the manifestation of "chronic" in vulnerability. The partial rule of law reflects power asymmetry in Belizean society, driven by the severe social, political, and economic elitism that has hobbled institutional development. This has been nothing less than catastrophic for development on Southside. The lack of financial and human resources and the predatory politics and endemic corruption have meant that even well-meaning individuals within state institutions are hamstrung, and the international community has, for all intents and purposes, given up.

Theory of Change: Reduce Chronic Vulnerability, Reduce Violence

Gang violence captivates. But if we are looking for a monster, it is poverty. "Taking on" gangs scores political points: roundups are quick, visible, and newsworthy, generating a veneer of political action wrapped in the rhetoric of being "tough on crime." For state institutions and politicians, it would require the political courage to look inward and dissect the state and government failures that have let socioeconomic destitution continue on Southside and recognize that their part of the social contract is unfulfilled. Gayle and Mortis (2010) correctly said, "[The government] must establish policies with year-by-year goals to reduce squalor.... This means planning ahead rather than reacting to problems" (p. 158), concluding, "social violence is a by-product of major social ills and so the suggestions are about fixing those social ills" (p. 330). That begs the question, Where is the welfare state?

The welfare state is nonexistent on Southside because of corruption, institutional ineptitude, and the grip of garrison politics. This is not a nuanced statement; it is an important starting point for change. Southsiders have been left behind, the inverse of the United Nation's rallying call to "Leave No One Behind" in the recent *Common Country Analysis* of Belize (United Nations Belize 2021, p. 96), which stated that "corruption ... is currently the greatest challenge to efficient, effective, and equitable governance in Belize" (p. 93). Numerous recommendations have been received over the years and not implemented because there are no checks and balances or effective oversight. The question then becomes, How do we strengthen accountability mechanisms, so the state performs better?

Given the post-1981 political track record in Belize, it would be naive to expect politicians, particularly those representing Southside constituencies, to willingly change. I am reminded of a quote from Darren McGarvey (2022), "For as long as there has been a democracy to participate in, working-class people and the poor have had to organize and fight for every right, every liberty and every other socioeconomic advance they got—never forget that" (p. 282). Four decades have passed since independence in Belize and people's basic needs are far from being met on Southside. There is, unfortunately, a mutually reinforcing harmony between chronic vulnerability and political predation, a vicious circle that has to be broken.

The PUP put together a #planbelize strategy that placed an emphasis on poverty reduction with a lengthy table of initiatives. Osmond Martinez from the Ministry of Economic Development said the aim was to deliver "fundamental rights for vulnerable populations."[2] Despite ingrained skepticism in government, there is a sense of a momentum shift. However, Belize has extremely challenging issues in terms of redressing its democratic deficit. The country is faced with limited resources and creaking institutions, particularly post-COVID-19, coupled with absolute poverty across a largely lawless Southside.

Political claims should always be taken with a grain of salt and, more often than not, represent rhetorical grandstanding rather than reality. However, one representative from the international community was particularly candid in their assessment of the current administration (2023). They noted that historically Belizean authorities have not been open but "the PUP are 100% totally different, it is a complete turnaround." They highlighted that policy had changed significantly and that "the PUP have different social objectives . . . and the PM has spoken clearly about the need to overcome poverty." I spoke to a national journalist for his take:

> I don't think it is all BS [regarding poverty reduction], but the results remain to be seen.
>
> There is an ongoing housing program. They have been providing low-income homes, concrete bungalows, what they call starter homes, which can be expanded. They've done . . . [about] 200–300 houses for single mothers, with children. A few men have received houses. I've been along to see those, so there is something to be said about the programs they are implementing and there does seem to be some focus on the poor.
>
> I was out last November [2022] with the Ministry of Infrastructure Development [and Housing] as they handed over supplies to people in need, and what was evident also, was how feeble the living conditions are in Belize City.
>
> Yes, for certain there is corruption happening, this is the nature of Belizean institutional politics, unfortunately. . . . I am certain and the public is too, that corruption is afoot and ever present. But they haven't been blatant or, daresay, caught yet. I can't recall any major scandal right off the top [of my head] in the last two years. But once that start to happen, that's the downward spiral for every party and government here in Belize. They haven't reached that point as yet. The admin is still young, they still have a lot of potential to shape themselves and create a different legacy than the administrations previous.

But how do Belizeans guarantee the long-term continuation of initiatives that reduce poverty? The answer lies in generating oversight mechanisms to press for transparency and accountability in state and government. Despite myriad challenges, in my personal experience there are numerous dedicated individuals within institutions that I have collaborated with in the past who are determined to have a positive impact on Southside. Agency is there. Structures are not. But this is not insurmountable.

The more the Southside population is empowered, beginning with their basic needs being met, the more they will break with the predatory politics they have been subject to historically. If the population is no longer starving, BZ$50 handed out at election time begins to look less attractive. The Belizean-style garrison politics exercised on Southside signals a total disdain for the social contract. Rebuilding that contract, starts with the welfare state, but that is a minimum requirement. Building trust, due process, functioning institutions, and all that this entails, must be the long-term and ongoing goal.

Beyond trade unions and a handful of women's organizations focused on gender-based violence, there is no discernible civil society organization in Belize. Even the University of Belize has negligible research that can be used to inform national policy making. Civil society is vital to speak truth to power and hold authorities accountable. There may be a supporting role the international community can play in developing such organizations, and the national government could develop a strategy to help CSOs and NGOs flourish. That said, they need to emerge organically from society, yet Belize is now over forty years old and still has no meaningful civic power. There is no easy answer to this question, but, optimistically, the disruption of chronic vulnerability and predatory politics should provide the conditions for this to germinate. As we have seen in Medellín, an active civil society played a key role in changing the face of the city. To promote civil society, the Public Defender's Office and Ombudsmen need support as an important interlocutor, and, speaking as an academic, the University of Belize clearly needs financial strengthening, particularly in postgraduate education, research, and academic positions, for more homegrown academics to emerge from the system. Too often the best-qualified cannot find secure university employment and migrate to the United States. The absence of published research on the socioeconomic challenges the country faces, by Belizean academic talent, is glaring.

Belizeans are angry with political dysfunction. Initially, I mulled the idea of proposing a form of UN oversight into corruption—such as the CICIG (International Commission against Impunity in Guatemala[3])—particularly as former Belizean politicians have now been designated on the U.S.'s Engel List. I would not discard this as an option, but it is a last resort that raises issues around sovereignty. The PUP's 2023 midterm report provided a road map presenting an opportunity for international community alignment and cooperation. The closed culture and weakness of institutions still presents a challenge. One diplomat said in 2022 that although the Ministry for Economic Development is "not good enough . . . we need a structure of how to coordinate and work with them," there *is* scope for working with the Ministry for

Human Development. Ambitiously, they continued that strengthening accountability and "a dialogue on transparency" would be a natural next step.

Tackling chronic vulnerability requires greater equity of economic opportunity. A Belizean who has worked with gangs for decades reflected that "90% of young kids on Southside will take up job opportunities if given them" (2016). But to create equity of opportunity, the elites in society have to be convinced that this is the right route to go, then actively support it. The case for support was made convincingly by Wilkinson and Pickett (2009) in their book *The Spirit Level*, a metastudy on inequality, which showed that *elites do better* in more equal societies. It is not a zero-sum game. Engaging elites and explaining that improving Southside through economic opportunities is in their own interests is the right strategic avenue to take. Notably, when the prison was taken over by the Kolbe Foundation nonprofit organization, it transformed from one of the worst to one of the best prisons in the region. This transition, and the Kolbe Foundation itself, was underpinned by the support of industrial elites. Or as Jenny Pearce said on a recent podcast, without the equitable distribution of economic opportunities, violence will inevitably continue, "which is frankly a terrifying prospect."[4]

Clearly, an equitable rule of law must be a consideration by the new government. Although it acted to strike down two hundred corrupt police officers in 2022, at the time of writing, none of them were in jail. The rule of law has not been wielded with the same vigor against corruption in government, state, or white-collar crime. There are no politicians in jail, making the police force culling another reminder that punishment is only exercised against the lower classes.

It is crucial to follow through on the anti-corruption measures in the 2023 midterm strategy and point the rule of law upward for once. Southsiders would be justified in asking, If the Gi3 special police unit was created to target gang members, where is the equivalent unit targeting corruption? In 1990s Argentina, a special anti-corruption unit was created called the Untouchables because they were endowed with significant political and legal power to investigate and make arrests. Until corrupt politicians, government officials, and civil servants face the real prospect of jail time, ordinary Belizeans would be correct in assuming "one rule for them, one rule for us," recalling the power of coloniality to "never go up against the master."

Finally, let us focus on gender. Gang interventions the world over tend to be gender blind and are most certainly masculinities blind. If we draw down from the theory of change presented here, "reduce chronic vulnerability, reduce violence," Southside impacts males and females differently. Some issues are, of course, shared, the all-too-common sexual abuse of both boys and girls growing up, for example, but gendered vulnerabilities are often widely divergent in gang-affected communities. Young men are vulnerable to gang recruitment, injury and disability, incarceration, and murder, and young women are more likely to be on the receiving end of sexual harassment and rape from gangs. Furthermore, barriers to the access of state services vary drastically according to gender, race, and class. The mere fact that someone lives on Southside means they find closed doors and dead ends on the occasions they do seek help, and young men, in particular, are stigmatized as "probably gang members" unworthy of support. When thinking about change, while basic welfare provision is universal, specific gender-based responses are needed on Southside to effectively tackle feminine and masculine vulnerabilities. If this can be achieved, gang recruitment will be diminished, and violence will be reduced sustainably.

Notes

PREFACE

1. British Academy and Leverhulme Trust Small Research Grants (2016). *From Transnational Crime to Local Insecurity: How Drug-Trafficking Penetrates Communities and Creates Violent Masculinities in Belize.* Award number SG160310.

2. "Gangs, Gangsters, and Ganglands: Towards a Global Comparative Ethnography," led by Professor Dennis Rodgers. Available at https://www.graduateinstitute.ch/research-centres/centre-conflict-development-peacebuilding/gangs-gangsters-and-ganglands-towards.

3. Anna Fazackerley. (2021). "This Happens in Brazil, Not Britain": Academics in Despair as Global Research Funds Pulled, *The Guardian*, London. Available at https://www.theguardian.com/education/2021/mar/19/this-happens-in-brazil-not-britain-academics-in-despair-as-global-research-funds-pulled.

4. *Joe Rogan Experience #1993—Josh Dubin & Bruce Bryan.* JRE Podcast. (2023, June 1). https://www.jrepodcast.com/episode/joe-rogan-experience-1993-josh-dubin-bruce-bryan/.

INTRODUCTION

1. Some of my colleagues and I have experienced participating in multilateral policy spaces covering not only Latin America and the Caribbean but also those with global reach. We have noted that discussions around homicide causality tend to be simplistic and disproportionately deduced from quantitative data alone (Baird, Bishop, and Kerrigan 2022).

CHAPTER 1

1. Quotations from interviews have been written phonetically where the interviewees spoke with a pronounced Creole accent. These tended to be young people and gang mem-

bers, while expert interviewees would typically "lighten their tongue" or "speak American" for the benefit of foreign ears.

CHAPTER 2

1. Statistical Institute of Belize. (2020). Census Report, Belmopan. Available at https://sib.org.bz/publications/census-reports/.
2. Carlos Martínez, Efren Lemus, and Óscar Martínez. (2023). Régimen de Bukele desarticula a las pandillas en El Salvador, *El Faro*, San Salvador. Available at https://elfaro.net/es/202302/el_salvador/26691/R%C3%A9gimen-de-Bukele-desarticula-a-las-pandillas-en-El-Salvador.htm.
3. Duane Moody. (2013). Throats of 4 Gang Members Slashed in Apartment, *Channel 5 Belize*. Available at https://edition.channel5belize.com/archives/80475.

CHAPTER 3

1. PMO Prophit (2023). Instagram. Available at https://www.instagram.com/pmo_prophit/.
2. See, for example, Nathaniel Janowitz. (2014). Belize's Island Paradise Is Caught Up in a Bloods vs Crips Floating Drug War, *Vice News*, New York. Available at https://www.vice.com/en/article/kz55b9/belizes-island-paradise-is-caught-up-in-a-bloods-vs-crips-floating-drug-war.
3. Isani Cayetano. (2021). Police and Drug Plane Landings, the Year in Review, *Channel 5 Belize*. Available at https://edition.channel5belize.com/archives/227598.
4. Nathaniel Janowitz. (2021). How the US Exported a Bloods and Crips Gang War to Belize, *Vice News*, New York. Available at https://www.vice.com/en/article/88ndmp/how-the-us-exported-a-bloods-and-crips-gang-war-to-belize.
5. As noted in the previous chapter, the 2022 flash incarceration of over seventy thousand poor young men in El Salvador, and a continuously extended state of emergency, has led to a collapse in homicide rates, but the sustainability and long-term impact of this extreme form of mano dura is seriously questioned.
6. Nathaniel Janowitz. (2021). How the US Exported a Bloods and Crips Gang War to Belize *Vice News*, New York. Available at https://www.vice.com/en/article/88ndmp/how-the-us-exported-a-bloods-and-crips-gang-war-to-belize.
7. 7 News Belize. (2012). Arthur Young Killed by Police: Was It Extrajudicial? Available at http://www.7newsbelize.com/sstory.php?nid=22270.
8. Aaron Humes. (2021). Commissioner: City's Most Well-Known Gangs at War; Police Will Be Right in the Middle, *Breaking Belize News*, Belize City. Available at https://www.breakingbelizenews.com/2021/05/14/commissioner-citys-most-well-known-gangs-at-war-police-will-be-right-in-the-middle/.
9. Personal correspondence via Twitter, April 28, 2023. Also, Ioan Grillo. (2021). *Slow the Iron River of Guns to Mexico*, *New York Times*. Available at https://www.nytimes.com/2021/02/20/opinion/international-world/guns-mexico.html.
10. Popularized in the Netflix documentary *Running with the Devil: The Wild World of John McAfee*, (August 24, 2022). Director Charlie Russell, Curious Films, U.K.

CHAPTER 4

1. Police Chancey (Official Video)—Etdan featuring TY. (2015). YouTube. Available at https://www.youtube.com/watch?v=RJ2I2X_HCVg.

2. Amandala. (2016). Hon. Patrick Faber's SUV Plunges into the Caribbean Sea, *Amandala*, Belize City. Available at https://amandala.com.bz/news/hon-patrick-fabers-suv-plunges-caribbean-sea/.

3. Love Staff. (2022). Video Showing Former UDP Leader Patrick Faber Head-Butting Woman Emerges, *Love FM*, Belize City. Available at https://lovefm.com/video-showing-former-udp-leader-patrick-faber-head-butting-woman-emerges/.

CHAPTER 5

1. The People's United Party (PUP). (2020). *Manifesto 2020–2025*, Belmopan. Available at https://web.archive.org/web/20211001123029/https://planbelize.bz/wp-content/uploads/2020/10/BLU-manifesto-eBOOK.pdf.

2. The People's United Party (PUP). (2022). Plan Belize Medium Term Development Strategy, 2022 to 2026, Belmopan. Available at https://7newsbelize.com/sstory.php?nid=64857.

3. Chris Must List. (2023). The Swamp People of Belize City! Available at https://www.youtube.com/watch?v=szTxdJAPEPk.

4. Adam Baird. (2022). Panel 20. Masculinidades en paz y conflicto, 6º Congreso de Construcción de Paz con Perspectiva de Género, Universidad Iberoamericana, Ciudad de México. Available at https://www.youtube.com/watch?v=VSDCudkqxfw&list=PLm3odcCjE04_x1_mM_B0Dgb4NYJgV3gEa&index=7.

5. Channel 5 Belize. (2018). Meeting on Masculinity and Male Violence, Belmopan. Available at https://www.youtube.com/watch?v=SroKQmvxSbg.

6. BBN Staff. (2021). Over 3,000 People Applying for Just over 200 Spaces in the Belize Police Department, *Breaking Belize News*, Belize City. Available at https://www.breakingbelizenews.com/2021/01/14/over-3000-people-applying-for-just-over-200-spaces-in-the-belize-police-department/.

7. Ana María Méndez Dardón. (2022). Engel List: What Is the United States Telling Central America? *WOLA*, Washington, DC. Available at https://www.wola.org/analysis/engel-list-what-is-the-united-states-telling-central-america/.

8. Office of the Spokesperson. (2022). Designation of Former Belizean Minister John Birchman Saldivar for Involvement in Significant Corruption, U.S. Department of State, Washington, DC. Available at https://www.state.gov/designation-of-former-belizean-minister-john-birchman-saldivar-for-involvement-in-significant-corruption/.

9. BBC. (2023) Jasmine Hartin: Socialite Spared Jail after Killing Belize Police Chief. Available at https://www.bbc.com/news/world-us-canada-65770626.

10. Channel 5 Belize. (2018). State of Emergency Lifted; Detained Inmates Share Their Stories upon Release. Available at https://www.youtube.com/watch?v=CtrZKY3yXnU; Channel 5 Belize. (2020). Gang Members Released from Detention after Thirty-Day Lockdown. Available at https://www.youtube.com/watch?v=sA-gvyAQ1bs.

11. Channel 5 Belize. (2022). ComPol Says No More Dialogue with Gang Members. Available at https://www.youtube.com/watch?v=RIUAVeHAwFA.

12. Channel 5 Belize. (2022). A Police Raid on Baptist Family Home Leaves Two Brothers Injured. Available at https://www.youtube.com/watch?v=XkLo6DwE5_4.

13. Vice. (2023). *Belize*, New York. Available at https://www.vice.com/en/topic/belize.

14. Ross Kemp on Gangs: Belize. (2008). Tiger Aspect Productions, London. Available at https://www.youtube.com/watch?v=tEqzbE753IY.

15. The World Bank. (2023). *Belize*, Washington, DC. Available at https://data.worldbank.org/country/belize.

16. The World Bank. (2023). *Gini Index—Belize*, Washington, DC. Available at https://data.worldbank.org/indicator/SI.POV.GINI?end=1999&locations=bz&most_recent_value_desc=true&start=1999&view=map.

17. UNDP Belize. (2013). Southside Youth Success Project Book Excerpt, Belmopan. Available at https://www.youtube.com/watch?v=P8tf_JamrlQ; Channel 5 Belize. (2012). 54 Young Men Graduate from the Southside Youth Success Project. Available at https://www.youtube.com/watch?v=9F3-Dcrn8PA.

18. Love Foundation. (2023). Education and Projects, Belize City. Available at https://lovefoundationbelize.org/education-and-projects/.

CONCLUSION

1. See the United Nations Office of the High Representative for the Least Developed Countries, Landlocked Developing Countries and Small Island Developing States. (2023). *Multidimensional Vulnerability Index.* Available at https://www.un.org/ohrlls/mvi.

2. Zoila Palma Gonzalez. (2023). #PlanBelize Medium-Term Development Strategy Launched, *Breaking Belize News*, Belize City. Available at https://www.breakingbelizenews.com/2023/01/23/planbelize-medium-term-development-strategy-launched/.

3. See Political and Peacebuilding Affairs. (2023). CICIG—International Commission against Impunity in Guatemala. Available at https://dppa.un.org/en/mission/cicig.

4. Jenny Pearce. (2023). 444: The Ruling Elites in Colombia, *Colombia Calling Podcast*, Bogotá. Available at https://colombiacalling.libsyn.com/444-the-ruling-elites-in-colombia.

References

Adler, A. (1928). *Understanding Human Nature*. Allen and Unwin.
Aguilar Umaña, I., and Rikkers, J. (2012). Violent Women and Violence against Women: Gender Relations in the *Maras* and Other Street Gangs of Central America's Northern Triangle Region. Interpeace. Initiative for Peacebuilding—Early Warning Analysis to Action. Available at https://www.interpeace.org/wp-content/uploads/2012/09/2012_09_18_IfP_EW_Women_In_Gangs.pdf.
Alexander, M. (2012). *The New Jim Crow: Mass Incarceration in the Age of Colorblindness* (Rev. ed.). New Press. Available at https://newjimcrow.com.
Alpers, P., and Picard, M. (2022). Belize—Gun Facts, Figures and the Law. Available at https://www.gunpolicy.org/firearms/region/belize.
Anderson, E. (2000). *Code of the Street: Decency, Violence, and the Moral Life of the Inner City*. W. W. Norton.
Anderson, P. (2012). Measuring Masculinity in an Afro-Caribbean Context. *Social and Economic Studies*, 61(1), 49–93. Available at http://www.jstor.org/stable/41803739.
Arciaga Young, M., and King, D. (2019). *Community Gang Assessment, Belize*. Inter-American Development Bank.
Arias, E. D. (2017). *Criminal Enterprises and Governance in Latin America and the Caribbean*. Cambridge University Press. Available at https://doi.org/10.1017/9781316650073.
Arias, E. D., and Barnes, N. (2016). Crime and Plural Orders in Rio de Janeiro, Brazil. *Current Sociology*, 65(3), 448–465. Available at https://doi.org/10.1177/0011392116667165.
Arias, E. D., and Goldstein, D. M. (2010). *Violent Democracies in Latin America*. Duke University Press.
Auyero, J. (2012). *Patients of the State: The Politics of Waiting in Argentina*. Duke University Press.
Auyero, J., Bourgois, P., and Scheper-Hughes, N. (2015). *Violence at the Urban Margins*. Oxford University Press. Available at http://www.amazon.co.uk/Violence-Margins-Global-Comparative-Ethnography/dp/0190221453.

Bagley, B. (2013). The Evolution of Drug Trafficking and Organized Crime in Latin America. *Sociologia, Problemas e Práticas*, 71, 99–123.
Baird, A. (2009). Methodological Dilemmas: Researching Violent Young Men in Medellín, Colombia. *IDS Bulletin. Violence, Social Action and Research*, 40(3).
Baird, A. (2011). *Negotiating Pathways to Manhood: Violence Reproduction in Medellin's Periphery*. University of Bradford. Available at http://hdl.handle.net/10454/5246.
Baird, A. (2012). The Violent Gang and the Construction of Masculinity amongst Socially Excluded Young Men. *Safer Communities: A Journal of Practice, Opinion, Policy and Research*, 11(4), 179–190.
Baird, A. (2015a). Duros and Gangland Girlfriends: Male Identity and Gang Socialisation in Medellín. In *Violence at the Urban Margins in the Americas* (pp. 112–132), J. Auyero, P. Bourgois, and N. Scheper-Hughes (Eds.). Oxford University Press.
Baird, A. (2015b). *Towards a Theory of Change for Social Cohesion and Community Safety*. United Nations Development Programme. Available at https://pureportal.coventry.ac.uk/files/3990485/BAIRD.
Baird, A. (2018a). Becoming the "Baddest": Masculine Trajectories of Gang Violence in Medellín. *Journal of Latin American Studies*, 50(1), 183–210. Available at https://doi.org/10.1017/S0022216X17000761.
Baird, A. (2018b). Dancing with Danger: Ethnographic Safety, Male Bravado and Gang Research in Colombia. *Qualitative Research*, 18(3), 342–360. Available at https://doi.org/10.1177/1468794117722194.
Baird, A. (2019). Dangerous Fieldwork. In *SAGE Research Methods Foundations*, S. Atkinson, A. Delamont, J. W. Cernat, Sakshaug, and R. A. Williams (Eds.). Sage. Available at https://doi.org/10.4135/9781526421036832584.
Baird, A. (2020a). From Vulnerability to Violence: Gangs and "Homicide Booms" in Trinidad and Belize. *Urban Crime—An International Journal*, 1(2), 76–97. Available at https://ojs.panteion.gr/?journal=uc&page=article&op=view&path%5B%5D=246&path%5B%5D=230.
Baird, A. (2020b). Macho Research: Bravado, Danger, and Ethnographic Safety. *LSE Blog*. Available at http://blogs.lse.ac.uk/latamcaribbean/2020/02/13/macho-research-bravado-danger-and-ethnographic-safety/.
Baird, A. (2021a). Man a Kill a Man for Nutin': Gang Transnationalism, Masculinities, and Violence in Belize City. *Men and Masculinities*, 24(3), 411–431. Available at https://doi.org/10.1177/1097184X19872787.
Baird, A. (2021b). The Fourth Corner of the Triangle: Gang Transnationalism, Fragmentation and Evolution in Belize City. In *Routledge International Handbook of Critical Gang Studies* (pp. 386–398), D. Brotherton and R. Gude (Eds.). Routledge. Available at https://doi.org/10.4324/9780429462443.
Baird, A., Bishop, M., and Kerrigan, D. (2022). Breaking Bad? Gangs, Masculinities and Murder in Trinidad. *International Journal of Feminist Politics*, 24(4), 632–657.
Baird, A., Bishop, M. L. and Kerrigan, D. (2023). Differentiating the Local Impact of Global Drugs and Weapons Trafficking: How Do Gangs Mediate "Residual Violence" to Sustain Trinidad's Homicide Boom? *Political Geography*, 106, 102–966. Available at https://doi.org/10.1016/j.polgeo.2023.102966.
Baird, A. and Rodgers, D. (2015, September 28). Are Latin American Gangs the New Revolutionaries? *ResearchGate.net*. Available at https://www.researchgate.net/blog/latin-american-gangs-revolutionaries.
Barker, G. (2005). *Dying to Be Men: Youth, Masculinity and Social Exclusion*. Routledge.

Beckles, H. (2003). Black Masculinity in Caribbean Slavery. In *Interrogating Caribbean Masculinities: Theoretical and Empirical Analyses*, R. Reddock (Ed.). University of the West Indies Press.

Belize Crime Observatory. (2020). *Annual Crime Comparative 2018–2019*. Government of Belize. Available at https://bco.gov.bz/crime-statistics/.

Bennett, I. A. B. (2017). Review: Gangs in the Caribbean: Responses of State and Society eds. by Anthony Harriott and Charles M. Katz, *Caribbean Studies*, 45(1–2), 245–250. Available at https://doi.org/10.1353/crb.2017.0009.

Berg, L.-A., and Carranza, M. (2018). Organized Criminal Violence and Territorial Control. *Journal of Peace Research*, 55(5), 566–581. Available at https://doi.org/10.1177/0022343317752796.

Bergmann, A. (2020). Glass Half Full? The Peril and Potential of Highly Organized Violence. *Revista de Estudios Sociales*, 73, 31–43. Available at https://doi.org/10.7440/res73.2020.03.

Beske, M. (2016). *Intimate Partner Violence and Advocate Response: Redefining Love in Western Belize*. Rowman and Littlefield. Available at https://rowman.com/ISBN/9781498503600/Intimate-Partner-Violence-and-Advocate-Response-Redefining-Love-in-Western-Belize#.

Biderman, C., De Mello, J. M. P., De Lima, R. S., and Schneider, A. (2019). Pax Monopolista and Crime: The Case of the Emergence of the Primeiro Comando da Capital in São Paulo. *Journal of Quantitative Criminology*, 35(3), 573–605. Available at https://doi.org/10.1007/s10940-018-9393-x.

Bloch, H., and Niederhoffer, A. (1958). *The Gang: A Study of Adolescent Behavior*. Philosophical Library.

Bolland, N. (1986). *Belize: A New Nation in Central America*. Routledge.

Bolland, N. (1997). *Struggles for Freedom: Essays on Slavery, Colonialism and Culture in the Caribbean and Central America*. Angelus.

Bolland, N. (2004). *Colonialism and Resistance in Belize: Essays in Historical Sociology* (2nd ed.). University of the West Indies Press.

Bourdieu, P. (1977). *Outline of a Theory of Practice*. Cambridge University Press.

Bourdieu, P. (1992). *The Logic of Practice*. Polity.

Bourdieu, P. (1996). *The State Nobility: Elite Schools in the Field of Power*. Polity.

Bourdieu, P. (2001). *Masculine Domination*. Polity.

Bourdieu, P., and Wacquant, L. (2004). Symbolic Violence. In *Violence in War and Peace: An Anthology*, N. Scheper-Hughes and P. I. Bourgois (Eds.). Blackwell.

Bourgois, P. (1995). *In Search of Respect: Selling Crack in El Barrio* (2nd ed.). Cambridge University Press.

Bourgois, P. (1996). In Search of Masculinity: Violence, Respect and Sexuality among Puerto Rican Crack Dealers in East Harlem. *The British Journal of Criminology*, 36(3), 412–427. Available at https://doi.org/10.1093/oxfordjournals.bjc.a014103.

Brereton, B. (2010). The Historical Background to the Culture of Violence in Trinidad and Tobago. *Caribbean Review of Gender Studies: A Journal of Caribbean Perspectives on Gender and Feminism*, 4, 1–15.

Brett, R. (2022). In the Aftermath of Genocide: Guatemala's Failed Reconciliation. *Peacebuilding*, 10(4), 1–21. Available at https://doi.org/10.1080/21647259.2022.2027660.

Briceño-Perriott, J., Olivera, F., and Esner, V. (2013). *Prevalence and Pattern of Drug Use in Third Year Belize City High School Students 2012–2013*. University of Belize, Belize City.

Bridges, T., and Pascoe, C. J. (2018). On the Elasticity of Gender Hegemony. In *Gender Reckonings* (pp. 254–274), J. W. Messerschmidt, P. Y. Martin, M. A. Messner, and R. Connell (Eds.). New York University Press. Available at http://www.jstor.org/stable/j.ctt1pwtb3r.21.

Briscoe, I., and Breda, T. (2020). A Bargain Worth Making? Bukele and the Gangs of El Salvador. War on the Rocks Media. Available at https://warontherocks.com/2020/12/a-bargain-worth-making-bukele-and-the-gangs-of-el-salvador/.

Brotherton, D. (2015). Youth Street Gangs: A Critical Appraisal. Routledge. Available at https://doi.org/10.4324/9780203727782.

Brotherton, D. C., and Barrios, L. (2004). *The Almighty Latin King and Queen Nation*. Columbia University Press. Available at https://doi.org/10.7312/brot11418.

Brotherton, D. C., and Gude, R. (2020). Social Control and the Gang: Lessons from the Legalization of Street Gangs in Ecuador. *Critical Criminology*. Available at https://doi.org/10.1007/s10612-020-09505-5.

Brotherton, D. C., and Gude, R. (2021). *Routledge International Handbook of Critical Gang Studies*. Routledge. Available at https://doi.org/10.4324/9780429462443.

Campbell, A. (1984). *The Girls in the Gang: Report from New York City*. Basil Blackwell.

Campbell, J. L. (1998). Reviewed Work—Embedded Autonomy: States and Industrial Transformation by Peter Evans. *Theory and Society*, 27(1), 103–108. Available at http://www.jstor.org/stable/658040.

Castells, M. (2000). *End of Millennium, The Information Age: Economy, Society and Culture, Vol. 3* (2nd ed.). Blackwell.

Chioda, L. (2017). *Stop the Violence in Latin America: A Look at Prevention from Cradle to Adulthood*. World Bank.

Cloward, R., and Ohlin, L. (1960). *Delinquency and Opportunity: A Theory of Delinquent Gangs*. Free Press.

Cobbina, J., Like-Haislip, T., and Miller, J. (2010). Gang Fights versus Cat Fights: Urban Young Men's Gendered Narratives of Violence. *Deviant Behavior*, 31(7), 596–624. Available at https://doi.org/10.1080/01639620903231522.

Connell, R. W. (2005a). *Gender and Power: Society, the Person and Sexual Politics* (2nd ed.). Polity in association with Blackwell.

Connell, R. W. (2005b). *Masculinities* (2nd ed.). University of California Press. Available at https://www.ucpress.edu/book/9780520246980/masculinities#about-book.

Connell, R. W. (2016). Masculinities in Global Perspective: Hegemony, Contestation, and Changing Structures of Power. *Theory and Society*, 45(4), 303–318. Available at https://doi.org/10.1007/s11186-016-9275-x.

Connell, R. W., and Messerschmidt, J. (2005). Hegemonic Masculinity: Rethinking the Concept. *Gender and Society*, 19(6), 829–859. Available at https://doi.org/10.1177/0891243205278639.

Connell, R. W., and Wood, J. (2005), Globalization and Business Masculinities. *Men and Masculinities*, 7(4), 347–364. Available at https://doi.org/10.1177/1097184X03260969.

Contreras, R. (2019). The Broken Ethnography: Lessons from an Almost Hero. *Qualitative Sociology*, 42(2), 161–179. Available at https://doi.org/10.1007/s11133-019-9415-5.

Cooper, A. (2009). Gevaarlike Transitions: Negotiating Hegemonic Masculinity and Rites of Passage amongst Coloured Boys Awaiting Trial on the Cape Flats. *Psychology in Society*, 1–17.

Crooks, H. (2010). *Crooks Report*. Belmopan. Government of Belize.

Cruz, J. M. (2014). Maras and the Politics of Violence in El Salvador. In *Global Gangs: Street Violence across the World* (pp. 123–144), J. Hazen and D. Rodgers (Eds.). University of Minnesota Press.

Cruz, J. M., and Durán-Martínez, A. (2016). Hiding Violence to Deal with the State: Criminal Pacts in El Salvador and Medellin. *Journal of Peace Research*, 53(2), 197–210. Available at https://doi.org/10.1177/0022343315626239.

Decker, S. H., and Pyrooz, D. C. (2015a). Street Gangs, Terrorists, Drug Smugglers, and Organized Crime: What's the Difference? In *The Handbook of Gangs*, S. H. Decker and D. C. Pyrooz (Eds.). Wiley.

Decker, S. H., and Pyrooz, D. C. (2015b). *The Handbook of Gangs*. John Wiley and Sons. Available at http://eu.wiley.com/WileyCDA/WileyTitle/productCd-1118726871.html.

de la Tierra, A. L. (2016). Essentializing Manhood in "the Street": Perilous Masculinity and Popular Criminological Ethnographies. *Feminist Criminology*, 11(4), 375–397. Available at https://doi.org/10.1177/1557085116662313.

Demombynes, G. (2011). Drug Trafficking and Violence in Central America and Beyond. In *World Development Report Background Papers*. World Bank. Available at https://doi.org/doi:10.1596/27333.

Denyer Willis, G. (2015). *The Killing Consensus* (1st ed.). University of California Press. Available at http://www.jstor.org/stable/10.1525/j.ctt13x1hrn.

Denzin, N. K., Lincoln, Y. S., and Smith, L. T. (2008). *Handbook of Critical and Indigenous Methodologies*. Sage.

Deosaran, R. (2017). Foreword. In *Crime, Violence and Security in the Caribbean* (pp. xviii–xx), M. R. Izarali (Ed.). Routledge. Available at https://doi.org/10.4324/9781315525778.

Dixit, M. (2012). Field Research in Conflict Zones: Experience from India and Sierra Leone. *International Studies*, 49(1–2), 133–150.

Doyle, C. (2019). Social Urbanism: Public Policy and Place Brand. *Journal of Place Management and Development*, 12(3), 326–337. Available at https://doi.org/10.1108/JPMD-01-2018-0006.

Drug Seizures Increase in Belize as More Cocaine Flows North. (2019). *Insight Crime*.

Dudley, S. (2011). Central America Besieged: Cartels and Maras Country Threat Analysis. *Small Wars and Insurgencies*, 22(5), 890–913. Available at https://doi.org/10.1080/09592318.2011.620806.

Dudley, S. (2020). *MS-13: The Making of America's Most Notorious Gang*. Hanover Square Press.

Durán-Martínez, A. (2015). To Kill and Tell? State Power, Criminal Competition, and Drug Violence. *Journal of Conflict Resolution*, 59(8), 1377–1402. Available at https://doi.org/10.1177/0022002715587047.

Durán-Martínez, A. (2018). *The Politics of Drug Violence: Criminals, Cops, and Politicians in Colombia and Mexico*. Oxford University Press.

Duriesmith, D. (2016). *Masculinity and New War: The Gendered Dynamics of Contemporary Armed Conflict* (1st ed.). Routledge. Available at https://doi.org/10.4324/9781315561493.

Durkheim, É. (2007). The Rules of Sociological Method. In *Classical and Contemporary Sociological Theory: Text and Readings* (pp. 95–102), S. Appelrouth and L. D. Edles (Eds.). Pine Forge Press. Reprinted from 1895.

Dziewanski, D. (2020). From East Harlem to Cape Town: Tupac Shakur's Legacy as a Globalised Oppositional Repertoire. *Ethnography*. Available at https://doi.org/10.1177/1466138120923372.

Edmonds, K. (2016). Guns, Gangs and Garrison Communities in the Politics of Jamaica. *Race and Class, 57*(4), 54–74. Available at https://doi.org/10.1177/0306396815624864.

Espange, M. (1999). *Les Transferts Culturels*. Press Universitaires de France.

Evans, L., and Jaffe, R. (2020). Introduction: Representing Crime, Violence and Jamaica. *Interventions, 22*(1), 1–7. Available at https://doi.org/10.1080/1369801X.2019.1659162.

Evans, P. (1995). *Embedded Autonomy*. Princeton University Press. Available at http://www.jstor.org/stable/j.ctt7t0sr.

Fabre, A.-S., Florquin, N., Karp, A., and Schroeder, M. (2023). *Weapons Compass: The Caribbean Firearms Study*. Available at https://www.smallarmssurvey.org/sites/default/files/resources/CARICOM-IMPACS-SAS-Caribbean-Firearms-Study.pdf.

Felab-Brown, V. (2020). *Bargaining with the Devil to Avoid Hell? A DISCUSSION PAPER ON NEGOTIATIONS WITH CRIMINAL GROUPS IN LATIN AMERICA AND THE CARIBBEAN*. Barcelona. Available at: https://ifit-transitions.org/publications/negotiations-with-criminal-groups-in-latin-america-and-the-caribbean/.

Feltran, G. (2020). *The Entangled City: Crime as Urban Fabric*. Manchester University Press.

Ferrell, J., and Wainwright, J. (2022). The Political Economy of Development in Belize under the People's United Party. *Economic History of Developing Regions*, 1–24. Available at https://doi.org/10.1080/20780389.2022.2057294.

Fexia, C. (2021). Transnationalism and Postnational Identities: The Three Lives of a Latin King. In *Routledge International Handbook of Critical Gang Studies* (pp. 298–315), D. Brotherton and R. Gude (Eds.). Routledge. Available at https://doi.org/10.4324/9780429462443.

Flores, J. (2009). *The Diaspora Strikes Back: Caribeño Tales of Learning and Turning*. Routledge. Available at http://www.myilibrary.com?id=170711.

Fontes, A. W. (2018). *Mortal Doubt: Transnational Gangs and Social Order in Guatemala City*. University of California Press.

Foucault, M. (2000). *Power: Essential Works of Foucault 1954–1984* (J. D. Faubion [Ed.], Vol. 3). Penguin Books.

Fowler, M. R., and Bunck, J. M. (2012). *Bribes, Bullets, and Intimidation: Drug Trafficking and the Law in Central America*. Penn State University Press.

Fraser, A. (2013). Street Habitus: Gangs, Territorialism and Social Change in Glasgow. *Journal of Youth Studies, 16*(8), 970–985. Available at http://www.tandfonline.com/doi/abs/10.1080/13676261.2013.793791.

Fraser, A. (2017). *Gangs and Crime: Critical Alternatives*. Sage.

Gaviria, V. (1990). *Rodrigo D: No Futuro*. Zona A Limitada.

Gayle, H. (2009). Young Boys Learning to Fear, Hate and Harm: A Recipe for Sustaining Tribal Political Violence in Jamaica's Garrisons. *IDS Bulletin, 40*(1), 53–62. Available at https://doi.org/10.1111/j.1759-5436.2009.00009.x.

Gayle, H., Hampton, V., and Mortis, N. (2016). *Like Bush Fire: A Study on Male Participation and Violence in Urban Belize*. Cubola.

Gayle, H., and Mortis, N. (2010). *Male Social Participation and Violence in Urban Belize: An Examination of Their Experience with Goals, Guns, Gangs, Gender, God, and Governance*. Ministry of Education.

Glebbeek, M.-L., and Koonings, K. (2015). Between Morro and Asfalto. Violence, Insecurity and Socio-spatial Segregation in Latin American Cities. In *Habitat International, 54*(1), 3–9. Available at https://doi.org/10.1016/j.habitatint.2015.08.012.

Goldstein, D. M. (2004). *The Spectacular City: Violence and performance in urban Bolivia, Latin America otherwise*. Durham: Duke University Press. Available at: http://www.loc.gov/catdir/toc/ecip0413/2004001305.html.

Grassi, P. (2021). Stuck in Between: A Former Marero in the "European Capital" of Salvadoran Gangs. In *Routledge International Handbook of Critical Gang Studies* (pp. 329–339), D. Brotherton and R. Gude (Eds.). Routledge. Available at https://doi.org/10.4324/9780429462443.

Greenblatt, S. (2009). *Cultural Mobility: A Manifesto*. Cambridge University Press. Available at http://www.cambridge.org/us/academic/subjects/anthropology/anthropology-general-interest/cultural-mobility-manifesto?format=HB&isbn=9780521863568.

Griffith, I. L. (1997). *Drugs and Security in the Caribbean: Sovereignty under Siege*. Penn State Press.

Grillo, I. (2023). *Blood Gun Money: How America Arms Gangs and Cartels*. Bloomsbury.

Gutierrez Rivera, L., Strønen, I., and Ystanes, M. (2018). *Coming of Age in the Penal System: Neoliberalism, "Mano Dura" and the Reproduction of "Racialised" Inequality in Honduras* (pp. 205–228). Available at https://doi.org/10.1007/978-3-319-61536-3_9.

Gutmann, M. C. (1996). *The Meanings of Macho: Being a Man in Mexico City*. University of California Press.

Hagedorn, J. (1998). Frat Boys, Bossmen, Studs, and Gentlemen: A Typology of Gang Masculinities. In *Masculinities and Violence* (pp. 152–167), L. H. Bowker (Ed.). Sage. Available at https://doi.org/10.4135/9781483328010.n8.

Hagedorn, J. (2008). *A World of Gangs*. University of Minnesota Press.

Hall, S. (2015). Creolité and the Process of Creolization*. In *Creolizing Europe*. Liverpool University Press. Available at https://doi.org/10.5949/liverpool/9781781381717.003.0002.

Hanson, R., Warchol, G., and Zupan, L. (2004). Policing Paradise: Law and Disorder in Belize. *Police Practice and Research*, 5(3), 241–257. Available at https://doi.org/10.1080/156142604200227585.

Hanzen, J., and Rodgers, D. (2015). *Global Gangs*. University of Minnesota Press. Available at https://www.upress.umn.edu/book-division/books/global-gangs.

Hari, J. (2015). *Chasing the Scream: The First and Last Days of the War on Drugs*. Bloomsbury. Available at https://search.library.wisc.edu/catalog/9910218616302121.

Harvey, D. (2013). The Right to the City. In *Citizenship Rights*, I. Štiks and J. Shaw (Eds.). Routledge. Available at https://www.taylorfrancis.com/chapters/edit/10.4324/9781315260211-20/right-city-david-harvey?context=ubx&refId=3589b0c1-442b-4830-9032-5e10f2bde7cf.

Haylock, N. (2013). *National Public Policy Proposal: Prevention of Youth-Involved Violence in Belize 2012–2022*. Belmopan. Belize Crime Observatory Press.

Heinonen, P. (2011). *Youth Gangs and Street Children: Culture, Nature and Masculinity in Ethiopia*. Berghan Books.

Hosein, G., and Parpart, J. (2016). *Negotiating Gender, Policy and Politics in the Caribbean: Feminist Strategies, Masculinist Resistance and Transformational Possibilities*. Rowman and Littlefield.

Hughes, L. A., and Broidy, L. M. (2024). Masculinities and Respect in the Group Context of Gangs. In *The Oxford Handbook of Gangs and Society* (pp. 395–412), D. C. Pyrooz, J. A. Densley, and J. Leverso (Eds.). Oxford University Press. Available at https://doi.org/10.1093/oxfordhb/9780197618158.013.12.

Hume, M. (2004). "It's as if You Don't Know, Because You Don't Do Anything about It": Gender and Violence in El Salvador. *Environment and Urbanization*, 16(2), 63–72.

Hume, M., and Wilding, P. (2015). "Es que para ellos el deporte es matar": Rethinking the Scripts of Violent Men in El Salvador and Brazil. In *Violence at the Urban Margins* (pp. 93–111), J. Auyero, P. Bourgois, and N. Scheper-Hughes (Eds.). Oxford University Press.

Hume, M., and Wilding, P. (2019). Beyond Agency and Passivity: Situating a Gendered Articulation of Urban Violence in Brazil and El Salvador. *Urban Studies, 57*(2), 249–266. Available at https://doi.org/10.1177/0042098019829391.

Hylton, F. (2007). Extreme Makeover: Medellín in the New Millennium. In *Evil Paradises: Dreamworlds of Neoliberalism* (pp. 152–163), M. Davis and D. Bertrand Monk (Eds.). New Press.

Igarape Institute. (2024). *Homicide Monitor*. Rio de Janeiro. Available at https://igarape.org.br/en/issues/citizen-security/homicide-monitor/.

International Narcotics Control Strategy Report. (2019). U.S. State Department. Bureau for International Narcotics and Law Enforcement Affairs. Available at https://www.state.gov/wp-content/uploads/2019/04/INCSR-Vol-INCSR-Vol.-I-1.pdf.

Jaffe, R. (2013). The Hybrid State: Crime and Citizenship in Urban Jamaica. *American Ethnologist, 40*(4), 734–748. Available at https://doi.org/10.1111/amet.12051.

Jaffe, R. (2019). Writing around Violence: Representing Organized Crime in Kingston, Jamaica. *Ethnography, 20*(3), 379–396. Available at https://doi.org/10.1177/1466138118818585.

James, C. E., and Davis, A. (2014). Jamaican Males' Readings of Masculinities and the Relationship to Violence. *Caribbean Review of Gender Studies: A Journal of Caribbean Perspectives on Gender and Feminism, 8*, 218–251.

Jensen, S. (2008). *Gangs, Politics and Dignity in Cape Town*. James Curry.

Jewkes, R., Morrell, R., Hearn, J., Lundqvist, E., Blackbeard, D., Lindegger, G., Quayle, M., Sikweyiya, Y., and Gottzén, L. (2015). Hegemonic Masculinity: Combining Theory and Practice in Gender Interventions. *Culture, Health and Sexuality, 17*(2), 112–127. Available at https://doi.org/10.1080/13691058.2015.1085094.

Johns, A. (2014). Bloods, Crips and Southern Cross Soldiers: Gang Identities in Australia. In *A Critical Youth Studies for the 21st Century* (pp. 299–316), P. Kelly and A. Kamp (Eds.). Brill. Available at https://doi.org/10.1163/9789004284036_022.

Kan, P. R. (2014). Malicious Peace: Violent Criminal Organizations, National Governments and Truces. *International Journal of Criminology and Sociology, 3*, 125–132.

Karandinos, G., Hart, L., Castrillo, F. M., and Bourgois, P. (2015). The Moral Economy of Violence in the US Inner City: Deadly Sociability in the Retail Narcotics Economy. In *Violence at the Urban Margins*, J. Auyero, P. Bourgois, and N. Scheper-Hughes (Eds). Oxford University Press. Available at https://doi.org/10.1093/acprof:oso/9780190221447.003.0003.

Kerrigan, D. (2016). "Who Ent Dead, Badly Wounded": The Everyday Life of Pretty and Grotesque Bodies in Urban Trinidad. *International Journal of Cultural Studies, 21*(3), 257–276. Available at https://doi.org/10.1177/1367877916674740.

Kerrigan, D. (2019). "She Look for It": Young Men, Community Violence, and Gender in Urban Trinidad. *Caribbean Journal of Criminology, 1*(4), 29–59.

Kerrigan, D., and Baird, A. (2024). Carceral Masculinities in the Caribbean. In *Routledge Handbook on Caribbean Studies*, P. Noxolo (Ed.). Routledge.

Knight, W. A. (2019). The Nexus between Vulnerabilities and Violence in the Caribbean. *Third World Quarterly, 40*(2), 405–424. Available at https://doi.org/10.1080/01436597.2019.1576518.

Levenson, D. T. (2013). *Adiós Niño: The Gangs of Guatemala City and the Politics of Death*. Duke University Press.

Maclean, K. (2015). Social Urbanism and the Politics of Violence: The Medellín Miracle. Springer International Publishing. Available at https://link.springer.com/book/10.1057/9781137397362.

Maguire, E. R. (2013). *Research, Theory, and Speculation on Gang Truces.* Woodrow Wilson International Center for Scholars. Available at https://www.wilsoncenter.org/sites/default/files/media/documents/event/Maguire PPX.pdf.

Mäki-Rahkola, A., and Myrttinen, H. (2014). Reliable Professionals, Sensitive Dads and Tough Fighters. *International Feminist Journal of Politics, 16*(3), 470–489. Available at https://doi.org/10.1080/14616742.2012.755834.

Martínez D'Aubuisson, O., and Martínez D'Aubussion, J. J. (2018). *El Niño de Hollywood: Cómo Estados Unidos y El Salvador moldearon a un sicario de la Mara Salvatrucha 13* (2nd ed.). Debate.

McGarvey, D. (2022). *The Social Distance between Us: How Remote Politics Wrecked Britain.* Ebury.

Méndez, M. J., and Van Damme, E. (2024). Studying Gangs in Central and South America: Reflections on Gender and Researcher Positionality. In *The Oxford Handbook of Gangs and Society* (pp. 329–350), D. C. Pyrooz, J. A. Densley, and J. Leverso (Eds.). Oxford University Press. Available at https://doi.org/10.1093/oxfordhb/9780197618158.013.27%0A.

Mendoza-Denton, Norma. (2008). *Homegirls: Language and Cultural Practice among Latina Youth Gangs.* Wiley-Blackwell.

Messerschmidt, J. W. (1993). *Masculinities and Crime: Critique and Reconceptualization of Theory.* Rowman and Littlefield.

Messerschmidt, J. W. (1997). *Crime as Structured Action: Gender, Race, Class, and Crime in the Making.* Sage.

Messerschmidt, J. W. (2018). *Hegemonic Masculinity: Formulation, Reformulation, and Amplification.* Rowman and Littlefield.

Miller, J., and Brunson, R. K. (2000). Gender Dynamics in Youth Gangs: A Comparison of Males' and Females' Accounts. *Justice Quarterly, 17*(3), 419–448. Available at https://doi.org/10.1080/07418820000094621.

Miller Matthei, L. (1998). Belizean "Boyz 'n the 'Hood"? Garifuna Labor Migration and Transnational. In *Identity in Transnationalism from Below* (pp. 270–290), M. P. Guarnizo and L. E. Smith (Eds.). Transaction.

Moncrieff Zabaleta, H. J., and García Ponce de León, O. (2018). Máscaras Masculinas de Violencia: Sociología visual de pandilleros en México. *Revista Mexicana de Sociología, 80*(2), 385–414.

Morrell, R., Jewkes, R., Lindegger, G., and Hamlall, V. (2013). Hegemonic Masculinity: Reviewing the Gendered Analysis of Men's Power in South Africa. *South African Review of Sociology, 44*(1), 3–21. Available at https://doi.org/10.1080/21528586.2013.784445.

Moura, T., Borde, E., Slegh, H., and Barker, G. (2022). Understanding Linkages: Conflict, Societal Violence and Masculinities in and outside of Wars. In *Untapped Power: Leveraging Diversity and Inclusion for Conflict and Development* (pp. 376–395), C. Koppell (Ed.). Oxford University Press.

Muggah, R., and O'Donnell, C. (2015). Next Generation Disarmament, Demobilization and Reintegration. *Stability: International Journal of Security & Development, 4*(1), 1–12. Available at https://stabilityjournal.org/articles/10.5334/sta.fs.

Muhammad, N. (2015). *Insights into Gang Culture in Belize: Essays on Youth, Crime, and Violence.* Reynolds Desktop.

Mullins, C. W. (2006). *Holding Your Square: Masculinities, Streetlife, and Violence.* Routledge.

Mullins, C. W., and Lee, S. (2019). "Like Make Up on a Man": The Gendered Nature of Gun Norms. *Deviant Behavior, 41*(3), 294–310. Available at https://doi.org/10.1080/01639625.2019.1565515.

Myrttinen, H., Khattab, L., and Naujoks, J. (2017). Re-thinking Hegemonic Masculinities in Conflict-Affected Contexts. *Critical Military Studies*, 3(2), 103–119. Available at https://doi.org/10.1080/23337486.2016.1262658.

Naef, P. (2018). Touring the "Comuna": Memory and Transformation in Medellin, Colombia. *Journal of Tourism and Cultural Change*, 16(2), 173–190. https://doi.org/10.1080/14766825.2016.1246555.

Noche y Niebla Magazine. (2002). *Caso Tipo No. 2 Comuna 13, La Otra Versión*. Revista Noche y Niebla. Bogotá. CINEP and Justicia y Paz. Available at https://www.nocheynie bla.org/wp-content/uploads/u1/casotipo/Comuna13.pdf.

OECD. (2020). *States of Fragility 2020*. Available at https://doi.org/10.1787/ba7c22e7-en.

Orozco Flores, E. (2013). *God's Gangs: Barrio Ministry, Masculinity, and Gang Recovery*. New York University Press.

Palillo, M. (2020). "He Must Be a Man": Uncovering the Gendered Vulnerabilities of Young Sub-Saharan African Men in Their Journeys to and in Libya. *Journal of Ethnic and Migration Studies*, 1–17. Available at https://doi.org/10.1080/1369183X.2020.1816813.

Panfil, V. (2021). Performance Narratives of Gang Identity and Membership. In *Routledge International Handbook of Critical Gang Studies* (pp. 556–566), D. Brotherton and R. Gude (Eds.).Routledge.

Pawelz, J. (2018). Hobsbawm in Trinidad: Understanding Contemporary Modalities of Urban Violence. *Conflict, Security and Development*, 18(5), 409–432. Available at https://doi.org/10.1080/14678802.2018.1511165.

Pearce, J. (2007). *Violence, Power and Participation: Building Citizenship in Contexts of Chronic Violence, IDS Working Paper*. IDS Participation Group. Available at https://assets.publishing.service.gov.uk/media/57a08c0840f0b652dd001080/WP274.pdf.

Pearce, J., and Velasco Montoya, J. D. (2022). *Élites, Poder y Principios de Dominación en Colombia (1991–2022): Orígenes, Perfiles y Recuento Histórico*. Available at https://www.lse.ac.uk/lacc/assets/documents/PEARCE-VELASCO-ELITES-Y-PODER-EN-COLOMBIA-1991-2022.pdf.

Pecaut, D. (1999). From the Banality of Violence to Real Terror: The Case of Colombia. In *Societies of Fear*, K. Koonings and D. Kruijt (Eds.). Zed Books.

Peirce, J. (2017). *Gap Analysis Report: Citizen Security in Belize* (May).

Pemberton, C., and Joseph, J. (2018). *National Women's Health Survey for Trinidad and Tobago*. Inter-American Development Bank. Availble at http://dx.doi.org/10.18235/0001006.

Peterson, D. (2018). Gender and Gang Involvement. In *Oxford Research Encyclopedia of Criminology*, H. N. Pontell (Ed.). Oxford University Press. Available at https://doi.org/10.1093/acrefore/9780190264079.013.448.

Pitts, J. (2008). *Reluctant Gangsters: The Changing Face of Youth Crime*. Willam.

Pitts, W. J., and Inkpen, C. S. (2022). Past and Present Trends in Gun Violence and Gangs and Their Implications in Belize: 2011–2020. In *Guns, Gun Violence and Gun Homicides: Perspectives from the Caribbean, Global South and Beyond* (pp. 211–228), W. C. Wallace (Ed.). Springer International Publishing. Available at https://link.springer.com/chapter/10.1007/978-3-030-84518-6_9.

Pyrooz, D. C., Densley, J. A., and Leverso, J. (Eds.). (2024). *The Oxford Handbook of Gangs and Society*. Oxford University Press. Available at https://doi.org/10.1093/oxfordhb/9780197618158.001.0001.

Quicker, J. C. (1983). *Homegirls: Characterizing Chicana Gangs*. International Universities Press. Available at https://books.google.co.uk/books?id=jXsmOwAACAAJ.

Quijano, A. (2000). Coloniality of Power and Eurocentrism in Latin America. *International Sociology*, 15(2), 215–232. Available at https://doi.org/10.1177/0268580900015002005.

Reddock, Rhoda. (2003). Men as Gendered Beings: The Emergence of Masculinity Studies in the Anglophone Caribbean. *Social and Economic Studies*, 52(3), 89–117. Available at http://www.jstor.org/stable/27865342.

Reynolds, L. (2011). *The Bloods and Crips: Belize's Deadly Gangs*. Available at https://digitalrepository.unm.edu/cgi/viewcontent.cgi?article=10855&context=noticen.

Riach, G. K. (2017). *An Analysis of Gayatri Chakravorty Spivak's Can the Subaltern Speak?* Macat Library.

Rodgers, D. (2017). Bróderes in Arms: Gangs and the Socialization of Violence in Nicaragua. *Journal of Peace Research*, 54(5), 648–660. Available at https://doi.org/10.1177/0022343317714299.

Rodgers, D. (2018). Drug Booms and Busts: Poverty and Prosperity in a Nicaraguan Narcobarrio. *Third World Quarterly*, 39(2), 261–276. Available at https://doi.org/10.1080/01436597.2017.1334546.

Rodgers, D., and Baird, A. (2015). Understanding Gangs in Contemporary Latin America. In S. H. Decker and D. C. Pyrooz (Eds.), *The Handbook of Gangs* (1st ed., pp. 478–502). Wiley-Blackwell. Available at https://doi.org/10.1002/9781118726822.ch26.

Roks, R. A. (2017). In the 'h200d': Crips and the Intersection between Space and Identity in the Netherlands. *Crime, Media, Culture: An International Journal*, 15(1), 3–23. Available at https://doi.org/10.1177/1741659017729002.

Roks, R. A., and Densley, J. A. (2019). From Breakers to Bikers: The Evolution of the Dutch Crips "Gang." *Deviant Behavior*, 41(4), 525–542. Available at https://doi.org/10.1080/01639625.2019.1572301.

Rozema, R. (2008). Urban DDR-processes: Paramilitaries and Criminal Networks in Medellín, Colombia. *Journal of Latin American Studies*, 40, 423–452.

Salazar, A. (1990). *No Nacimos Pa'Semilla*. CINEP.

Sanatan, A. (2018). *How Masculinity Becomes a Weapon*. TedX. Available at https://www.academia.edu/38452820/How_Masculinity_Becomes_a_Weapon_TEDx_Port_of_Spain.

Sandberg, S. (2008). Street Capital: Ethnicity and Violence on the Streets of Oslo. *Theoretical Criminology*, 12(2), 153–171. Available at https://doi.org/10.1177/1362480608089238.

Sartre, J.-P. (1948). *Les Mains Sales*. Gallimard.

Savenije, W., and van der Borgh, C. (2015). San Salvador: Violence and Resilience in Gangland: Coping with the Code of the Street. In *Violence and Resilience in Latin American Cities*, Kees Koonings and D. Krujt (Eds.). Zed Books.

Scheper-Hughes, N. (1993). *Death without Weeping: The Violence of Everyday Life in Brazil*. University of California Press. Available at http://www.ucpress.edu/book.php?isbn=9780520075375.

Scheper-Hughes, N., and Bourgois, P. I. (2004). Violence in War and Peace: An Anthology. In *Blackwell Readers in Anthropology*. Blackwell. Available at http://www.amazon.com/gp/reader/0631223495/ref=sib_rdr_toc/104-3701959-9035149?_encoding=UTF8&p=S006&j=0#reader-page.

Schuberth, M. (2016). Beyond Gang Truces and Mano Dura Policies: Towards Substitutive Security Governance in Latin America. *Stability: International Journal of Security and Development*, 5(1), 1–20. Available at https://stabilityjournal.org/articles/10.5334/sta.450.

Shabazz, R. (2009). "So High You Can't Get over It, So Low You Can't Get under It": Carceral Spatiality and Black Masculinities in the United States and South Africa. *Souls*, *11*(3), 276–294. Available at https://doi.org/10.1080/10999940903088309.

Shammas, V. L., and Sandberg, S. (2016). Habitus, Capital, and Conflict: Bringing Bourdieusian Field Theory to Criminology. *Criminology and Criminal Justice*, *16*(2), 195–213. Available at https://doi.org/10.1177/1748895815603774.

Shoman, A. (1987). *A History of Belize in 13 Chapters* (1st ed.). Angelus Press.

Shoman, A. (2011). *A History of Belize in 13 Chapters* (2nd ed.). Angelus Press.

Singh, K. (1984). *Race and Class Struggles in a Colonial State: Trinidad 1917–1945*. University of Calgary Press.

Sjoberg, L., and Gentry, C. E. (2007). *Mothers, Monsters, Whores: Women's Violence in Global Politics*. Zed Books.

SpearIt. (2011). Gender Violence in Prison and Hyper-Masculinities in the 'Hood: Cycles of Destructive Masculinity. *Journal of Law and Policy*, *37*, 89–147.

Spivak, G. C. (1988). Can the Subaltern Speak? In *Marxism and the Interpretation of Culture*, C. Nelson and L. Grossberg (Eds.). Macmillan.

Statistical Institute of Belize. (2021). *Abstract of Statistics*. Belmopan. Government of Belize.

Sukhu, R. L. M. (2012). Masculinity and Men's Violence against Known Women in Trinidad—Whose Responsibility? *Men and Masculinities*, *16*(1), 71–92. Available at https://doi.org/10.1177/1097184X12468102.

Sullivan, J. P. (2006). Maras Morphing: Revisiting Third Generation Gangs. *Global Crime*, *7*(3–4), 487–504. Available at https://doi.org/10.1080/17440570601101623.

Taussig, M. (2003). *Law in a Lawless Land: Diary of a Limpieza in Colombia*. University of Chicago Press. Available at http://press.uchicago.edu/ucp/books/book/chicago/L/bo3680337.html.

Theidon, K. (2007). Transitional Subjects: The Disarmament, Demobilization and Reintegration of Former Combatants in Colombia. *International Journal of Transitional Justice*, *1*(1), 66–90. Available at https://doi.org/10.1093/ijtj/ijm011.

Theidon, K. S. (2014). *"How Was Your Trip?": Self-Care for Researchers Working and Writing on Violence* (DSD Research Papers on Research Security No. 2). Social Science Research Council. Available at https://kimberlytheidon.files.wordpress.com/2014/04/dsd_researchsecurity_02_theidon.pdf.

Thompson, M. S. (2019). Cultivating "New" Gendered Food Producers: Intersections of Power and Identity in the Postcolonial Nation of Trinidad. *Review of International Political Economy*, 1–27. Available at https://doi.org/10.1080/09692290.2019.1663748.

Thrasher, F. M. (1927). *The Gang: A Study of 1,313 Gangs in Chicago*. University of Chicago Press.

Tomlinson, J. (2003). Globalization and Cultural Identity. In *The Global Transformations Reader: An Introduction to the Globalization Debate* (2nd ed.) (pp. 269–277), A. G. McGrew and D. Held (Eds.). Blackwell.

Townsend, D. (2009). No Other Live: Gangs, Guns and Governance in Trinidad and Tobago. In *Small Arms Survey*. Graduate Institute of International and Development Studies.

Trotman, D. V. (1986). *Crime in Trinidad: Conflict and Control in a Plantation Society, 1838–1900*. University of Tennessee Press.

UNDP. (2012). *Caribbean Human Development Report 2012: Human Development and Shift to Better Citizen Security*.

UNDP. (2014). *Southside Youth Success Project: Pathways to Employment for At-Risk Young Men Training and Apprenticeship Programme Report*. Belmopan.

UNICEF Belize. (2011). *The Situation Analysis of Children and Women in Belize 2011: An Ecological Review*.

United Nations Beilze. (2021). CCA: Common Country Analysis. Available at https://belize.un.org/en/150296-united-nations-belize-common-country-analysis-cca-2021.

UNODC. (2007). *Crime and Development in Central America: Caught in the Crossfire*. Available at https://doi.org/ISBN 978-92-1-030038-4.

UNODC. (2012). *Transnational Organized Crime in Central America and the Caribbean: A Threat Assessment*. Available at https://www.unodc.org/documents/data-and-analysis/Studies/TOC_Central_America_and_the_Caribbean_english.pdf.

UNODC. (2018). *Statistics*. Available at https://www.unodc.org/unodc/en/data-and-analysis/statistical-activities.html.

UNODC. (2019). *Global Study on Homicide 2019—Homicide: Extent, Patterns, Trends and Criminal Justice Response*. Available at https://www.unodc.org/documents/data-and-analysis/gsh/Booklet2.pdf.

Vandenberghe, F. (2008). Deleuzian Capitalism. *Philosophy and Social Criticism*, 34(8), 877–903. Available at https://doi.org/10.1177/0191453708095696.

van der Borgh, C., and Savenije, W. (2019). The Politics of Violence Reduction: Making and Unmaking the Salvadorean Gang Truce. *Journal of Latin American Studies*, 51(4), 905–928. Available at https://doi.org/doi:10.1017/S0022216X19000890.

Venkatesh, S. (2008). *Gang Leader for a Day: A Rogue Sociologist Takes to the Streets*. Penguin.

Vernon, S. (2000). *In-Transit: The Story of a Journey*. Angelus.

Viveros Vigoya, M. (2001). Contemporary Latin American Perspectives on Masculinity. *Men and Masculinities*, 3(3), 237–260.

Viveros Vigoya, M. (2002). *De Quebradores y Cumplidores: Sobre hombres, masculinidades y relaciones de género en Colombia*. Universidad Nacional de Colombia.

Viveros Vigoya, M. (2018). Race, Indigeneity, and Gender. In *Gender Reckonings* (pp. 90–110), J. W. Messerschmidt, P. Y. Martin, M. A. Messner, and R. Connell (Eds.). New York University Press. Available at http://www.jstor.org/stable/j.ctt1pwtb3r.11.

Warnecke-Berger, H. (2017). Forms of Violence in Past and Present: El Salvador and Belize in Comparative Perspective. In *Politics and History of Violence and Crime in Central America* (pp. 241–279). Palgrave Macmillan US. Available at https://doi.org/10.1057/978-1-349-95067-6_9.

Warnecke-Berger, H. (2019). *Politics and Violence in Central America and the Caribbean*. Palgrave Macmillan. Available at https://doi.org/10.1007/978-3-319-89782-0.

Warren, K., Anderson, C., Ayres, T., Kerrigan, D., Cameron, Q., and Moss, K. (2021). Confronting Silences Haunting Guyana's Juvenile Justice System. *Caribbean Journal of Criminology*, 3(1), 10–39. Available at https://www.dylankerrigan.com/uploads/2/4/3/4/24349665/confronting_silences.pdf.

Wennmann, A. (2014). Negotiated Exits from Organized Crime? Building Peace in Conflict and Crime-Affected Contexts. *Negotiation Journal*, 30(3), 255–273. Available at https://doi.org/10.1111/nejo.12060.

Whiteacre, K., and Miller, A. J. (2017). *Oral History in Belize Central Prison*. University of Indianapolis. Available at https://www.academia.edu/35370170/Oral_History_in_Belize_Central_Prison.

Whiteacre, K., and Miller, A. (2018). Rehabilitation and Social Distance in the Belize Central Prison. Belize National Research Conference. Belmopan. Available at https://www

.researchgate.net/publication/323734940_Rehabilitation_and_Social_Distance_in_the_Belize_Central_Prison.

Wilkinson, R., and Pickett, K. (2009). *The Spirit Level: Why More Equal Societies Almost Always Do Better*. Penguin Books.

Wolf, S. (2015). *"¿Hay terroristas en El Salvador?"* Distintas Latitudes. Available at http://www.distintaslatitudes.net/hay-terroristas-en-el-salvador.

Wolf, S. (2017). *Mano Dura: The Politics of Gang Control in El Salvador*. University of Texas Press. Available at https://utpress.utexas.edu/books/wolf-mano-dura.

World Bank Group. (2020). *Strategy for Fragility, Conflict, and Violence 2020–2025*. Available at https://documents.worldbank.org/en/publication/documents-reports/documentdetail/844591582815510521/world-bank-group-strategy-for-fragility-conflict-and-violence-2020-2025.

World Bank Group and United Nations. (2018). *Pathways for Peace: Inclusive Approaches to Preventing Violent Conflict*. World Bank. Available at http://hdl.handle.net/10986/28337.

Young, M., and Woodiwiss, M. (2019). Organised Crime and Security Threats in Caribbean Small Island Developing States: A Critical Analysis of US Assumptions and Policies. *European Review of Organised Crime*, 5(1), 85–117. Available at https://uwe-repository.worktribe.com/output/849208.

Zilberg, E. (2011). *Space of Detention: The Making of a Transnational Gang Crisis between Los Angeles and San Salvador*. Duke University Press.

Zubillaga, V. (2009). "Gaining Respect": The Logic of Violence among Young Men in the Barrios of Caracas, Venezuela. *Youth Violence in Latin America: Gangs and Juvenile Justice in Perspective*.

Index

accountability, 44, 129, 133, 139, 143, 163, 169, 170, 172
activism, 38, 55, 133
addiction, 64, 162
Adler, Alfredo, 15, 16
African, 7, 10–12, 16–18, 21, 25, 31, 43, 59, 97, 129; Afro-Caribbean, 13, 97; Afro-indigenous, 7, 27
Aguilar Umaña, Isabel, 15, 125
Alexander, Michelle, 25–26, 61
Arciaga Young, Michelle, 8, 71, 77, 82, 84, 85, 89, 126, 144
Arias, Desmond, 18, 53, 66, 72
Ashcroft, Michael, 42, 60, 140
Auyero, Javier, 9, 137

Barrow, Dean, 43, 49, 54, 59, 62, 63, 96, 134, 139, 145
Battle of St. George's Caye, 11
Belize Central Prison, 24–27, 52, 60–61, 77, 86, 106, 140, 143, 158, 166; inmates, 60, 77, 158; Wagner's Youth Facility, 60, 106, 107, 119
Belmopan, 10, 23, 24, 35, 38, 70, 86, 130, 131, 138, 142, 176, 177
Bergmann, Adrian, 54, 72, 100
Bishop, Matthew, 10, 12, 15, 18, 38, 54, 69, 73, 103, 175

Bloods and Crips, 2, 5–8, 13, 17–19, 21–34, 37, 48, 50, 53, 57, 62–67, 73, 76–80, 82, 84–90, 92–103, 125–126, 134, 141, 166–168; colors gangs, 7, 29, 30–31, 99–100, 110
BMCMS (Behavior Modification and Conflict Management Service), 84, 144–148, 159
Bolland, Nigel O., 7, 10–12, 38–39, 41, 45, 47, 57, 97, 139
Bourdieu, Pierre, 42–44, 102, 104, 125, 143; *libido dominandi*, 125
Bourgois, Philippe, 9, 15, 16, 38, 112
Briceño, Johnny, 40, 154
Briscoe, Ivan, 72, 81, 93, 182
British, 4, 7, 10, 11, 23, 28–29, 37–38, 41–42, 59, 140, 148; Convention of London, 11
Brotherton, David, 2, 3, 14, 15, 24, 64, 71, 79, 98, 146
Bukele, Nayib, 56–57
Bunck, Julie Marie, 4, 67, 72, 74, 76–77, 140

CARSI (Central America Regional Security Initiative), 114, 159
Castells, Manuel, 61, 141
Caye Caulker, 11, 39, 71, 74–75, 91
Chetumal border, 141, 161
children, 5, 24–25, 39, 42, 53, 58, 64, 81, 86, 88, 91, 99, 101, 105–107, 111–112, 114–125,

children (*continued*)
130, 135, 151–152, 157, 161, 170; abuse and vulnerability, 114–119; childcare, 125, 159; fostering, 116, 117, 118, 151, 156, 159
chronic vulnerability, 1–3, 9–10, 17, 20, 22, 27, 33, 37–38, 50, 55, 61, 65, 93, 94, 101, 111, 125, 128, 130, 162, 165–172
Colombia, 16, 43, 57, 64, 67, 68, 73, 92, 111, 121, 178, 180, 183, 188–191
colonialism, 4, 6–7, 10–13, 17, 23, 27–28, 29, 37, 38, 41, 42, 49–50, 59, 61, 65, 79, 83, 102, 136, 139, 163, 165, 167, 168; anticolonial, 37, 41; decolonialization, 12, 42, 45; postcolonial, 13, 17, 31, 36, 42, 44, 61, 102, 103; power of coloniality, 10, 29, 172
Commonwealth, 4, 23
Connell, Raewyn, 14–15, 17, 31, 102, 104, 133
corruption, 30, 37–38, 40, 43, 45–48, 57, 60, 75, 96, 104, 129–130, 137–139, 140, 142, 152, 155, 160, 162, 168–172; anti-corruption, 172; kickbacks, 75, 129, 138
courts, 40, 59, 64, 76, 141, 158
creolization, 18, 19, 93–95, 97, 168; *Kriolization*, 18
Crooks Report, 57, 141, 144
CSOs, 160, 171; civil society, 130, 133, 160, 171
cultural vulnerability, 29–30, 112
CYDP (Conscious Youth Development Programme), 8, 62, 64, 84, 144, 145

D'Aubuisson, Óscar, and D'Aubuisson, Juan José, 22, 23
demobilization, 63, 64, 146, 187, 190
deportation, 7, 23–25, 27
dignity, 104, 112, 126, 164, 168; esteem, 15, 31, 112, 117, 121, 168
disenfranchisement, 5, 14, 16, 22, 31, 35, 48, 54–55, 65, 167
dominant discourse, 128, 130
drugs, 1–5, 9–10, 18, 19, 22, 25–26, 53, 56, 67–77, 83, 88, 90, 93, 99, 102, 118, 123, 125, 140, 142, 146–149, 162, 168; anti-drug policy, 25; cartels, 67, 72, 81, 141; crack-cocaine, 79; drug-trafficking and transshipment, 1–5, 10, 18–19, 53, 57, 65–68, 72–77, 82, 83, 93, 140, 146, 162, 168; war on drugs, 25; zero-tolerance, 22, 26
Durán-Martínez, Angélica, 53, 67, 72, 78
Durkheim, Emile, 9, 141

Ecuador, 64, 146, 182
elitism, 6, 7, 12, 13, 36, 39, 42–48, 54, 55, 74, 93, 129, 133, 135, 130, 140, 143, 152, 163, 166–168, 172
El Salvador, 1, 4, 22, 23, 27, 39, 53, 56, 72
Engel list, 140, 171
Espange, Michele, 30, 184
Europe, 24, 69, 73, 74; Eurocentrism, 29
Evans, Lucy, 9, 18, 71, 133

family, 2, 12, 15, 18, 24, 36, 39, 42–44, 49–50, 53, 55, 57, 62–63, 72–77, 81–84, 92–93, 105, 107, 109, 115, 121, 127–128, 130, 135–140, 149–152, 157; fathers, 16, 73, 91, 103–111, 115, 119, 121, 125, 152; mothers, 77, 80, 84, 86, 91, 101, 105, 108, 115–118, 121, 124, 137, 152, 157, 170
Feltran, Gabriel, 54, 57, 67, 72, 79, 184
femininities, 3, 17–19, 95, 101–102, 119, 121, 125, 159, 168, 173; vulnerability, 3, 19, 95
Ferrell, Jacob, 36, 41–42, 44–45, 140, 184
Fontes, Anthony, 16, 55
former gang members: *Messiah*, 89, 95–96, 104, 112–114, 126; *Mr. T*, 42, 48, 50, 52, 54, 58, 98, 99, 100, 105, 118, 131, 135, 136, 146, 162; *JK*, 88–89, 95–96, 99, 112–114, 126

gangbanging, 70, 86, 99, 108, 114
gang members: *Angel*, 21, 28, 32, 52, 63, 64, 70, 78–92, 99, 111, 116; homeboys, 13, 88; homegirls, 14, 187, 188; hangers-on, 131, 155; hard-core, 30, 64, 106, 121, 131, 124; *Irving*, 106–111, 114; *Shorty*, 24, 50, 52, 59, 70, 77, 78, 84–88, 93, 99, 124, 126, 131, 134, 135, 137–142, 163; *Vartas*, 52, 53, 88–90, 93, 96, 100, 104, 106, 124, 135, 139, 145, 148, 149, 150, 168; *shottas*, 18, 19, 78, 80, 100, 102, 103, 106, 125
gang negotiations, 19, 34–36, 61, 62, 64, 80, 84, 131, 144–146
gangs: adaptation, 19, 94–126; crackdowns and mano dura, 8, 19, 27, 34–36, 56–58, 61, 62, 80, 81, 104, 145; fragmentation, 5, 8, 18–19, 22, 36, 53–54, 67, 78, 80–84, 90–94, 99, 100, 167; *lumpengangstas*, 54, 55, 139; syncretistic, 2, 5, 14, 18–19, 93–100, 112, 126, 168; turf, 2, 50, 73, 84, 93, 110
gangs on Southside: Bac-a-Lan, 13, 84, 90, 103, 128, 145; Belize City, 84t; Gaza, 58, 85, 90, 99–100; George Street Bloods, 8,

32–33, 53–58, 62, 73, 76, 81–82, 86–92, 99–100, 105–106, 123, 132, 167; George Street Next Generation (GNC), 106, 111; Ghostown, 87; Jungle, 6, 91; Majestic Alley Crips, 6, 8, 28, 32–33, 52, 63, 78, 85, 91, 138, 161, 167; PIV (People in Violence), 58, 64, 84, 87–90, 100
gang transnationalism, 1–2, 7, 8, 14, 17, 19, 21–23, 28, 31, 33, 98, 102; mara salvatrucha, 2, 6, 8, 18, 21–23, 27, 32, 56, 72, 81, 92, 93, 100, 132; posttransnational gangs, 18, 19, 94, 95, 126, 168; gang-deportation model, 21
Gayle, Herbert, 7, 8, 18, 39, 57, 58, 60, 77, 82, 84, 105, 113, 115, 116, 119, 120, 121, 129, 136, 137, 140, 141, 142, 143, 144, 148
gender, 1, 3, 14, 17, 18, 20, 22, 31, 33, 101, 104, 106, 111, 112, 164, 168, 171–173; gender-appropriate, 101; gender-disaggregated, 126; gender-segregated, 104; gender-sensitive, 3, 16; gendered vulnerability, 31
generals, 8, 18, 33, 53, 54, 58, 61, 64, 67, 78, 79, 80, 81, 82, 86, 98, 103, 105, 106, 109, 134, 167
ghettos, 29, 32, 37, 60, 61, 84, 88, 99, 102, 111, 118, 125, 126
Gini coefficient, 55, 151, 163
Gi3, 8, 57, 61, 145, 150, 172; GSU, 8, 34, 57, 58, 104
Goldstein, Daniel, 66, 80
Grillo, Ioan, 82
grindin', 111, 112, 114
Guatemala, 1, 3, 4, 22, 27, 29, 39, 40, 55–56, 67, 74, 76, 82–83, 90, 142
Gude, Raphael, 2, 3, 15, 24, 64, 71, 79, 146
guns, 5, 6, 32, 67, 68, 78–83, 88, 93, 103, 110, 124, 126, 142, 147, 165

Hagedorn, John, 15, 18, 24, 31
Hartin, Jasmine, 140, 141
Hattieville, 60, 124
Haylock, Nicole, 8, 84, 104
Herbert, George, 53, 73, 76, 81, 92, 106
homicide boom, 1, 5, 8, 19, 35–36, 53, 66–67, 71, 76–79, 93, 106, 165, 167
Honduras, 4, 7, 11, 22, 23, 27, 37, 38, 56
Hume, Mo, 16, 124
Hurricane Hattie, 7, 8, 23
hustlin', 11, 32, 79, 95, 126, 141

IDB (Interamerican Development Bank), 71, 144, 163
independence, 4, 7, 13, 28, 32, 37–46, 51, 129, 139, 169; postindependence, 13, 34–37, 41–48, 167, 168
indigenous, 40, 50, 96

Jabbar, 52, 62, 95, 97, 105, 106, 124, 132, 135, 136, 138, 143, 163
Jamaica, 2, 8, 11, 30, 37, 52, 57, 59, 67, 90, 94–97, 99–100, 126, 168; Jamaicanized, 52, 93–94, 112
Janus face, 19, 35, 36, 55, 61
Jewkes, Rachael, 17, 102

Kemp, Ross, 148
Kerrigan, Dylan, 9, 10, 12, 13, 15, 18, 37, 38, 54, 59, 69, 73, 103
Kolbe Foundation, 60, 172

Latinization, 39, 40
Latin Kings, 2
Levenson, Deborah, 17, 23, 56, 186
logging, 11, 12, 36, 37, 49
London Bridges, 17, 128

Magnitsky list, 140
malnutrition, 58, 115, 148, 153; hunger, 115, 119, 121, 156; starvation, 115, 132, 171
marijuana, 13, 32, 35, 41, 59, 66, 69–71, 76–78, 90, 92, 98, 99, 103, 109, 141–142, 147, 152, 161, 168; *Belizean Breeze* strain, 69–71; decriminalization, 35, 59, 70, 141; *Kush* strain, 70, 141, 161
masculinities, 1, 3–6, 13–20, 22, 30–34, 93–95, 101–105, 111–112, 114, 117, 121, 125–126, 130, 133, 155–156, 159, 164, 166, 168, 173; "badness", 17, 106, 111; hegemonic masculinities, 14–19, 93–94, 102, 114, 125; ganging/gangland masculinities, 18, 95, 106; male on male violence, 105, 113, 116; masculine capital, 102, 112, 114, 125, 126; masculine vulnerability, 3, 14, 19, 30–33, 94, 101–114, 156, 166, 168; masculinist approaches, 16, 101, 114; "strategic essentialization" of, 114; transnational masculinity, 14, 17, 19, 22, 31, 33, 166
McGarvey, Darren, 144, 169
Medellín, 5, 16, 53, 64, 66, 67, 72, 73, 90, 92, 105, 107, 111, 120, 121, 133, 146, 147, 171

Mendoza-Denton, Norma, 14, 98, 187
Mesopotamia, 50, 62, 134
Messerschmidt, James, 15, 17, 18, 102, 104, 124
mestizo, 7–8, 39–40, 82, 97
Mexico, 3–4, 9, 16, 22, 24, 67–68, 70, 73–74, 76, 82–83, 129, 130, 141, 161; Mexican Mafia, 22
migration, 7, 21–23, 27–29, 39, 129, 171
militarization, 8, 56, 57
Muhammad, Nuri, 8, 13, 29, 30, 31, 33, 53, 58, 59, 62, 64, 73, 79, 84, 97–99, 106, 111, 133
Myrttinen, Henri, 16, 17

neoliberalization, 13, 17, 36, 45, 102
NGOs, 62, 146, 153, 160, 171
Nicaragua, 22, 23, 72
Northern Triangle countries, 4, 7, 8, 32, 56, 56, 80, 179
Northside Belize City, 31, 43, 44, 50, 104, 137

OECD, 3, 10, 167, 167, 188
Ombudsman, 57, 139, 142, 171

partial rule of law, 20, 47, 130, 131, 139, 143, 163, 168
patriarchy, 13, 17, 19, 104
Pearce, Jenny, 9, 43, 127, 165, 172
Peirce, Jenifer, 4, 8, 59, 84, 144
#planbelize, 127, 169
Pleasers, 121–122, 125
police, 57–62, 73–77, 81–85, 89–91, 95–97, 128–132, 140–147
positionality, 112, 129, 187
PUP, 7, 8, 37, 38, 40–51, 55, 58, 76, 127, 128, 130, 134, 140, 144, 145, 154, 160, 169, 170, 170, 171
Pyrooz, David, 15, 24, 72

Queen Elizabeth II, 4, 50, 100, 134

race, 9, 12, 18, 21, 22, 29, 33, 39, 40, 42, 48, 49, 61, 139, 165, 166, 167, 173; racial-spatial, 61; racialized, 59, 163, 167, 168; racism, 12, 25, 26, 43, 49
Rampart district, 22, 26
rap, 21, 80, 89, 95, 96, 100, 112, 124
Reagan, Ronald, 25
recommendations, 139, 144, 169

reconfiguration, 20, 102, 165, 166
revolution, 133, 139; rebellion, 15, 16, 18, 30, 55, 98, 133
Rodgers, Dennis, 15, 16, 23, 28, 56, 71, 72, 133, 175
rule of law, 8, 20, 35, 38, 47, 56, 81, 130–131, 139–143, 163, 166, 168, 172

Scheper-Hughes, Nancy, 9, 38
self-harm, 118, 119; suicide, 113, 119
Shabazz, Rashad, 60, 61, 61, 88
Shammas, Victor, 15, 102
Shirley, 130, 135, 139
Sjoberg, Laura, 16, 101, 190
slavery, 10–13, 18, 27, 36–38, 43, 45, 61, 65, 128, 136; barracks, 36, 49, 128, 134, 138, 158; houseslaves, 11, 13, 36, 48, 49; fieldslaves, 11, 13, 36, 48, 49, 55, 65, 130, 136, 143, 163, 167, 168; indentureship, 10, 59
smuggling, 5, 31, 73, 83
social terrain, 1–5, 14, 30, 33, 35, 68, 88, 93, 95, 101, 111
Spain, Treaty of Madrid, 11–12
Spivak, Gayatri Chakravorty, 46, 49, 130
stigmatization, 113, 153, 173
structure and agency, 14–16, 31, 101, 111, 122, 125, 171
subaltern, 46, 48, 50, 52, 54, 130
subculture, 22, 80, 104
subjugation, 13, 44, 55, 65, 125, 135, 136, 167
subordination, 13, 14, 16, 17, 31, 33, 44, 48, 52, 54, 102, 104, 128
swamplands, 4, 6, 10, 13, 36, 84, 148, 150
symbolic violence, 42, 143
SYSP (Southside Youth Success Project), 20, 84, 99, 114–116, 120, 131, 137, 144, 151–164

transhistorical, 9, 12, 17, 37, 61, 102, 167
trauma, 64, 78, 84, 104, 106, 110, 116, 118, 147, 151, 162; *demons*, 92, 107, 115–116, 119, 129, 137, 150, 162
Trinidad and Tobago, 10, 37, 47, 54, 73

UDP, 8, 35–38, 40, 42–55, 58–59, 62, 81, 134–135, 140, 144–147, 154, 159–160
United Nations, 3, 131, 171; UNDP, 3, 59, 68, 114, 119, 130, 133, 155–159, 167;

UNICEF, 6, 13, 156; UNODC, 3, 27, 67–68, 72, 83, 93

Venkatesh, Sudhir, 15, 77
victimization, 3, 14, 111–113, 122–125, 143, 149; victimhood, 16, 149
violence: chronic, 4, 9–10, 15, 18–19, 55, 65, 101, 165; disorganized, 19, 36, 66–67, 78, 167; escalation, 19, 66–93, 145; fratricide, 133
Vybz Kartel, 99, 100

Wacquant, Loïc, 26, 42, 143
Wainwright, Joel, 41, 42, 44, 45, 140, 184
Warnecke-Berger, Hannes, 6, 13, 23, 27, 28, 32, 39, 41, 44, 45, 46, 48, 57, 76, 98, 140
Washington, Raymond, 25
Williams, Stanley "Tookie," 25

youth, 5, 8, 14, 20, 28, 30–31, 39–40, 47, 60, 62, 70, 84–87, 91, 95, 98–101, 104–107, 113, 130–137, 141, 144, 147, 151, 155–158, 160; adolescents, 105

Adam Baird is a Researcher at the United Nations Institute for Disarmament Research. He is the coeditor of *Paz, paso a paso: Una mirada a los conflictos colombianos desde los estudios de paz.*